At twenty-five Cicero successfully defended a man "framed" on a parricide charge and a woman whose property was confiscated by the dictator Sulla. Thirty-nine years later he was murdered by the henchmen of Antony and Octavian, and his head and hands were placed on public view in the Roman forum.

The reason for Cicero's murder can be found in the passionate defense of law and freedom that characterized his life work. His orations against Verres forced a corrupt Roman governor into precipitous exile. The Catilinarian orations exposed an infamous conspiracy and prevented the overthrow of the government by an army of assassins. Whether defending a minor poet, accusing Antony of treachery, or exposing the gangsterism of Catiline and Antony, Cicero stands unrivaled as a man of letters and a defender of human liberties.

Palmer Bovie's new translation, supplemented ⬛⬛⬛⬛⬛⬛⬛⬛⬛⬛⬛⬛, offers a ⬛⬛⬛⬛⬛⬛⬛⬛⬛ s times, and ⬛⬛⬛⬛⬛⬛⬛⬛ a dynamic p⬛⬛⬛⬛

Other Ancient Classics in MENTOR Editions

CICERO

NINE ORATIONS AND THE DREAM OF SCIPIO

Newly Translated, with an Introduction, by *Palmer Bovie*

A Mentor Book
Published by The New American Library, New York and Toronto
The New English Library Limited, London

MENTOR TRADEMARK REG. U.S. PAT. OFF. AND FOREIGN COUNTRIES
REGISTERED TRADEMARK—MARCA REGISTRADA
HECHO EN CHICAGO, U.S.A.

MENTOR BOOKS are published *in the United States* by
The New American Library, Inc.,
1301 Avenue of the Americas, New York, New York 10019,
in Canada by The New American Library of Canada Limited,
295 King Street East, Toronto 2, Ontario,
in the United Kingdom by The New English Library Limited,
Barnard's Inn, Holborn, London E.C. 1, England

PRINTED IN THE UNITED STATES OF AMERICA

INTRODUCTION

The nine orations and the Dream of Scipio that I have translated for this volume follow the main stages of Cicero's public career and show several different sides of his rhetorical art. In the individual introductions to each work I review the historical circumstances surrounding its composition; here I wish only to discuss some of the common features of this collection as a whole. It represents primarily Cicero's public life as a statesman and speaker. He was both a man of action and a man of letters, and these works all illustrate the way in which literature can be a political force. Cicero was what he spoke, and more than most artists he lived what he wrote. Even though we are not here concerned with his literary criticism, philosophical essays or voluminous correspondence, in the speeches alone, we can readily identify the personality of a confident Roman statesman and literary scholar. As a representative cross-section of his professional accomplishments in the law courts, before the public gathered in the forum or in the Assembly, in the presence of his fellow Senators, these nine orations are, nevertheless, only a small part of the some eighty or more works in this style which

Cicero produced between his twenty-sixth and sixty-third year. When we take into account the period of his exile and the years he professed to be in retirement from public life, this average rate of production of formal, crafted, literary prose itself speaks for the powerful use of a politically engaged mind.

The orations disclose Cicero's working methods as a trained public speaker and his intellectual horizons as a practical humanist. He likes to defend, for example, but also relishes the opportunity to attack his opponents. He is as aggressive as a modern literary critic when he turns the tables on an adversary on a point affecting the Roman state and its ideals, or some crucial dispute over principles and values. Cicero's method is often to seize the initiative, but then to retire long enough to mount a defense in depth before returning to the attack. He seems to have an instinct for sensing the interplay of forces of aggression and of defense contained in the art of rhetoric as fundamental matters of contrast and balance in human expression. In attacking Verres, for instance, Cicero puts a luster on the positive side of efficient provincial administration by scoring off Verres' malign injustices. In defending Caelius, he brings into bold relief the savagery of Clodius and the sinister influence of the indomitable Clodia. Revenge against his tormentor Clodius was clearly called for, but the undermining of Clodia was due, perhaps, to a subtler psychological frustration by a woman a man could not conquer, but only despair of. In any case, the occasion for attack in the one instance is also used as an opportunity for effective defense, the occasion for defense in the other as the time for a counter-offensive.

Steeped in the patterns and practices of professional rhetoric—to such an extent that he also freely wrote volumes about the technique, the art, and its implications—Cicero created novel results within the form and forged a highly individual style. Speeches before the court became colorful, imaginative, minor prose epics. In the section of the speech against Verres here translated—comprising only eighty of the four hundred pages he wrote in preparing this one case—Cicero is busy, like any lawyer, burying the defendant under mountains of factual evidence. But in "Concerning the Statues," he also brings his literary art to the defense of the fine arts by composing a kind of descriptive catalogue of the Verres collection,[1] identifying many of the artifacts, as well as

[1] The cheerful modern Italian word "cicerone" is defined as, "a guide who shows and explains the antiquities, etc., of a place."

commenting on the paintings and statues. What this proves in the oration is that Verres is no connoisseur, but a violent bungler of values. Snarling and vindictive as Cicero's tone often becomes in this work, the oration is not a harangue, or a crushing summing up of Verres' villainy. It is rather the story of a compulsive art thief.[2] Beside an actual Roman magistrate so obsessed, the rape of Proserpina—which Cicero takes time to narrate at some length—looks like an endearing myth. Cicero's *De Signis* has become the rape of Verres.

In the speech in defense of Caelius, Cicero is as free with the *confirmatio*, another standard feature of rhetorical structure, as he is with *narratio*. The corroboration of proofs becomes a spirited sociological essay that demonstrates Caelius' right to be a normal young man. The oration is turned into a sketch of the younger generation, whose members are, the speaker finds himself casually suggesting, entitled to some pleasure and excitement. The Roman father's dour dignity is good publicity, but even Terence in his winning comedies had long since shown the danger of believing one's own publicity. Now, Caelius had quite a session with Clodia and her crowd—but why hound him further for that entanglement with such a bitch—excuse me, I meant to say witch? It's all over and done with, except, of course, for the seething fury of a woman scorned, that is obviously the motive behind this prosecution. Cicero talks artlessly on, on the subject, around it, about it. The listener discovers a defending attorney who is not paternal or patronizing, but affable, experienced, familiar with young people and their problems, prompt to distinguish between vice and folly.

The speech for Archias readily discloses the patterned structure that Cicero the rhetorician knew by heart, as a musician knows his key relationships, and always used, but in his own way. The *exordium*, or beginning, states the problem before the court, but also articulates Cicero's personal interest in the case. The *propositio* is emphatically stated in one sentence that includes its overstatement. Of course, Archias is legally entitled to citizenship. But even if he were not, I would easily convince you he ought to be made a citizen! There follows next the *narratio*, epitomizing Archias' career in forty lines. The *confirmatio*, comprising a full two-thirds of this speech, is a defense of two kinds, and a corroboration of two things. The evidence for Archias' legal claim to citizen-

2 A fascinating, modern account of the same syndrome, concerning Field Marshal Goering and his appraisers, is given in Janet Flanner's (Genêt) essay, "The Beautiful Spoils."

ship is neatly and factually marshaled, but there is also an
opportunity for a dissertation on eloquence. Here Cicero
becomes, it seems to me, pompous and highhanded in his
praise of the liberal arts and in his pitch for culture. He
glories in the glory of literary immortality. It is all rather
sweeping and self-approving. But then, a speech in praise of
eloquence has its psychological pitfalls. In the short *peroratio*
that concludes the defense, Cicero leaves the humanist poet
on a rather high plane, somewhat like an elevator operator
who brings his passenger to the top of the building and takes
the car down again empty. We appreciate his remarks and
admire his fervor, and, of course, can concede him the
factual evidence. But the disquieting thought occurs, that if
the liberal arts and the culture they confer are so divine,
they need not be harped on in such grossly mortal and
keyed-up language.

An orator must deliberately exaggerate, reiterate, and
overstate his case. Like a teacher, he is a man who talks too
much. The aim is to let the message linger long enough to
lodge in the hearer's ears. We always find Cicero ready to
glory in his Latin, directing a broad stream of prose at a
skillfully chosen target. Like a medieval monk, he can make
the rafters ring with genitive plurals. He can bounce sibilant
superlatives off the sides of the Senate house. He can pound
the ears of the Assembly with a staccato fire of verbs, or
relax them with the great supple contours of the periodic
sentence, the significant verbs stacked successively at the
end of the accumulating clauses. He is, for my taste, "a bit
too positive in his opinions," as Swift describes the ship's
captain in the Fourth Book of *Gulliver's Travels,* and this
was for Cicero, as it was for the captain, "the cause of his
undoing, as it hath been of many." I suppose that the
oratorical momentum carries the speaker on too far in his
desire to direct our attention overwhelmingly to the issues
contained in the argument.

Also, like a crafty pundit writing for the newspaper
world of today, or like a classroom lecturer, Cicero is a
resourceful ontheotherhandy man. In the defense of Murena
we hear that it is the professional soldier, not the artist-
statesman, who deserves an accolade from a nation like
Rome's. The military man is far superior in every way to the
mundane lawyer, or political orator. In this speech, at which
scholars say, "even Cato laughed," Cicero launches a fiendish
parody of the archaic mannerisms of the law and its arcane
jargon: a kind of voodoo-it-yourself scheme for wasting time

and money. The great soldier and leader, on the other hand, represents the acme of Roman achievement. Cicero reminds us of a point worth emphasizing, however obvious, that a man with an army behind him cuts a rather impressive figure as a candidate for public office. In the oration for Murena, Cicero the lawyer manages a skillful addition to his portrait of the sinister Catiline, which is of course entirely relevant to the critical atmosphere. On the other hand, it was something of a tour de force for Cicero, seven years later, to insert the sympathetic sketch of Catiline's character in the oration for Caelius. And in the Murena again, Cicero the consul, confronting a sober crisis in Rome, badgers the Stoics and their austere, heroic pride. He must have caught the prosecutor Cato quite off guard in composing a delightful criticism of the self-righteous Stoic ethic.

The Catilinarian orations are overly familiar and have suffered the fatal afterlife of many masterpieces by becoming schoolbooks. But a conspiracy against the state and its laws, in the name of a revolution that is aimed nakedly and solely at exploiting the citizens, is worth reading about, in school or out. These four speeches are grand opera. The case is well-proven by factual evidence, but what Cicero does in addition is dramatize the fundamental issues. He had long since learned by heart the orator's code: "to instruct, to please, to move the passions." Now, he practices the principles with all his heart and mind. The result is an unleashing of the speaker's imagination. Like Henry James, Cicero has a strong capacity for "the imagination of disaster." Consistently, rhythmically, he reviews the picture of Rome falling in flames to the fury and the swords of the conspirators. Can a noble state—he makes his hearers ask this question of themselves—perilously balanced on the cumbersome machinery of law and order, withstand the savage attack of men intoxicated by the will to take it over for themselves? One cannot read these orations without being haunted by the vision of Rome's fall, without feeling the mind seared by the literal flames Cicero picturesquely imagines. In fact, the conspirators had actually organized the strategic assignment of fire points in different sections of the city, where the panic-inducing conflagration could be set off simultaneously. The master plan, as Cicero evokes it, makes the conventional picture of Nero in a later epoch dwindle to the insignificance of cocktail hour variations on "Smoke Gets in Your Eyes." But, by his imagery of fire, by his noble personification of the guardian gods of Rome at bay, by his visions of the frenzied populace at the mercy of their exploiters, Cicero knows how to make his hearers feel the disaster in their bones. It is no mere rhetorical trick either: it is inflaming "the passions," with a vengeance.

There are numerous elements giving aesthetic variety, contrast, balance to the speeches against Catiline, but any intelligent reader can be trusted to discover their delights and take from them what instruction he may want to use. Cicero trusted his Roman audience implicitly.

In translating these speeches, my main purpose has been to let Cicero speak for himself. Just how well the bridge to Cicero's voice can be built anew in modern English is not easy to judge. I have taken a middle ground between the formal, strict prose of earlier translators, and the temptation to make it all crisp. Even so, I think I have been sometimes inconsistent, writing long, armor-plated sentences that read with some difficulty. Occasionally, I have broken Cicero's characteristically long sentences into shorter compact ones. Throughout, I have tried to use a modern English vocabulary that is equivalent to the meaning of Cicero's words, although not parallel to his polysyllabic diction. By trying to be both formal and, where called for, informal, the translation may, at times, sound as if it were grounded on the principle a political candidate once announced, promising that "he would steer a narrow course between impartiality and partiality in office." But throughout this new translation, I have tried to listen carefully to Cicero, and to hear as clearly as I could in my world what he was saying to his.

In the autobiographical passage from the *Brutus* quoted on pages 309 and 310, Cicero discusses what he learned from his teacher, Molo of Rhodes.

> His principal trouble with me was to restrain the luxuriancy of a juvenile imagination, always ready to overflow its banks, within its due and proper channel. Thus, after an excursion of two years, I returned to Italy, not only much improved, but almost changed into a new man. The vehemence of my voice and action was considerably abated; the excessive ardour of my language was corrected. . . .

But when we read Cicero's orations again today, we are still astonished by the luxuriancy of an imagination always ready to overflow its banks, by an excessive ardor. The melodramatic refrains make us wince. The tendency to exaggerate claims, and elevate abstract premises to giddy heights, produces a kind of moral vertigo in the skeptical modern mind. I have wondered whether the language of American advertising, predicated on unguarded superlatives and ambiguous total statements, might not be the best equivalent for some of Cicero's fortissimo passages. I have also wondered whether the propaganda harangues rehearsed before vast audiences by communist orators, suffocating criticism, and inducing a Pavlovian belief-response, would not be suited to the occasions where Cicero dogmatizes incredibly. But I have tried to avoid both the deceiving decibels of some such call to arms as "The Coming Victory of the Peoples' Revolutions" by Defense Minister Lin Piao, and the murderous lyric of a song for carbonated syrup, bidding its bewildered listeners to "Come Alive!"

Cicero's rhetorical style is eminently suited to the ear, by definition, and he will, I think, find hospitality among modern readers caught in a flood tide of "communication" that is an experience in listening and hearing, even more than reading. For readers, he stands out as a prolific prosateur and voracious literary enthusiast. In the years of his retirement, for example, he composed five detailed studies of the art of rhetoric so amply argued and specifically illustrated as to form a genuine branch of literary criticism. They still have much to tell the world about the problems of persuasive speaking; today this is again, as it was in classical Greece and Rome, a controversial sphere, the human arena where a public skill can be used, or abused, expertly.

During the period when Cicero took refuge in his books, he also wrote historical treatises, like *The Republic, The Laws,* and at least twelve major philosophical essays. Like the Greek statesman he admired unreservedly, Demosthenes, Cicero put his public career at the disposal of the state and used it for the defense of the constitutional democracy that he believed offered mankind the best opportunity for life.

Unlike Demosthenes, Cicero was also a free-lance humanist and a writer of books. He delighted in the exercise of his literary gifts. He enjoyed being famous and wealthy. The thirty-seven books of correspondence alone, show to what extent he remained intelligently active, in close communication with all the glorious men of his day and with many rather more appealing inglorious men and women in the Roman world. In the energetic practice of the liberal arts, he had learned how to make his voice heard. From his interest in literature, this versatile humanist created books for later readers.

NINE
ORATIONS

Against Verres, IV

INTRODUCTION

At the age of thirty-seven, Cicero undertook the prosecution of Gaius Verres in 70 B.C., the year of the consulship of Pompey and Crassus. In the previous decade, Cicero had distinguished himself as an advocate and orator by his speeches in defense of Quinctius (81), Sextus Roscius (80), and Quintus Roscius (76), but the case against Verres brought him more forcefully into the public eye and gained him wide popular support. It represented the triumph of legal procedure and justice over corruption and abuse of political office, and also resulted in Cicero's victory over the most eminent advocate of the day, Hortensius, who had agreed to defend Verres. Cicero had prepared his case carefully, and so effective was the first part of his presentation that the defense withdrew; and Verres went into exile, as was the defendant's prerogative at any time until the verdict was announced. The speeches that Cicero had prepared for the second part of the case were therefore never delivered publicly in the forum, but he had copies made of them to be circulated among influential circles in Rome, whose readers would then have other copies made. And so, we still possess today virtually all of Cicero's words in this one case, which alone fill four hundred pages.

When he was asked by all the leading representatives of the main cities of Sicily, except Messana and Syracuse, to act as their prosecuting attorney in a suit against Verres for extortion, misappropriation of funds, and expropriation of valuables, and consented to take the case, the first battle Cicero had to fight was for the right to represent them. Verres' side had become alarmed at the choice of so talented and hardworking a person ("it was the first trace of fear Verres ever showed," Cicero observes), and tried to plant their man Quintus Caecilius Niger, a swarthy Sicilian, as their rival contestant; a preliminary hearing was held to decide whether Cicero or Caecilius had the better claim to try the case. Cicero's speech, *In Q. Caecilium Divinatio* (*Against the Selection of Q. Caecilius [Niger] as Prosecutor*), the first oratorical item on the Verrine agenda, gained him the right to undertake the prosecution and thereby match his skill against Hortensius. Delaying tactics were then introduced by the powerful group of nobles, including members of the Scipio and Metellus families, who were Verres' adherents. If the trial could be dragged out until the following year, the chances of Verres' acquittal would be greatly increased, for at that time, Metellus and Hortensius would be the consuls, and Metellus' brother the *praetor urbanus* (the chief magistrate in the city of Rome), before whom cases of extortion were heard. Cicero was allowed one hundred and ten days in which to prepare his case, but with dispatch and energy completed the gathering of evidence and examination of witnesses in Sicily in fifty days, and returned home with the documentary proof he needed to support his charges. The cities of Sicily had cooperated with him fully in the course of these investigations, even the officials of Syracuse, who had supplied him with valuable information and state records, despite the obstructions of Metellus, then the Roman praetor. Only Messana still maintained its support of Verres. Cicero makes a point of analyzing the reasons for Messana's intransigence, in the fourth oration of the second part of the case, which I have translated, beginning and ending his speech with the problem of Messana and its citizens, the Mamertines, and reserving a climactic position for Syracuse. The next step Cicero took to offset his opponent's delaying tactics was to deliver a very short opening speech, packed with summary evidence and clearly outlining the main charges he was prepared to prove with detailed corroboration from witnesses and sworn testimony. The eighteen pages of this speech constitute the first part of the case, the *actio prima*, now the second item on the literary agenda of Cicero's case against Verres. After it was delivered in the forum before the presiding judge Glabrio and the extortion court composed exclusively of members of the Senatorial class, and in the presence of Hortensius and Verres, the defense threw in the case, realizing that Cicero's charges and the evidence supporting them could never be refuted. Verres went into exile at Marseilles, where he remained for the rest of his life, and a fine was imposed on him amounting to two or perhaps two and a half times the amount of his extortions.

There are five more speeches in this body of work, the ones that Cicero wrote for publication, which constitute the second part of the case, or *actio secunda,* and it is the fourth in this series which I have translated, *De Signis,* "Concerning the Statues," which deals principally with Verres' theft of works of art from temples and private homes in Sicily. Like the others, it evokes the scene of the court in session as if the trial were still in progress. Cicero addresses Verres in person by name or by a barrage of epithets; one of the recurrent devices Cicero uses to create the effect of an immediate and dramatic presence is to point to the defendant by means of the snarling demonstrative pronoun, "iste," "that man over there"; "the person in question"—when Cicero hissed it—"that rat" —when Cicero growled and spat it out. The noun *verres* in Latin also means wild boar, and Cicero is willing to remind his hearers that the person in question is a swine, piggish in his self-interests, and mud-caked in his habits as well as boorish in his tastes. Cicero's attacks are so flamboyant, his style of prosecution so concentrated, and the fire he trains on Verres' atrocious behavior so withering that we are at times appalled beyond belief. We wonder whether, if reading *De Signis* is an education in itself, it is not that form of education which has been defined as "casting false pearls before real swine." Still, to read the oration through from beginning to end is to see that Cicero had a genuine and important case to present, and that in several different ways his decision to accept the Sicilians' suit against Verres meant seizing an opportunity to wage a war of words in defense of social justice, political responsibility, and the rights of Roman citizens and of Roman subjects.

For one thing, the Senate itself was on trial in an action like this extortion case. A decade earlier, Sulla had placed this permanent court for cases of extortion exclusively in the hands of members of the Senate, who compose the "gentlemen of the jury" sitting as judges here whom Cicero addresses. But Cicero, like Pompey and Crassus, the consuls of the year, although by now a Senator himself, was sympathetic toward the Equestrian Order, whose members had so far been excluded from this court and from other positions of power. Cicero throughout his life took a consistent and lively interest in the struggle between the nobility and the "businessmen" who, like himself, did not trace their ancestry to aristocratic origins, but who undertook active careers in the Roman state and who wanted to serve the state and have a voice in its policies. It is significant that later in this same year a law was passed requiring the Senate to share the membership in the extortion court with the knights, and with another group from a non-noble order.

Ever since Rome had begun to acquire provinces—and Cicero reminds us that Sicily was the first, the most strategic, and the most productive in natural resources and revenue—the opportunity for a Roman governor going out to administer the province as propraetor, to amass a fortune at the expense of the inhabitants, had been a notorious political temptation. If a consul, after his year's term in the nation's highest office, could embark on a lucrative tour of duty as a provincial governor, a lesser magistrate like Verres, should such an appointment fall to him, might also turn the business to good advantage. Were he called to account for his actions, the official might count on the court as one monopolized by Senators, members of his own class, to be lenient; and he could also buy his way out. Verres had built up an enormous fortune by extorting money and treasure from Sicily, amounting in fact to a long-range social security program for himself in the form of three fortunes: "putting the proceeds of the first year into his own pocket, handing over the second year's to his advocates and supporters, and reserving the third year's, the fattest and richest of all, wholly for the jury" (*Actio prima*, 14.20).

If the Roman rule and its expanding empire became the kind of tyranny Verres' praetorship demonstrated, it would end by provoking fear, hatred, and resistance, instead of respect and cooperation. If the courts of justice were weak and the juries and judge venal, the vaunted Roman ability to advance law and order and promote social justice would be thoroughly undermined. If the provinces were chaotically plundered, they would become a liability, rather than an asset, to the Roman state and its needs for income and material resources. If a few individuals grew enormously rich by impoverishing multitudes, the economic realities of political injustice would end by pitting the poor against the rich. If the aristocracy fell down in their duty, conscientious citizens,[1] from the ranks of the Equestrian Order or elsewhere, would of necessity lead the fight against dishonest administration, and if Rome were to maintain and justify her power, they would have to win the fight.

In all the Verrine orations these issues are at stake, and Cicero recurs to them throughout each of the separate parts of the elaborate case he prepared. The Fourth Speech of the Second Action, which I have translated here, is somewhat lighter and more varied than the others, because of the subject matter, and because Cicero often adopts a more relaxed tone than the furious intensity which is heard almost exclusively in the other speeches. He ridicules Verres' pretensions, and the horrible examples paraded before our ears have to do, after all, with things rather than people, in good part. It is as if Cicero knows that we could hardly believe our ears when we learn, as he has learned, how foolish and grotesque a creature the nobles have inadvertently unleashed on the provinces.

The oration, like the others, takes a main subject for presentation, as reflected in the title editors have given it, *De Signis (Concerning the Statues)*, or, the works of art stolen by Verres from temples and homes in Sicily. Around this main charge are developed many specifications, and the whole account is divided into sections, where separate cities, regions, and persons Verres robbed are dealt with. The speech is filled with episodes and incidents, and a vast array of details showing what form Verres' compulsion to have these art treasures took at various times and places. Cicero seems to be narrating a kind of epic, the saga of an unscrupulous "counter-hero," the corrupt Roman governor, compulsively bent on looting the province he was sent to safeguard. The malign genius of Verres is also seen in some of its melodramatic aspects, by means of the dialogues and scenes wherein we watch him at work overruling the wishes of his subjects and in the very act of taking their possessions from them. As Cicero's investigations had proved to furnish him with a nearly incredible detective story, so his rhetorical re-enactment of the material provides us with many dramatic moments when a thief is caught in the act. Many of the descriptive details,

---

[1] For instance, in Chapter 70 of the fifth oration against Verres, Cicero writes: *non idem licet mihi quod iis qui nobili genere nati sunt, quibus omnia populi Romani beneficia dormientibus deferuntur.* (I am not quite in the position of those born of a noble family—on them are showered all the honors of the Roman people even when they are asleep.)

moreover, drive home the force of the main charge far better
than logical summation could. From Cicero's words we get
an actual picture of Verres wrapped in his dark tunic and
dark praetorian cloak sitting for hours on end in his manu-
factory at Syracuse while his hired and impressed goldsmiths
melt down and recast the silver plate stolen from Sicilian
householders. We weigh the evidence in terms of the un-
forgettably huge transport vessel that Verres had constructed
at Messana, for the sole purpose of carrying back to Rome
the bulky cargo of valuables he had acquired over the three-
year period of his praetorship. We measure the ingenious
cruelty of the defendant in terms of the sight of the innocent
Sopater lashed naked astride the bronze equestrian statue of
the great benefactor of the Sicilians, Marcellus, in the freezing
winter rain, for resisting the governor's will. And, as Cicero
narrates the many different episodes in the saga of the stealing
of the statues of the gods, we sense that, just as the Sicilians
seemed to feel when they reported these events to Cicero,
it is the gods themselves, not mere works of art, that are
being trundled off, and persecution of spirit that is taking
place. We are brought into the presence of melancholy and
tragic blasphemy, and confronted with a man Juvenal was to
refer to nearly two centuries later as "*sacrilegus Verres*."

Cicero has also given the subject of this oration a clever
turn that rescues it from the mere annals-of-crime category
of a famous case involving theft of works of art. Like the
other speeches comprising the *actio secunda*, this one is a
way of informing us about Verres' art of theft. In the others,
we are told, successively, about Verres' greedy exploitations,
first in his tenure of the quaestorship and of the praetorship
of the city, before his appointment in Sicily; then about the
way he stole or expropriated money by confiscating legacies
in Sicily, and, in general, about his way of ruining a province
he was meant to be running—using the role of judge to decide
damages in his own favor, for example. In the third speech,
Verres' art of stealing the taxes the Sicilians were required
to pay Rome is discussed in great detail; in the fourth, the
statuary. In the fifth, his art of stealing the rights of Roman
citizens, and subjecting them to appalling punishments, is
brought out as a kind of climax, *De Suppliciis (Concerning
the Torments)*—which also would be an apt title for the
whole effect of Verres' twisted art of administering a province by theft and bringing to it not justice but *supplicium:*
torture, torment.

Unique interest in this oration is generated by its many

references to famous works of art. Cicero pretends to be only moderately informed on the subject and possessed of only average taste. But as we know from his own references in his letters to his collection of works of art, and can easily judge from the breadth of his interest in everything that concerns literature, art, and philosophy, he was a keen æsthetician. The fourth oration is, itself, a catalogue of masterpieces, many of them quite fully described, and all of them dealt with with an art-historian's care for identification and attribution. Despite Cicero's self-deprecation about his knowledge, the ironic stroke that puts Verres to the most disadvantage is the revelation of his foolish ignorance of art. He had the ingenuity to employ two art experts to help advise him on what to steal, but they could deceive him at will if they needed ready cash. Verres' blindspot is that he was incapable of imagining that art was priceless. To him, it was only something to be invested in and to be invested with—for he realized how much he could impress others by owning it. He failed utterly to grasp the possibility that it might be valued for itself, and this was his ultimate undoing, for the Sicilians were stung to reprisals by his arrogant seizure of what they treasured in their hearts. So Cicero's story that begins in a private chapel in Messana with the theft of things both beautiful and sacred and ends in the populous capital of Syracuse with acts of grosser sacrilege tells of the Nemesis of art taking revenge upon its hypocritical worshiper.

The aftermath of Cicero's case against Verres can be swiftly told. Twenty years later, at the age of fifty-one, Cicero was appointed proconsul of Cilicia and governed his province with a justice and efficiency that has been unanimously acclaimed. In 43 B.C., the year that Cicero was assassinated by hired killers under orders from Antony, Verres was killed by agents of Antony at Marseilles in a quarrel over a statue they were sent to take from his possession.[2]

---

[2] Verres took with him into exile at Marseilles some of the works of art he had collected while in office. There was a story that Antony had put Verres' name on the proscription list because he would not hand over to him his Corinthian vessels (Pliny, *Hist. Nat.* 34 .2; Seneca, *Suasor.* 6). It is hard to see why otherwise Antony would have singled out the former governor of Sicily as a proscribed enemy. The story also says that Verres died bravely, and had already heard of the death of Cicero, on December 7 of the same year.

Part Two of the Action Against Verres

SECTION IV   THE ART TREASURES STOLEN BY VERRES
(DE SIGNIS)

1 [3]   I come now to what Verres calls his "consum-
ing interest in art," what a sympathetic friend of
his might describe as his weakness and aberration, and
the Sicilians call highway robbery. I am not sure what
name to attach to it, so let me merely lay the case before you to judge on its own terms rather than by its
name. Familiarize yourselves with the type of thing it
is, gentlemen of the jury,[4] and you will probably have
little difficulty in applying the appropriate name to it.
I simply state that there was not in all of Sicily, this
wealthy and ancient province with its many towns and
many prosperous families, a single silver vase, a Corinthian or Delian jar, a jewel or a precious stone, a
single statue, bronze, marble, or ivory, that Verres did
not inquire into, personally inspect, and if it appealed
to him, steal. Perhaps that sounds like rather a large
claim; but hear what I have to say. It is not in order
to add more words to the subject, or to emphasize the
enormity of his malefactions, that I include everything.
When I say that he left nothing whatsoever of this sort
of material in the entire province, I want you to realize
that I am speaking plain Latin, not the technical language of an attorney. To put it even more plainly: he
left not a single thing that happened to come to his
attention or fall under his eyes, in any public place or
any private residence, in sacred shrines, in the personal
possession of a Sicilian or or a Roman citizen, nothing
private or public, sacred or secular, in all of Sicily.

What better place to begin, than with that city
which was united to you by affectionate cultural ties?
Which should I choose, rather than the one that has

---

[3] The numbers in the margin refer to the corresponding pages
of the Latin text.
    [4] *iudices:* "Gentlemen of the jury" is the traditional way to
translate this word, which literally means both "judge" and "jury-
man."

found so many admirers among you? Then, it will be
easier to perceive what you, Verres, stand for in the
eyes of those who detest and charge and prosecute you,
after you have been exposed as a person who robbed
your good Mamertine citizens in your perverse, methodical way. As all who have visited Messana can
readily acknowledge, Gaius Heius is a Mamertine citi-   2
zen, an accomplished man, and a leader in the community in all things. His residence is, if not the best
house in Messana, certainly the best known to us
Roman citizens, to whom its hospitable doors stand
ever open. Before Verres arrived in the city, this
residence was so magnificently furnished as to be a
handsome embellishment of the city. Messana itself,
beautifully situated, and graced with fine walls and a
commanding harbor, was of course left quite empty
and bare of the works of art that struck Verres' fancy.
In Heius' house, there was a private chapel, which had
been carefully kept up by one generation of the family
after another in reverent care. It contained four su-
premely beautiful statues of excellent workmanship,
which any of us idiots (as Verres would call us) might
appreciate as readily as that gifted and shrewd connoisseur himself. One was a marble Cupid from Praxiteles' hand. (In the course of investigating Verres'
crimes, I have became only too familiar with the names
of these artists.) The same sculptor, I believe, executed
the Cupid carved in a similar style which is now at
Thespiae, and which, in fact, constitutes the sole reason
for visiting Thespiae.⁵ There seems to be no other good
reason for going to that particular town in Boeotia. Our
great general Mummius, when taking away from the
Thespians art treasures housed in the temple of Felicity,
and some other secular statues in the town, did not
touch this marble Cupid, most sacred to the Thespians.
   But to return to the private chapel in Heius' home   3

⁵ The Cupid of Thespiae was donated to the city by Phryne, the
mistress of Praxiteles (fl. 340 B.C.); there was also a statue of
her there. The emperor Caligula (37–41 A.D.) was the first to
remove the statue of Cupid from Thespiae. Claudius (41–54) gave
it back, but Nero (54–68) carried it off again. It was apparently
destroyed at Rome in a fire in the time of Titus (79–81). The
Thespians still clung to their divinity, after a fashion, for Meno-
dorus, an Athenian, made them a copy of Praxiteles' statue. This
figure was seen by Pausanias on his journeys in the second century A.D.

where, as I say, the marble Cupid was: across the room, there was an excellent bronze Hercules, said to be the work of Myron,[6] and certainly similar in style to his. Before these gods were small altars which would signify to anyone the religious character of the sanctuary. Also in the chapel were two bronze statues of a pair of maidens known as the *"Canephorae,"*[7] or Basket-Bearers, supporting sacred objects on their heads with upraised arms, like the maidens of the porch of the Erechtheum in Athens.[8] Who was the artist of these authentic antique bronze Canephorae? Who was it again? Yes, indeed, that's quite right; they were said to be the work of Polyclitus.[9] Whenever a Roman arrived in Messana he made a pilgrimage first off to these figures, which were on view daily for all visitors to see, and Heius' house became a showpiece of the city as much as a proud possession of its owner. Gaius Claudius, whose tenure of the aedileship we remember as having been marked by expensive and impressive exhibitions, made prolonged use of the loan of the Cupid to enhance, for the sake of the immortal gods and the Roman people, our own forum. As a guest of the Heius family and as a patron of the Mamertine

---

6 Myron was one of the great sculptors of Athens' fifth century; his most famous work (which we know only through Roman copies) is the *Diskobolos* (the "Discus Thrower"), c. 460–50 B.C.

7 The "Canephorae," in real life, also walked in ritual processions. It was on such a day, Ovid writes in *The Metamorphoses,* that Mercury saw them, and fell instantly in love with Herse:

> *Illa forte die castae de more puellae*
> *Vertice subposito festas in Palladis arces*
> *Pura coronatis portabant sacra canistris.*
> (II. 711–13)

. . . It was the holiday
That feasted Pallas when her girls walked out
Bearing their secret gifts in flowered caskets,
Head-high, to fill her temple with their treasures; . . .
(Translated by Horace Gregory,
Ovid: The Metamorphoses. New York:
New American Library, Inc., 1960.)

8 Temple on the Acropolis, built c. 420–06 B.C. One of its porches has karyatids, maidens acting as columns, supporting the roof structure on their heads.

9 Polyclitus of Argos was another renowned Greek sculptor of the fifth century. His two most famous works (surviving only in Roman copies) are the *Doryphoros* (the "Lance-Bearer") and the *Diadoumenos* (the "Youth Binding a Fillet Round His Head").

people, he availed himself of the privilege of borrowing the statue and was careful to return it to its owners. And more recently, aristocrats of this sort, gentlemen of the jury—but why should I say even "recently," when we have seen them among us here and now during the days just preceding this trial?—have contributed largely to the elegance of our forum and public buildings, not indeed by means of loot stolen from the provinces, but by the treasures bestowed on them by their friends, and the gifts showered on them by their hosts, not things purloined by criminal no-goods. Characteristically, they have restored the statues and objects of art to their owners; such materials were not spirited away from the cities of our friends and allies to their own homes on the pretext of a four-day festival ordained by the ædiles. All the statues I have been speaking of, gentlemen, Verres absconded with from Heius' private chapel. Not a one did he leave in place, I remind you; nor anything else, for that matter, except a very old wooden effigy of, I believe, the Goddess of Good Fortune. He preferred not to harbor that in his own house.

By the faith of gods and men, what have we here? *4* What motive underlies this brazen behavior of his? No one ever came to Messana without going to visit the statues I refer to before you, Verres, made them invisible. As many Roman praetors and consulars as visited Sicily in peacetime, or again as many as in war, and as many men of every sort and condition (not even mentioning those good and true persons impelled by respect for religion), so many of them, so greedy for gain, so unscrupulous, so audacious as they were—not one of them thought himself so high and mighty as to ask for, to take, or to touch anything in that chapel. And so, I suppose Verres will just make off with whatever beautiful object he may happen to come across anywhere? Will he let no one else have anything? Will his one house include so many other wealthy homes? And did none of his predecessors lay hands on these things, expressly in order that Verres might have the privilege of stealing them? Gaius Claudius Pulcher[10] returned the works he had taken on loan for his exhibition, just so that Verres might proceed to steal them?

[10] Gaius Claudius Pulcher, aedile in 99 B.C., was the first, according to Pliny, who ornamented the stage scene with paintings.

But that figure of Cupid was not in the least interested in being housed with a pimp and in a residence that was definitely more a house than a home. Cupid was perfectly content where he was, in his ancestral sanctuary. He knew perfectly well he had been passed on to Heius by his forefathers as a sacred legacy. He had no intention of asking to be the heir of a whore.

But why do I inveigh against him in such bitter language, when I am sure to be refuted by one simple phrase? "I bought it," states Verres. Immortal gods, what an admirable defense! What we sent to the province, then, was a buyer, a merchant decked out in the imperial insignia and carrying the axes of power, to purchase all this art work, statuary, painting, silver and gold, ivory, jewels, and leave nothing for anyone else! Clearly this is meant to be his defense against everything: he bought it. First, then, if, as you wish, I may grant that you bought it all, inasmuch as you have adopted this sole excuse, let me just ask what kind of courts of justice you think we have at Rome? You don't seriously think that it would be permitted to you, in your praetorial powers and imperial authority, to purchase so many extremely valuable objects, indeed, everything that was of any value, in the whole province?

5   Notice, gentlemen, the scrupulous concern of our ancestors, even though they did not anticipate anything of quite this sort, in foreseeing some possibilities of venality. They thought that no one setting out for a province, invested with ambassadorial or imperial powers, would be so mindless as to buy silver plate (it was furnished to him at public expense), or clothing (which was furnished to him by law). They did think he might buy slaves; we all use them and they are not supplied to us at public expense. And so *they ruled against such purchases except to replace a dead one.* And suppose the servant had died here at Rome? No, it would not then be legal to replace him by a slave bought abroad; only if he had died in the place where his master was.[11] For they did not intend for you, Verres, to outfit a home for yourself in the province, but rather, to furnish your services, as it were, to the province you were

11 Athenaeus tells a story of Scipio Africanus taking only five slaves with him when he went abroad on a public mission; one of these having died, he wrote to his friends to buy another and send the replacement to him.

supposed to govern. And what was their principal motive in legislating so precisely against our purchasing powers in the provinces? They knew that it would constitute purloining rather than purchasing, that it would be more of a theft than a sale, if the seller was not allowed to sell just as he wanted. They knew that, if some official in the provinces invested with imperial authority wanted to buy an object he saw in someone's house or shop and were permitted to do so, he could get it at whatever price he wished, whether the thing were for sale or not.

Someone may now object: "You mustn't treat Verres this way. You shouldn't investigate his acts in terms of our ancient and traditional principles. Grant him the point that he made purchases and complaints were not made about it, that he bought so methodically as not to force an unwilling buyer to sell because of his official position, that he bought nothing under pressure." All right, I will so proceed. Let us suppose that Heius had something to vend: if he received the price he was asking for it, I will desist from asking why you bought it.

How, then, shall we proceed? Do we introduce **6** the usual arguments in a case of this kind? I suppose we must inquire as to whether Heius was, in fact, in debt, and had held an auction. And, if he did so, whether he was in such dire financial straits and immediate need, so hard pressed for money as to strip his ancestral sanctuary and make merchandise of his ancestral gods. However, I observe that the gentleman in question did not hold an auction; he sold nothing except the produce of his farms. He was not in debt; in fact, he had a considerable amount of cash out on loans that could always be called in. And even if the situation were the opposite of what I state it was, he would still not have sold precious treasures that had been in his family for so many years and reposed in his ancestral sanctuary.

Could he, perhaps, have been persuaded to do so because of the large sum of money involved? It is, of course, unlikely that a wealthy and upright man like Heius would put consideration of money above the claims of piety made upon him by the monuments of his forebears. Let us see how much money was actually involved that might induce Heius, a wealthy man and exempt from all traces of greed, to go against his normal human inclination to be conscientious and reverent. No doubt, Verres, you told him to record the transaction as follows:

ALL THESE STATUES[12] BY PRAXITELES, MYRON, POLYCLITUS SOLD TO VERRES FOR 6500 SESTERCES[13]

And he duly entered that item on his accounts. Will the clerk of the court please read it aloud? (Pause.) Thank you. How gratifying! I hear the names of these famous artists, which most men raise to the skies, and am delighted to think that they have fallen so low in the estimate of Verres. A Cupid of Praxiteles for 1600 sesterces![14] Surely, this is the origin of the proverb, "I had rather buy it than beg for it."

7   Now someone may ask, "But do you really rate it at so high a price?" Well, I am not setting a price according to my own methods or experience in these matters; I think it must be looked at to see what the value is in the opinion of those well versed in art, and in terms of how much such works usually sell for, what price they would fetch if sold legally and openly, and then in terms of the value Verres himself attaches to it. Had he thought the Cupid actually worth only 400 denarii,[15] he would not have incurred the danger of inviting so much criticism and vituperation as has come his way because of it. And who of you after all does not realize the value usually placed on these fine objects? We see a bronze statue at an auction knocked down for some 40,000 sesterces. If I wanted to name the names of men who have paid this kind of price or a higher one, could I not easily do so? The main limitations on the price of such objects are the limits to one's cupidity for them. If you mean to put a ceiling on the price you must put some limit to your desire for the thing. And so I can observe that Heius did not, either of his own free will, or because of financial diffi-

12 The general word for sculpture of any kind, including busts and reliefs, is *signum*. The word *statua* is used for a figure that is cast, or worked with the chisel, of the complete human form, life-size, or larger.
13 Roughly $320 (sesterce = five cents); in other words, a ridiculously small sum.
14 Roughly $80.
15 400 denarii = 1600 sesterces.

culties, or because of an irresistible price, feel induced to sell these statues. Rather what happened was that by your pretense of purchasing, through the application of force and fear, and by flaunting your official authority, you simply wrenched them and stole them away from a man who, with so many of his friends and associates, was committed by the Roman people not only into your power, but into your safekeeping.

And what, gentlemen, could more suit my wishes in this prosecution, than to have Heius himself assert the same things that I have been enumerating? Nothing, naturally. But I imagine we ought not to wish for so difficult an eventuality. Heius is a Mamertine citizen. The city of Messana stands alone by virtue of having offered a public panegyric to Verres. Among all the other citizens of Sicily, Verres is an object of loathing; only to the citizens of Messana has he been the subject of some praise. And Heius is, of course, the principal spokesman in the delegation sent here to vouch for Verres, the others being also eminent Mamertine citizens. While under official instructions, he will hardly air his personal grievances. Although I realized that fact perfectly well, gentlemen, I still went ahead with my case and brought Heius into the first hearing; and did that, moreover, without inviting any danger, for what answer could Heius make, even if he turned out to be unlike himself, a dishonest person? Could he have said that the statues in question were all safe at home, his home, that is, not Verres'? If some depraved, stupid, careless creature were committing perjury, he might say that he had the objects for sale and had sold them at the desired price. But the most respected man in the city, concerned that you have the true impression of his good character and reliability, said, first, that he spoke in commendation of Verres because he had been so instructed by the officials of the city council to do so. Next, he testified that he had not had these objects on sale in any way, shape, or manner, and that, had he been allowed to follow his own wishes, he could never have been persuaded by any means whatsoever to sell the things in his chapel which he had inherited as a legacy from his forefathers.

Well, why do you sit there, Verres? What are you waiting for? What can you say, surrounded as you are and hemmed in by citizens from Centuripa, Catina, 8

Halaesina, Tyndaris, Henna, Agyrium, and the other cities of Sicily? Messana, which you liked to call your other homeland, your Messana, I say, has also surrounded you, the accomplice of your crimes, the witness of your lusts, the receiver of your stolen goods. An irreproachable man from that city has been sent here, as a delegate from his home, to appear at this trial at the head of the delegation sent to commend you publicly. Those are his orders and his instructions. Although, gentlemen of the jury, you, of course, recall what he said when he was asked about the large freighter:[16] that it had been built at public expense, that a Mamertine Senator had been put in charge of its construction, by authority of the city. As a private citizen, Heius takes refuge among you, gentlemen of the jury, and relies on the process of law, that great citadel for our allies, by which this court is established and conducted. Although there is a law against extortion, he is not suing to reclaim the money, which, even though it has been extorted from him, he is not greatly concerned over. What he does demand from you is the return of his ancestral gods. Have you no shame, Verres? No respect, no conscience? You lived in the home of Heius, you saw him daily performing the ritual duties to the gods in the chapel. He is not worried about the money invested in the acquisition of such treasure, and is not seeking to reclaim it. You may keep the Canephorae if you wish: only restore to Heius his household deities. And because he spoke of this, because after a moderate length of time, as an ally and friend of the Roman people, he voiced his complaints to you in a mild way, because he was utterly scrupu-

---

16 Juvenal classes *sacrilegus* Verres with Antonius and Dolabella as notorious for carrying off in their ships more spoils in time of peace than generals after a conquest:

                                                    (VIII. 105–7)

   inde Dolabella atque hinc Antonius, inde
   sacrilegus Verres referebant navibus altis
   occulta spolia et plures de pace triumphos.

. . . But later there was Dolabella, and next
Antonius, then sacrilegious Verres to load the decks
Of huge freighters with smuggled spoils—more trophies of
   peace
Than of war . . .

                         (Translated by Hubert Creekmore, *The*
                         Satires of Juvenal. New York: New
                         American Library, 1963.)

lous in his religious concern, not only when asking to have his fathers' gods back, but also when giving testimony under oath, I would have you know this: one of the representatives from Messana has been sent back to the city, the very man who was put in charge of the construction of the freighter at public expense, to request the Senate that Heius be ignominiously punished.

You madman, what could you have been thinking 9 of? Gaining your goofy goal? Were you completely unaware of the great respect his fellow citizens have for Heius, of the influence he wields? But let's assume that you did succeed somehow, let's assume that the Mamertines did bring some serious charge against Heius: what value would lie in a commendation from people who imposed a penalty on a man who always spoke the truth when he gave evidence? Is it, in fact, praise, at all, when the one asked to furnish it must do wrong? Well? Are not any who praise you actually my witnesses, rather than yours? Heius has offered the panegyric, and, apparently, he has thereby committed a grave error. I will produce others who will be seen to refrain freely from speaking insofar as they can, and to speak begrudgingly when they must. And will they deny that this huge freighter was constructed at Messana? Let them, if they can. Will they deny that a Mamertine Senator was officially appointed to supervise this project? Would that they could! There are some other matters, too, which I prefer to hold in reserve, so that my opponents will have as little time as possible to react to them and swear to their falsity. Will this praise then be placed on the credit side of your ledger? Will these men come to your aid with their great influence, who could neither help you if they wanted to, nor ought to if they wished? They are men on whom, as private individuals, you have heaped many wrongs and slanders, and in whose city you have completely disgraced many a family forever by your infamous evil habits of debauchery. You maintain that you have rendered them many public services—not, however, without great damage to the state and the province of Sicily. They were supposed to supply the Roman people, and used to, with 15,000 bushels of wheat; by your arbitrary ruling, they were relieved of that obligation. And so our state was wronged, because you decreed for one city that our rights need not be respected. And,

of course, all of Sicily was also hit hard by your ruling, because the quantity in question was not deducted
from the total amount the province was obliged to furnish, but, in fact, only transferred to the cities of
Centuripa and Halesa, whose people had been exempt
from that required duty. They then had to carry a
heavier burden than they could. Also, in accordance
with our treaty, it was your duty to supply a ship. But
you waived that necessity for three years. And, during
those years, you never asked for one soldier. You dealt
with the situation as pirates will, who—despite being
the declared enemies of civilized men—select some
favorites, and, not only let them off, but even shower
them with loot, especially the people who possess a
conveniently located town where they can frequently,
and at times necessarily, lay to with their ships.

10   The Asian city of Phaselis, which Servilius[17] took,
had not previously been a haunt of Cilician pirates; the
Lycians, a Greek people, inhabited it. But it was located
so prominently on the seacoast that the pirate bands
sailing from Cilicia inevitably skirted it on their way
out to sea, and, on their return, were likewise borne
back in upon it. So, the pirates formed ties with the
town, at first by trading there, and then by making
partners of the townspeople in the disposing of their
stolen goods. Neither was the city of the Mamertines
previously a place with a dubious reputation. A city
that impounded the baggage of our consul, Gaius
Cato,[18] was indeed unfriendly to outlaws. For Cato was
an irreproachable and powerful person, and, even
though a man of consular rank, was sentenced to pay
a fine—the great Cato, a descendant of two most-dis-
tinguished men, L. Paulus and M. Cato, and the son
of Scipio Africanus' sister. The damages he was required to pay amounted to 18,000 sesterces. The
Mamertines were enraged at this man,[19] they who often
spent more money than the sum fixed for the settlement of the suit against Cato, on a banquet for Timar-

---

[17] Publius Servilius Vatia fought successfully against the Med-
iterranean pirates in 78–76 B.C. No doubt referred to by Cicero
because Servilius was one of the *iudices* present.

[18] Gaius Cato, a grandson of the Censor. After being consul in
114, he was appointed proconsul for the province of Macedonia;
he received money improperly there and was tried, convicted, and
fined.

[19] I.e., Cato.

chides.[20] But Messana, this austere city of the Mamertines, became the Phaselis of that predatory Sicilian pirate, Verres. Everything he swiped from different places was carted off to Messana and left there for safekeeping. What needed to be kept out of sight his accomplices among the townspeople hid away, and, by their help, he could manage to have the things he wanted stockpiled in secret and then shipped out unobtrusively. Finally, he had a huge freighter built and outfitted by the Mamertines, to be sent to Italy laden with his stolen goods. In return for such services, he exempted the citizens from military service, from supplying labor, and from paying taxes for a period of three years. For these three years, then, they were the only people not merely in Sicily, but, I would say, in all the world, to be free and without obligations, released and excused from taxes, trouble, and tribute. This, no doubt, accounts for those typically Verrine diversions, such as occurred, for instance, at the banquet when Verres ordered Sextus Cominius to be dragged in by the feet, and tried to hurl a goblet at him. Verres then ordered Cominius to be taken by the neck, dragged away from the party, and bundled off into irons. This was the origin, also, of the cross on which he raised a Roman citizen in full view of a host of onlookers. He would never have dared do this anywhere, except among those people with whom he had entered into partnership for carrying out his robberies and crimes.

And even so, do you citizens of Messana come to praise someone? And by what authority—one you exercise over the Senate, or over the Roman people? **11**

Is there a city, not only in our own provinces, but in the remotest regions, so powerful or so free, so vast and barbaric, or is there a king in existence anywhere who would not cordially receive a Senator of the Roman people under his roof and into his home? It is considered an honor to do so, not only for the person in question but also, first and foremost, for the Roman people, by whose grace we have arrived at this senatorial order, and next, for the influence of the order itself: were the Senate not to carry great prestige among our allies and among foreign nations, where would the influence of our imperial name be? But the Mamertines

20 A freedman of Verres, and his henchman.

refrained from extending me any kind of official welcome. To say "me" is not significant; but not to receive a Senator of the Roman people is to deny respect, not to the man, but to the order. The lavish and spacious dwelling of Gnaeus Pompeius Basiliscus opened wide its doors to Tullius himself, where I, of course, would have stayed, even had I been offered your hospitality. And there was the house of the Percennii, a most praiseworthy family, also now called by the name of Pompeius, where my cousin Lucius stayed at their eager invitation. But so far as you citizens of Messana were concerned, the Senator of the Roman people might just as well have spent the night in the street. No other city ever acted like that. "But you were bringing a friend of ours up for trial." Will you then interpret my professional activities as a private citizen so as to lower my status as a Senator? Well, I can lodge this complaint against you, should you ever want to bring in an action on your own behalf before that order, an order which you alone seem to hold in contempt. Furthermore, what kind of an image do you think you present in the eyes of the Roman people? Why did you not tear down that cross, wet with the blood of a Roman citizen, and standing at the harbor of your city, cast it into the deep, and purify the whole area before approaching Rome, before coming into the presence of this body? A monument to Verres' atrocity was erected on the allied and peaceful soil of the Mamertines. Was your city specially selected, the first one visitors to Sicily see, so that they might behold the cross of a Roman citizen[21] before they could see anyone disposed to friendship with the Roman people? Are you in the habit of showing it to the people of Regium,[22] whose city you are jealous of, and likewise of indicating to your own townspeople just how much they have to lose by joining forces with you and how they ought to scorn you? Is that why you let them see that justice in your city is dealt out by means of that instrument of torture?

[21] The man crucified was one P. Gavius of Cosa in Samnium, in northeastern Italy. Verres imprisoned him in the Syracusan quarries, but he escaped to Messana where he publicly protested his Roman citizenship. He was crucified at Messana behind the city. Later Verres ordered he be moved to the sea front.

[22] Regium faced Messana across the narrow channel between Sicily and southeast Italy, now the Straits of Messina.

And now, what have you to say about a different item on the agenda? Well? Do you know of the Attalic cloth,[23] the tapestry known throughout Sicily as the possession of Heius? Did you happen to forget to buy that item? You could have done so in the same way you did for the statues. Or did you not save the accounts? Ah, here is something the madman overlooked: he thought it would be less obvious if something were missing from the armoire where household stores were kept, than if it were missing from the chapel. But how did you make off with these goods? I cannot tell the story more plainly than Heius has. When I questioned him as to whether anything else among his goods had ended up at Verres' place, he said that Verres had sent him a message to convey the tapestry to him at Agrigentum. I then asked whether he had sent it or not. He answered that he had done the required thing when he heard the word of the praetor, and had sent the material. I asked about the condition in which it had been returned. Heius said that as yet it hadn't been. Ah, the statement produces some laughter among the people present at the hearing, and all are astonished at your deeds. Did it never enter your head, Verres, to have it put on record that he had sold you this cloth for 6,500 sesterces? Were you afraid that your debts would grow too large if those 6,500 sesterces were credited to you for material you could easily sell for 200,000? That is the value, believe me. And then you would have enough cash to meet the costs of your defense, and no one would ask how much was involved in the transaction; if only you could say that you bought it, you could readily enough defend your case and your acts to anyone you wished. But, as it is, you now have no means of disentangling yourself from this expensive cloth.

And here is another item. Are you prepared to say whether you bought, or simply confiscated, from Phylarchus of Centuripa, the wealthy aristocrat, those beautifully decorated breastplates which are said to have once belonged to King Hiero?[24] When I was in

---

23 *Attalica peripetasmata* were draperies embroidered with gold which one of the Attali rulers of Pergamum introduced, or, encouraged the manufacture of. This "cloth of gold" was used to cover banquet couches.

24 Hiero the younger, son of Hierocles, king of Syracuse from 270 to 216 B.C.

Sicily, I heard the story one way from the Centuripans,
another way from others, and it was far from clear just
what did happen. They were saying that you had confiscated these metal trappings from Phylarchus of
Centuripa, just as you had also done with other fine
things from Aristus of Panhormus, and, as a third
instance, from Cratippus of Tyndaris. For even if
Phylarchus had sold them, you did not, as you had
promised you would, return them, after you became
the defendant in this case. But, because you saw that
many people knew about the incident, you thought
that if you gave them back he would have less respect
for you, and the theft itself would be just as liable to
be used against you in evidence. So you failed to return the stuff. When he was on the stand, Phylarchus
said that he had known about your "weakness" (as your
friends like to call it) and had tried to conceal the
breastplates from you. When he was summoned, he
told you he did not have them, but that they had been
left with another person, that they might not be found.
So shrewd was Verres' instinct, however, that he could
see right through the person who was keeping them to
where the things themselves were hidden. Then, Phylarchus could not deny that he had been found out, and
the metal trappings were acquired from their owner
against his wishes and without any payment.

13   Now, gentlemen of the jury, it will be worth your
while to notice the method Verres has developed for
finding all these precious objects and looking them over
carefully. There are two brothers from the town of
Cibyra, Tlepolemus and Hiero, one of them formerly
a modeller in wax, the other a painter. Both had run
away from home upon being suspected by their fellow
citizens of having robbed a shrine of Apollo, fearful
of facing the punishment that law and justice would
mete out to them. They had learned of Verres' interest
in their special knowledge when Verres came to Cibyra
(as you heard witnesses say earlier) with false promissory notes.

So, when they ran away, they hurried to him while
he was still in Asia. He took them in and made much
use of their talents, busy as he was, at that juncture,
pillaging and purloining on a large scale in his role as
official state envoy. These are the men referred to in

the account books of Q. Tadius,[25] who records that he "gave them to some Greek painters, at the order of Verres." Verres took the brothers with him to Sicily, by now well tried and tested in their work as art detectives. And after they arrived there, these "bloodhounds," or "hunting dogs," as you might call them, scented out all the treasures, with a remarkable instinct for finding anything there was to find. They would get wind of one valuable piece by threatening someone, of another by making promises, of another by terrorizing some slaves, of another by approaching some freedmen, of another by making use of a friend, of another by exploiting an enemy. Whatever caught their fancy was as good as gone. And people whose plate had been asked for had not a single thought in mind but to trust that it would not find favor in the eyes of Tlepolemus and Hiero.

And now, a further item for the agenda, gentlemen. I remember my friend Pamphilus of Lilybaeum, my host there, and a member of one of the leading families of the city, telling me that when Verres forcibly confiscated a hydria[26] he owned, massive and splendid in design, a prime example of the work of Boëthus,[27] Pamphilus returned home, downcast, seething in his heart, to think that such a hydria, handed down in his family from father to father, brought out on festive occasions to regale guests with—that such a hydria had simply been taken away from him. "I was sitting at home dejectedly," Pamphilus told me, "when, suddenly, one of his slaves of Venus[28] came running up, with an order for me to take my embossed drinking cups to the praetor at once. I was terribly upset," he went on, "for I had a matching pair. I ordered them both brought out, so that nothing else could appear as eligible for their acquisition list, and took them with me to the governor's residence. When I arrived, the governor was resting, but those brothers from Cibyra

14

---

25 A relative of Verres on his mother's side. No connection with P. Tadius, Verres' legate in Sicily.
26 A three-handled water jug, having one large handle on top for pouring, and two smaller ones further down, by which one lifted the hydria to place it on the head for carrying.
27 Boëthus of Carthage (fourth century B.C.) was a *caelator*, or worker in silver.
28 Verres used attendants of the temple of Venus Erycina as his public servants.

were strolling about, and when they saw me, they said,
'Where are your drinking cups, Pamphilus?' Sick at
heart, I held them out. They found nothing but praise
for them. But I started protesting that I would have
nothing of value left if those cups were taken from me,
and, when they noticed how upset I was, they asked,
'What will you give us to keep him from confiscating
them?' Well, they demanded 600 sesterces, and I said I
would pay it. Just then the governor bawled out from
inside the house to bring him those cups. The brothers
started telling the governor that they had thought, because they'd heard about them somewhere, that the
cups were worth something. But the information was
worthless, the whole business a mess, the item not
worthy of forming part of Verres' collection of silver.
He, in turn, said that that was just how it looked to
him, too." And so it was, that Pamphilus went back
home carrying his priceless cups. Well, even I, by
Hercules, before I learned the truth, even though I know
the matter is quite trivial, I used to admire Verres'
actual taste in matters of art, and this in a man who
had, I knew, nothing like a cultivated man's taste for
anything.

15   Then, for the first time, I realized that the brothers
from Cibyra were his eyes for detecting (and his
hands for stealing) art objects. So eager is he to
be thought a keen critic and shrewd connoisseur of art
and its value, however, that only the other day (note
the utter aberration of the man), having obtained a
three-day postponement of his trial, despite the fact
that he appeared to be a man already convicted and
condemned, early in the morning on the day of the
circus games, he went to the home of Lucius Sisenna,[29]
a prominent person in the city, where the festive board
was spread, and the silver plate set out on display.[30]
As befits his rank and dignity, Sisenna's residence was
thronged with leading citizens, and Verres went over to
the table and began studying the silver intently, looking

[29] Lucius Cornelius Sisenna, who was praetor in 78 B.C., was
known as an orator and a historian. He was a supporter of Verres.
[30] An *abacus* was a board, or slab of marble, or something of
the sort that would serve as a sideboard on which plate could be
arranged. Verres took all the plate just as it was laid out on the
abacus. In Chapter 59, there is a mention of "Delphic tables,"
mensas Delphicas, which were slabs of marble resting on some
kind of support that were also used as sideboards.

over each and every piece, eyeing the display at his leisure. The others present were astonished at such foolhardiness, the fact being that his standing accused of overweening avarice made this behavior all the more suspicious. Some of the guests were also taken aback at his sheer senselessness, wondering how such thoughts as he was indulging in could enter the mind of a man about to undergo trial in three days, and when so many witnesses had already spoken at the hearing. The servants of Sisenna who had heard about the testimony given against Verres did not take their eyes off him, or their fingers off the silver. Now, of course, it is the part of a wise judge to draw a large inference from small things, as regards the degree of continence or lust in a man. What defendant, even one enjoying a three-day stay of the proceedings—but, in fact, in most men's opinions, as good as convicted already—would not refrain from handling (and carefully inspecting, no less!) the silver plate in the thronged quarters of Sisenna's home? Well, this defendant could not and would not: and will anyone consider him, when he was the governor of a province, as being capable of restraining either his hands, or his desires for, the silver of the Sicilians?

But, to return to Lilybaeum after this digression in my speech, I want to mention a man there by the name of Diocles Popilius, the son-in-law of the Pamphilus whose hydria was stolen. Diocles had vases displayed on his sideboard: Verres went off with them all. He may, of course, claim that he bought them, and, in view of the rather large scale of this theft, I suppose some accounts may have been kept. He ordered Timarchides to make an estimate of the silver in the manner one would, if he were to make some trivial gift to an actor. And, even though I may have been somewhat in error for having joked at such length about your purchases, Verres, and in asking whether you bought this or that item, or not, and what you paid for it, I can settle this specification with a word. Show me the written account on which you have recorded the purchases of silver plate you made in the province of Sicily, and the place you got each piece, and the amount you paid for it. What has happened to the records? Perhaps, I ought not ask you for the accounts, but should have them now in my custody and so produce

16

them. You say, though, that you did not keep any records for these three years. But just furnish the one I am after, pertaining to the silver plate; I will see to the rest. "I have no written list and cannot show it to you." Well, then, what does that signify? What do you think these judges will infer from that? Even before your governorship began, your home was filled with extraordinarily beautiful statues; there were many pieces scattered among your villas, and many left with friends for safekeeping; many had been handed on to other people as gifts and donations. The accounts show that not one of these statues was bought. And now, the fact is that all the silver plate has been taken out of Sicily, with nothing left in the possession of any owner who wanted it to be his. The baseless defense is trumped up that the governor bought all that silver plate, but that alleged fact cannot be proved by means of any record of any transaction. If, on the records you can produce—however you may be keeping them, for there is no account, and, moreover, for the period during which you made the bulk of your "purchases," as you claim— you can show no account whatsoever of the transactions, do you not think it is obligatory that you be found guilty on the basis both of the records you can present and of those you cannot?

17   You took whatever you wanted from Marcus Coelius at Lilybaeum, a Roman Knight and an exemplary young man; you showed no hesitation in depriving Cacurius of all his furniture; and Cacurius was another fine person, energetic and alert, congenial, tried and true; as for Lutatius Diodorus, you carried off his very beautiful and grand cedarwood table,[31] this from a person on whom Roman citizenship had been conferred by Sulla, thanks to representations made on his behalf by Quintus Catulus, and you performed the feat in the clear sight of all the inhabitants of Lilybaeum. Of course, I have no objections to make to your having plundered and bilked of his goods another character who was the very image of yourself, Apollonius of Drepanum, the son of Nico, who now goes by the name

---

31 *Mensam citream*, i.e., a table of the wood of the *citrus*, probably a kind of cypress or cedar. Later Lucan, in the *Pharsalia*, expressed the mania for rare fruit and rare furniture by observing that, "We ransack the forests of the East not only for delicacies for our tables but also for tables for our delicacies."

of Aulus Clodius. You got all his silver, but I don't even care to mention the fact. He hardly took it amiss, indebted as he was to you for former services: you came to his rescue when he was bankrupt, with his neck in the noose, and went even shares with him in the property he had duped his wards of in Drepanum. I am, in fact, delighted that you took something from him; it was one of your finer hours. On the other hand, you really should not have walked off with that statue of Apollo belonging to Lyso of Lilybaeum, an eminent man with whom you had been staying as a house guest. You claim that you bought it? I realize that; for 600 sesterces, no doubt. Yes, I'm sure you did. "I will produce the records." Still, I think you ought not to have done it. And will you say that those hydrias, decorated with figures of Lilybaeum, were bought from Heius, the ward under the protection of Gaius Marcellus, from whom you had already taken a large sum of money, or will you admit that these vessels were taken by force?

But why do I collect all these instances of his perfectly average—if perfectly perverse—pilferings, which seem only to illustrate his ability as a thief and the losses inflicted on his victims? Hear instead, gentlemen, if you will, of an episode that will demonstrate how violent a compulsion and how real a form of madness Verres labored under, rather than being simply greedy. Diodorus of Malta[32] has already given evidence before you. He lived in Lilybaeum for many years, and was a man with a fine home, as well as one who was cheerfully and proudly welcomed in the homes of others because of his excellent character. Verres was informed that Diodorus owned some very fine examples of chased silver work, among them the cups called "Thericlian,"[33] from the hand of Mentor[34] himself, wrought with consummate workmanship. When he heard about this, Verres himself became so wrought up with the desire, not only of seeing them, but of adding them to

18

[32] Malta was under the praetor of Sicily.

[33] Thericles was a maker of earthen vessels in the time of Aristophanes. Cups made in imitation of his were called Thericlian —although in his style, they were often of other materials: wood, silver, glass.

[34] Mentor was a worker in silver, the most celebrated of all the Greek artists of his class. Pliny states (*H.N.*33.12) that his works perished, either in the conflagration of the temple of Diana (in 356 B.C.), or in that of the Roman capitol.

his collection, that he summoned Diodorus into his presence and asked outright for the cups. Diodorus, who was rather proud of owning these cups, answered that they were not in his residence at Lilybaeum but had been left with a relation in Malta. Verres thereupon dispatched some agents to Malta and wrote to some of the Maltese citizens to instruct them to search out these cups; he also asked Diodorus to send a letter to the relation. He could not wait to see these goblets. Diodorus, a thrifty and painstaking person, who, after all, wanted to retain possession of his property, wrote the relation to say to Verres' agents that he had just a few days earlier sent the goblets off to Lilybaeum. And Diodorus, meanwhile, disappeared, preferring to be away from his home rather than present and presiding over the liquidation of his beautiful chased silver. When Verres heard about that he became so furious that everyone thought he had gone stark raving mad. Unable to take the silver away from Diodorus, he went around saying that he himself had been robbed by Diodorus of some very fine specimens of silver. He threatened the absent Diodorus; he ranted and raved; at times, he could not keep back his tears. We have heard in the legend of Eriphyle how the queen was so taken with desire when she saw the famous golden necklace, studded with precious stones, that she betrayed her husband's life. Like hers was Verres' insatiable desire for these goblets, but his was even more fierce and foolish, because she lusted for something she had seen, whereas his desires were fanned to a fever pitch by something his eyes had never encountered, but only his ears had heard of.

19   Verres ordered a search conducted for Diodorus throughout the province. But Diodorus had already packed up and moved camp. Verres thereupon hit upon this plan for recalling him somehow to Sicily, if a mad impulse can be called a plan. He appointed one of his "dogs" to subpoena Diodorus of Malta as the defendant in an accusation involving a capital offense. Of course, it seemed absurd, at first, to everyone that Diodorus could be such a one, being the most peace loving and quiet sort of person, free from not only all manner of crime, but even from any suspicion of wrongdoing. Soon, of course, it became perfectly apparent that the whole thing derived from the inciden

of the silver goblets. Verres lost no time having the prosecution set in motion; and this was, I think, the first time he allowed the name of an absent man to be filed in an accusation. The affair attained widespread publicity throughout Sicily, to the effect that people could be prosecuted simply because the governor had designs on their chased silver, and that charges were filed against them not only when they were present to answer them, but even when they were absent. At Rome, Diodorus assumed mourning garb and went about consulting his friends and patrons, informing them of the details of the incident.

Meanwhile, angry communications reached Verres from his father and from his friends, telling him to watch his step this time, saying that the suit against Diodorus was notorious and working him harm. If he were not careful, they wrote, this one affair would surely ruin him; he must be out of his mind. At this time, Verres still thought of his father as of the ranks of men, if not of parents; and he had not prepared the material for the trial at all adequately. Also, it was his first year on duty in the province and he was not yet, as he was by the time the case of Sthenius came around, stuffed with cash. And so his eagerness was held in check, not by any sense of shame, but by fear and anxiety. He did not dare condemn Diodorus in his absence, and struck his name from the lists of defendants. Meanwhile, Diodorus was in exile from his residence and from the province for the better part of the three years that Verres was governor. The affair ended by convincing others, Romans as well as Sicilians, that, since Verres had gone so far with his compulsive greed, no one could expect to hold on to, or keep possession of, anything that might happen to have appealed, however slightly, to Verres.

When people realized that the upright man, Quintus Arrius, whom they had been eagerly awaiting, would not replace Verres, they resigned themselves to the fact that nothing could be kept under wraps, or so effectively hidden as not to lie helplessly open to his avarice and be his for the plucking. And promptly enough, he took from Gnaeus Calidius, a gracious and eminent Roman Knight, one whose son moreover was well known to Verres as a Senator of the Roman people and a magistrate, an equestrian group of silver

20

statues that had once been the property of Quintus
Maximus. Oh, I beg your pardon for that misstatement,
gentlemen: not "took from," but "bought from," I
should have said. I apologize for putting it that way.
Now, Verres can boast of riding high on those
statuesque steeds. "I bought that item, paying cash for
it." Yes, I believe you. "Accounts will show the sale
recorded." Of course they will: just let me see the
accounts. Provided that I have the chance to see these
accounts, you may clear yourself of this charge
concerning Calidius. But, nevertheless, I wonder what it
was that Calidius was complaining of at Rome, when
he said that he was scornfully treated by you, by you
alone, after many years of being in business in Sicily,
that he was contemptuously handled and exploited by
you, as were the rest of the Sicilians? Why was he
declaring that he would sue you for recovery of his
silver, if he had voluntarily sold it to you? How could
you manage, moreover, not to return the things to
Calidius, especially since he was such a close friend
of your defender, Lucius Sisenna, when you had restored their property to all of Sisenna's other friends?
I think you cannot deny that, because of the representations of your friend Potamo, you returned his
silver to Lucius Curidius, an exemplary man, but not
one whose prestige was greater than that of Gnaeus
Calidius. It was this case that made the others more
difficult for you. For, although you had firmly promised
to several that you would restore their property, after
Curidius had testified under oath to your having returned his, you put an end to such restoration, because
you perceived that you had lost the purloined goods,
but had not been able to escape the evidence introduced
against you. By all the other governors Gnaeus Calidius
had been allowed to retain possession of his exquisitely
made silver, and so make use of it to provide from his
household resources an attractive and handsome dinner
setting for a visiting magistrate or superior officer. On
many occasions men of importance and influence were
entertained by Calidius, and none were so crazy as to
walk off with his ancestral silver, or so shameless as
to ask him to sell it to them. Just imagine, gentlemen,
the unbearable pride of a provincial governor who might
say to one of the respectable, wealthier citizens: "Sell
me those chased silver vessels." It would be tantamount

to saying: "You are not really worthy of them, they are such unusually fine pieces; they ought, rather, to be in the collection of a truly worthy person like me." And so, Verres, you are more deserving than Calidius? Of course, I won't compare him in life and reputation with you—there being no basis on which such a comparison might be made—but let me compare him with you only in that imaginary dimension where you, Verres, think you are superior. You bribed agents to canvas for you to ensure your election as praetor, at the price of 80,000 sesterces; you bought off an accuser with 300,000 to quash his charges. Is this the reason that you, a noble, look down on the Equestrian Order contemptuously? Is that why it seemed to you outrageous for Calidius to possess something you liked?

Verres has been bragging for a long time about this negotiation with Calidius, telling everyone that he bought the things. But what have you to say, Verres, about the censer belonging to Lucius Papirius, that most outstanding, trustworthy, and respectable member of the Equestrian Order—did you buy that also? When he gave evidence, Papirius stated that you had asked to see it, and then returned it to him with the carved mountings torn off—which establishes the fact, gentlemen, that the man is intellectually stimulated, not just greedy, since here it was an interest in the expert workmanship of the decorative parts (not in the silver itself) that clearly was involved. Nor is this the exclusive example of such noble restraint on Verres' part; he followed the same procedure in dealing with all the censers in Sicily. It may be hard to believe how many of these censers, and what famous specimens, there were in the province. And, no doubt, when Sicily was at the height of its prosperity, and abounded in wealth and resources, there were many fine workshops on the island. For, before Verres' tenure as governor, there was not a home somewhat well off in which there could not be found such things as silver dishes with decorative medallions and figures of the gods, silver bowls used by the women in performing rituals, and a censer, even though there may not have been much else in the way of silver plate. These things were, moreover, executed in a classic style of exquisite craftsmanship; one would be led to believe that the Sicilians had, at one time, owned many other things of equal value, but, that incurring their loss through changed fortunes, they still retained the objects associated with religious worship. I have just stated, gentlemen, that there were many things, in general, in the possession of the Sicilians; but I also affirm that not one is left. How can this be? What monstrous creature have we loosed upon this province? Does it not look to you as if he wanted, when he returned to Rome, to satisfy the lust not of just one man, not of his own eyes only, but the frenzied desires of every lustful man, this creature, who would unleash his Cibyratic hounds, the moment he reached a town, to search out and locate everything? If they discovered some large vessel, they fetched it to him happily; if it was some lesser trophy which had been flushed out of hiding, they took them as small game: dishes, cups, censers, anything at all. Can you not imagine how the women cried, and what laments they raised, in the midst of all this? It may seem trivial to you, but did not these depredations set in motion a frenzied and powerful sorrow, especially in the hearts of the women, when the very objects they customarily handle for the purposes of religious rituals were torn from their hands, the ancestral possessions which always had been in the family from generation to generation?

22   But do not think you must wait, gentlemen, while I go from door to door describing each and every one of these offenses, pointing out that he took such and such a bowl from Aeschylus of Tyndaris, this or that dish from Thraso, also of Tyndaris, that censer from Nymphodorus of Agrigentum. When I present my witnesses from Sicily, let Verres choose any one of them at random, and I will question him about dishes, goblets, censers. There will be not one fairly well-to-do home, much less any single town, that has been left undamaged by Verres' injustice. If he went to a banquet and saw some chased silver plate there, he could not, gentlemen, keep his hands off it. Let us take the instance of Gnaeus Pompeius Philo of Tyndaris, who gave a dinner for Verres in his villa. Roman citizen that he was, he did what the Sicilians would not dare do, and imagined he would not suffer for it: he brought out a dish with engraved figurines of surpassing design on it. As soon as Verres saw it, he did not hesitate to remove from his host's dinner table that noble mark of the gods' presence on this hospitable occasion. What

I said earlier about Verres' self-restraint, however, holds true here, for, once he had ripped off the silver figures, he returned the rest of the dish and manifested no craving for it. Shall I instance more? Did he not do the very same thing to Eupolemus of Calacta, an aristocrat closely linked by ties of friendship to the Luculli, and now serving in the army under Lucius Lucullus? When he dined with Eupolemus, the latter had set out plain silver without any reliefs on it, so that he might not be relieved of it, but there were two large cups of moderate size with figures on them. Verres, as if he were the master of ceremonies at the feast who would not be dismissed from the scene without a present, then and there, in the presence of the other guests, pulled the figures loose and appropriated them.

I will not try to enumerate every single one of his exploits; that would neither be necessary nor possible. I merely set before you some of the chief examples of each major type of thing within the whole range and variety of his wickedness. He never conducted himself in these matters as if he might someday be called to account for them, but always went right on ahead, as if he would never have to stand trial, as if he thought somehow that the more he stole, the less risk he would run, were he brought to judgment. He made no effort to disguise these actions I am referring to behind a screen of friends or accomplices, but proceeded openly, from his vantage seat of power and authority.

When he arrived in Catina, a prosperous town and a commanding and influential one, he ordered the proagorus, that is, the chief magistrate, Dionysiarchus, brought to him. He unashamedly instructed Dionysiarchus to see that all the silver in the possession of every citizen of Catina be searched out and conveyed to him. And did you not hear Phylarchus of Centuripa, the leading citizen there by virtue of wealth, character, and class, assert under oath that Verres had given him the very same sort of commission, ordering him to identify and convey to Verres all the silver in that city, which was by far the largest and wealthiest city in all of Sicily? When Verres issued the same kind of orders at Agyrium, all the Corinthian vases there were transported to Syracuse by the agency of Apollodorus, whose testimony you have also heard. But the classic example of this craft of convenient confiscation occurred at

23

Haluntium. When our diligent and painstaking praetor hove into sight of that city, he was disinclined to enter it, because of the steep and difficult ascent. So, he summoned Archagathus of Haluntium, one of the finest men, not only in his own city, but in all of Sicily, and instructed him to see that every piece of chased silver (and of Corinthian ware, too) was brought down from the city to the seashore. Archagathus climbed back up the hill into the town, a good man who wanted only to be cherished and respected by his fellow man, now heartsick to be the bearer of this commission from Verres. He publicly announced his instructions, telling all the citizens to produce whatever they possessed. There was widespread anxiety; that tyrant was near at hand, waiting for Archagathus and the silver, lolling about in his litter down below the little town, by the side of the sea. You can readily imagine the great confusion, the cries of protest, the loud laments of the womenfolk! To be at the scene would make one think that the city had been captured in war, and the Trojan Horse brought right through its walls. Vessels were forcibly carried out, lacking their cases or covers, some torn right out of the hands of the women who were clutching them; doors were hurled open and locks smashed. And what else would you expect? Even in time of war, when armor is requisitioned from private citizens, they are reluctant to donate it, although they realize it is wanted for the cause of the common welfare. You would hardly expect anyone to furnish the precious engraved silver from his own house, for another to make off with, without experiencing the deepest distress. But everything was brought down to the seashore, where the Cibyratic brothers were called into action, rejecting a few pieces, but stripping all that passed their scrutiny of its figures or embossed portions.[35] And then the people of Haluntium returned home bearing their plain silver plate, denuded of all its endearing ornaments.

24   Did a broom[36] ever sweep so clean as this Verres

---

[35] *Iis crustae aut emblemata detrahebantur:* "the coverings or figures were torn off them." Many of the things that Verres laid his hands on were not solid metal, but had a case or covering of metal. He took this off, and, if there were *emblemata*, or figures, attached to the surface, he took them.

[36] *Broom: everriculum*, literally "drag-net," used here as if it were a diminutive of *Verres*.

swept through his province, gentlemen? After all, he swiped everything and cleaned the place out. Other officials have been known to be somewhat free with public funds, during their term of office, by subterfuge; or they have even robbed private citizens, by subterfuge again; they have been convicted for it. My role as investigator here is actually a very modest one: the real sleuths are they who have traced the plunderings of these others by getting wind of some scent or picking up the tracks, however lightly imprinted on the trail. What do we do with our swine Verres, who wallows ecstatically in the mud, until it is all too obvious to us where his fat traces are? It is not much of a job to come up with incriminating evidence against a man who, casually passing by some place or other, has his litter set down for a few moments and ransacks a whole city of its possessions, without any faking of his motives, but simply by asserting his authority and issuing a ukase.

In the present instance, curiously enough, in order to say that he had purchased the goods, he ordered Archagathus to pay some cash in exchange to the former owners of the silver, for the sake of appearances. Archagathus did find a few persons who were willing to accept some cash, and paid it to them. But, even so, Verres somehow failed to reimburse Archagathus for those expenses. Archagathus intended to sue for the money in Rome, although Gnaeus Lentulus Marcellinus dissuaded him from it, as you have heard him testify. Will the clerk of the court please read the testimony of Archagathus and Lentulus?

And so, that you do not think it was without reason that Verres wished to accumulate such a stock of silver figures, notice, gentlemen, in what high regard he held you, and the opinion of the Roman people and their judicial procedure, and the witnesses from Sicily, and the merchants there. After he had amassed such a great quantity of ornaments, as not to have left a single one in the hands of its owner, he had a huge workshop constructed in the palace at Syracuse. For all the world to see, he ordered all the metal workers, artisans, carvers, and goldsmiths to be brought there; and had, also, quite a few in his own hire. He organized a great number of men and kept them busy for eight months uninterruptedly working only on gold vessels. During

that period, he had the figures which he had detached
from the dishes and censers so cleverly re-worked, and
so cunningly re-shaped into golden vessels and goblets,
that you would think they had been designed for just
this purpose. And he, the governor, who says that,
thanks to his unceasing vigilance, peace was maintained
in Sicily, used to spend the greater part of the day
seated there in the workshop, clad in his dark tunic
and dark cloak.

25   I would not venture into matters like these,
gentlemen of the jury, were it not such common knowledge that you might claim to have heard more about
the man from the conversation that is generally cir-
culating than you have heard from me in this trial. Is
there anyone, indeed, who has not heard about this
famous workshop, and of its golden manufactures, and
of Verres, a veritable fixture there in his dark tunic
and dark praetorial cloak? Name whom you will of the
inhabitants of Syracuse, and I will put him on the stand;
not a one will you find but will say that he has either
heard of it or seen it. *O tempora, O mores!*[37] I need not
go into ancient stories. Many of you have heard of
Lucius Piso,[38] the father of the Lucius Piso here present,
who was a praetor in Spain, where, by mischance, he
was slain. One day, on duty, during a military drill of
some sort, he managed to break and crush his gold
ring. When he decided to replace it, he had a goldsmith
called before his praetorial bench in the forum at
Cordova, and there weighed out to him the precise
amount of gold required, in the presence of onlookers.
He told the jeweler to set up his workbench right there
on the spot and cast the ring, in the presence of those
same bystanders. Well, perhaps, it might be said, he was
being a bit too scrupulous, and, perhaps, that is so, but
it is as far as we could go in blaming him. His attitude

[37]What times! What moral standards! One of the most famous
of Cicero's expressions (see *In Cat.* I, 1, 1.11); its underlying implications might not unjustly be used to characterize Cicero's
moral scheme.

[38] His grandfather, also Lucius Piso, was consul in 133 B.C.
The first to sponsor a law against extortion, his son was praetor
in Spain in 112 B.C. Forty-two years later, at the time of this trial,
this grandson was a colleague of Verres and *praetor peregrinus;*
he tried to effect redress for some of the grievances resulting from
Verres' edicts, according to Cicero's account in the *Actio Secunda,*
Book I, Ch. 46.

was perfectly appropriate for the son of Lucius Piso, the first person who sponsored the law against extortion and embezzlement. It is absurd to mention Verres in the same breath with Piso the Thrifty, but you can see the world of difference between them: Verres, busy making buffets to be filled with gold vessels, did not care the least what anyone thought of him, not only in Sicily, but also in a court of law at Rome. Piso wanted all Spain to know, to the half ounce, how much gold was being put into a praetor's ring. Verres is as aptly named the Swine, as Piso the Thrifty.

I cannot include all the exploits of Verres in the   26 course of this speech; nor, indeed, remember them all; I am only eager to touch on their various types, as, just now, in mentioning the incident of Piso's ring, I was put in mind of something I had utterly forgotten. How many respectable men do you think had rings torn from their very fingers by Verres? He had no compunction in doing so, whenever the jewel, or the setting of a ring on someone's finger, happened to tickle his fancy. You may find the following incredible, but it is such notoriously common knowledge that, I daresay, Verres will not deny it. A letter came from Agrigentum for his interpreter Valentius; Verres noticed the shape of the seal and was much impressed by it. Asking where it came from, he was told Agrigentum, and promptly wrote off to the men he employed there, telling them to have the ring brought to him without delay. In accordance with his instructions, the ring that made that seal was forcibly taken from the hand of Lucius Titius, a Roman citizen and the head of a family.

Verres' gross desires quite stagger the imagination. For example, he wanted to furnish three hundred couches, elegantly covered, and all the other decorations for a banquet, for the various rooms in his house in Rome, as well as the rooms in all of his villas; so, he began, systematically, to organize so many of these couch coverings that there was not a single well-to-do household in Sicily in which an upholsterer's shop was not set up for his purposes.

A woman of Segesta named Lamia, a wealthy and noble citizen, happened to have many looms at her disposal in her residence. So, for three years, she did nothing but make robes and woven cloth for him—and only of dyed purple materials. And there were Attalus, a wealthy citizen of Netum, Lyso of Lilybaeum, Critolaus of Enna, Aeschrio of Syracuse, Cleomenes, Archonidas, and Theomnastus of Helorus. The day will run out before the list of names can come to an end. Verres, himself, provided the purple extract for the dye, his friends only supplied the labor, no doubt. I believe him. As if I didn't have enough evidence against him in the mere fact that he had so much to give in exchange, and wanted, for it, to obtain so much material! He, himself, admits that he used his friends to perform this kind of work for his sole advantage. But do you think that bronze frames for couches, or bronze candelabra, were turned out at Syracuse during the whole of those three years for anyone but him? Oh, of course, he purchased them. I'll buy that. But, I merely wish to lay the facts before you, gentlemen, to inform you of his actions in the province as its governor, so that he does not seem to have been delinquent in his duty or to have skimped on the accoutrements necessary for a person in highest authority.

27   Now I come to a matter which is not theft, or avarice, or simple greed, but, rather, something that seems to include every kind of wickedness in it, an inherently nasty piece of business; in the course of which, the immortal gods were blasphemed, the dignity and prestige of the Roman people undermined, a bond of hospitality betrayed and exploited, and all the kings truly friendly to us, and the nations under their power and sway, alienated from us by Verres' nauseous conduct. As you know, the kings of Syria, the young sons of Antiochus,[39] were recently at Rome, which they visited on a mission not about their kingdom of Syria, where they had legitimate inheritance from their paternal ancestors, but to assert their claims on the kingdom of Egypt, which they thought properly belonged to them and to their mother, Selene. Their plea was obstructed by the current crisis in our affairs and could not reach the Senate for the necessary discussion, so they then departed for their ancestral kingdom of Syria. One of them, the one named Antiochus, wishing to make the return journey by way of Sicily, traveled to Syracuse and arrived there during Verres' praetorship.

[39] Antiochus and Seleucus were the sons of Antiochus Eusebes. The elder of the two, Antiochus Asiaticus, afterward was deprived of the Syrian throne by Pompey the Great.

On this occasion, Verres thought he had fallen heir to a fortune, when there came into his territory (and into his clutches) a man, he had heard, possessed of many precious things, and whom he would have imagined in any case to be rich. He overwhelmed the young man with gifts for his use at home: oil, wine, wheat from the plentiful supply paid in as tribute to Rome. Then he invited the young king to dinner at the governor's residence, arraying the banquet room with a lavish show from his vast and beautiful collection of silver. (At this time, he had not yet gone into the manufacture of golden vessels.) Verres went to great lengths to make sure that nothing was missing from the arrangement that might distinguish the most luxurious banquet. Well, why go into further detail? The young king departed, much impressed by the stylish and rich manner in which he had been received. Then he, in turn, invited the governor to dinner, and displayed all his treasure including a vast quantity of silver goblets, and quite a few of gold, brightly studded with settings of precious stones, as is the custom among the royalty of Syria. One of the wine containers was shaped in the form of a ladle, wrought entirely from a single precious stone, with a golden handle; this is the piece you have already heard described by an unimpeachable witness, Quintus Minucius. Verres lingered over each single thing, taking a vessel up in his hands, admiring it, descanting on its beauty, and the young king was gratified to think that his little dinner party had found favor with, and brought pleasure to, the praetor of the Roman people. After it was over, Verres could think of nothing, as the facts subsequently showed, but how to get rid of the king, sending him well fleeced and robbed of his goods out of the country. He sent to ask for another chance to look at the vessels he had found particularly beautiful among the king's possessions, explaining that he wanted to show them to his silversmiths. The young king, knowing nothing as yet of Verres' nature, gladly and innocently handed them over. Verres also sent for that ladle carved from one single jewel, saying that he desired to study it more carefully. It, too, was packed off to him.

Hear the rest of the story, gentlemen, one not unfamiliar to you, and not told for the first time here to you or the Roman people, one well known now to

foreign nations even at the farthest ends of the earth.
These two kings had brought with them to Rome, as
an intended present, a candelabrum[40] wonderfully
wrought of precious stones in an unparalleled design,
to place in the Capitolium.[41] Finding that the reconstruction of the building was not yet completed, they decided
against its installation, and against publicly exhibiting
it, feeling that it would make all the finer an impression
when, ultimately, it could be placed in the sanctuary of
Jupiter Greatest and Best, and would be the focus of
even more excited admiration, if it burst all at once
upon the people's vision in novel glory. They, therefore,
decided to take the candelabrum back home to Syria
with them, until they received the news that the great
statue of Jupiter Greatest and Best was to be dedicated;
thereupon, they would dispatch escorts to convey it
along with other gifts to Rome and donate this superb
object of unmatched beauty to the Capitolium. Somehow or other, this matter came to Verres' ears, even
though Antiochus had kept the candelabrum out of
sight, not out of fear or suspicion, but that too many
people might not have a chance to set eyes on it before
it came into the possession of the Roman people. Verres,
of course, immediately asked the king, in profuse and
elaborate language, to send the candelabrum to his
residence, saying that he wanted to feast his eyes on it
and would ensure that no one else would be allowed to
view it. Antiochus, as young as he was royal at heart,
had no inkling of Verres' contemptible motives; he told
his servants to wrap the candelabrum up securely and
convey it, in utter secrecy, to the governor's residence.
After they arrived with it, and set it before him, whip-
ping off the drapes, Verres went into ecstasies about the
magnificence of this treasure, incomparably worthy of
the kingdom of Syria, splendidly appropriate to their
royal munificence, immensely becoming as a gift intended for the Capitolium. It, indeed, was so gloriously
designed from the rarest and most precious jewels, and
intricately worked, as to be equally valuable, both as

40 The candelabrum was only ornamented with precious stones
(*gemmae*); its base was made of gold.
41 The temple of Jupiter Capitolinus was accidentally burned
in 83 B.C. Sulla began its restoration, but did not live to see the
work completed. It was dedicated by Quintus Catulus in 69 B.C.

a superb work of art and as an invaluable treasure; and, conceived in so grand a design and shape, that anyone could see it had been made expressly for the temple of the highest god, not for use of man. When he had gazed on it for what seemed a reasonable length of time, the servants of the king started to wrap it up again to take back. Verres stopped them, saying that he eagerly desired to have it by him a while longer, for he was by no means finished looking at it. He told them to return and leave the candelabrum with him. And so, the servants of the king returned empty-handed to Antiochus.

At first, the king entertained no fears or sus- **29** picions; a day went by, then another, several more: still the candelabrum had not been returned. Antiochus sent a message to Verres courteously requesting that the treasure be sent back, but Verres told the messengers to come back at another time. Then, Antiochus himself called on Verres and asked him directly to return it. You know the man's face and the insolent look he wears. He realized perfectly well the fact, which he had heard from the king himself, that this treasure was destined for Jupiter Greatest and Best, and was being reserved for the exclusive possession of the Roman people; and yet, he, then and there, began to entreat in all seriousness that it be given to him as a present. Antiochus protested that he could do no such thing, because of his reverence for Capitoline Jove and his regard for the opinion of the many men who already knew his intentions for the donation of this great work of art. Then Verres started threatening the king in no uncertain terms. Perceiving that he could get no farther with threats than he could with his entreaties, he peremptorily ordered the young man to be out of the province by nightfall. The pretext Verres gave was, that he had heard that Syrian pirates were making their way toward Sicily. The king, in the midst of the largest assembly place in Syracuse, in the forum (and I point this out so that no one will accuse me of discussing some obscure charge or fabricating the events from mere suspicions), standing there in the forum, I repeat, of Syracuse, weeping and calling on gods and men to witness, he began publicly lamenting the theft of this candelabrum from him by Gaius Verres, the candelabrum fashioned from precious stones that was intended

for the Capitolium, that was to stand as a monument
to the Roman people, in their most splendid place of
worship, of his friendship and alliance with them. He
avowed, in the course of this public complaint, that
he would not bother over the several other valuable
works of gold and precious jewels that had been in his
possession and were now in Gaius Verres' larder; but
to have the candelabrum stolen from him was a low
underhanded trick. Although the candelabrum had
long since been consecrated in his brother's and his own
mind and heart, he, nevertheless, wanted to state
publicly, in that gathering of Roman citizens in the
forum of Syracuse, that he was giving and donating it,
offering, dedicating, and consecrating it to Jupiter
Greatest and Best; furthermore, that he was now calling on Jupiter, himself, to witness the sacred and solemn
intention he professed.

30   Who would have the voice, the lungs, the strength
adequate to a sustained expression of this singularly
gross dereliction? Here was the young king Antiochus,
who, only recently, had passed two whole years among
us with his royal retinue and princely ornament in
Rome, a man who was the friend and ally of the
Roman people, whose father had been a most loyal
adherent of ours, whose grandfather and distant ancestors had been in the most distinguished line of the
kings of Syria—being unceremoniously thrown out of
a province that was under the jurisdiction of the Roman
people. Can you not see what effect this episode would
have on other foreign nations, and conceive of how it
would look to the eyes of others in the farthest regions
of the world, when they heard that a king had been
insulted by a praetor of the Roman people, a guest
robbed, a friend and ally of the Roman people sent
packing? Rest assured, gentlemen, that your name and
that of the Roman people will be as one, to provoke
hatred and resentment among foreign nations, if so
manifest a wrong as this inflicted by Verres goes unpunished. All men will then conclude, especially
because we have already acquired a reputation for
exploitation and greed through the behavior of Romans
in the provinces, that the criminal affront in this case
is offered them, not only by Verres, but also by any and
all who may see fit to condone his conduct. There are
many monarchs, many free polities, and many private

yet powerful, wealthy individuals who have the definite
intention of contributing to the beauty of our Capitolium
in a similar way, as would be altogether appropriate
to the high significance of this hallowed place and to
the grandeur of our empire. Should they find that this
tampering with a kingly donation has met with your
strictest censure, they will conclude that such gifts as
they would present, and the homage they would willingly pay to you and to the Roman people, are gra-
ciously welcome. But, if the news should reach them,
that you have taken no action against this willful and
grievous damage done to an irreproachable and noble
young king, they will hardly be so mindless as to devote money, time, and effort to produce offerings that
will seem negligible in your eyes.

I appeal to you, Quintus Catulus, in this very   *31*
place, when I speak of your splendid and beautiful
work of reconstruction on the Capitoline Hill and
especially in the Temple of Jupiter Greatest and Best.
You must be more that a magistrate in this matter:
you must employ the powers of an aggressive prosecutor. By the good trust of the Senate and the Roman
people, your own status is involved with that temple,
and, when the temple is newly consecrated, your name,
too, will be registered in the everlasting memory of
men. You ought to assume the burden of this case so
that the Capitolium, restored more gloriously than ever,
may be even more copiously arrayed than it was. And
the fire will appear to have been sent from heaven, not
to bring ruin to the Temple of Jupiter Greatest and
Best, but to create a finer and more splendid dwelling
for him. You have heard the testimony of Quintus
Minucius; how king Antiochus stayed at his home in
Syracuse; how he knew that the candelabrum had been
taken to Verres' residence, and had not been returned.
You heard, and you will hear further, from the assembled mass of the Roman citizens at Syracuse, their
statements that the candelabrum was dedicated in their
presence and vowed to Jupiter Greatest and Best by
King Antiochus. If you were not a judge, and you
received information about this matter, it would be
your clear duty to investigate it, to prosecute the case,
and reclaim the treasure. Therefore, I have no doubts
about what your attitude should be in this prosecution as
a judge: you should act, more than anyone else, as a

more driving prosecutor and attorney than I, myself, am.

32   Besides, can anything seem more shamefully intolerable than this to you, gentlemen of the jury? Will Verres have, in his home, the candelabrum of Jupiter, wrought of gold and precious gems? Will a beautiful object, whose light should reflect glory on the dwelling of Jupiter Greatest and Best, be the centerpiece on the banquet table for *his* parties, and grace the lurid scene of *his* debauchery? Is the lovely treasure that was meant to enhance our Capitolium to take a place alongside the other ancestral treasures he has looted from Chelidon, in the house of this depraved sensualist? Do you imagine that he will ever hold anything in awe or reverence—the man who thinks he will not incur punishment for having done so monstrous a wrong, he who dares come into this court, where he cannot turn to Jupiter Greatest and Best and ask for his help—as other men do in such circumstances? He is a man the immortal gods, themselves, are suing to reclaim their property from, in the court of justice instituted to benefit mankind, where they mean to recover the things he extorted from them. Is it any wonder that he stole from Minerva at Athens, Apollo at Delos, Juno at Samos, Diana at Perga, and trespassed against many other gods in addition to these, throughout all of Greece and Asia, when he could not keep his hands off of our own Capitol? The great temple, which private citizens seek to decorate, and will continue to do so, out of their own riches, Gaius Verres refused to allow to be decorated by a king.

And so, after he had formed the idea of dereliction on this scale, there was no religious or sacred object in all of Sicily for which, afterward, he had the slightest respect. During his three years in that province, he acted in such a way, that he was thought of as having declared war, not only against men, but also against the gods.

33   Segesta is one of the historic towns of Sicily, gentlemen, claiming to trace its origins back to the time of Aeneas, who touched here on his flight from Troy. The Segestans are, therefore, not only a people in friendly alliance with us, but consider themselves related and directly linked to the Roman people. In former days, when this town was at war with Carthage

in its own name and on its own initiative, the city was taken and sacked by the Carthaginians; as the spoils of victory, its art treasures were carried off to Carthage. One of their prime possessions was a bronze statue of Diana, an object of venerable religious significance and a masterpiece of the archaic style.[42] When the Diana was taken to Carthage, it merely changed places and worshipers, while preserving its aura of venerability, for its surpassing beauty seemed (even to the enemy!) to inspire the holiest sentiments of worship. Several ages later, when Publius Scipio overcame Carthage, he demonstrated in that victory the desire to have justice done to the Sicilians, and ordered that all their possessions be restored to them, for he realized fully how long and how often Sicily had been the victim of Carthaginian aggression. (I cite this action, in part, to illustrate the character and ideals of such a leader as Scipio, so that you may take deserved pleasure in your native Roman models of character, and judge the incredible arrogance of Verres with the more intense detestation the comparison evokes.) Scipio assured the Sicilians that all the possessions which had belonged to the different cities would be restored to them. Consequently, some things which had been taken from Himera, which I have spoken of previously, were returned to the people of Thermae, other things to the people of Gela, other things to the people of Agrigentum. Among the latter, incidentally, was the famous bronze bull of Phalaris, the cruelest of the instruments of torture devised by this notorious tyrant; the form of punishment was to have a man sealed up alive in the interior of the great bronze bull, and then, to apply intense heat to the bronze. When Scipio gave this artifact back to the Agrigentines, he is reported to have said that, it would be only fair for them to consider whether it was more advantageous to them to subject themselves to their own rulers, or to cooperate with the Roman people, in view of the reminder of the savagery of their native rulers, in the form of that very monument, and the leniency of the Romans who restored their possessions to them.

[42] The archaic style in sculpture covers the period roughly from 600 to 490 B.C. The archaic style is characterized by a) a movement toward more naturalistically life-like representations, b) a lively vitality, more unrestrained, less controlled than the purely classical, and c) most of all, a cheerful, ebullient smile worn by all: gods, maidens, slaves.

34   At the time of these events, great trouble was taken
to have the Diana I mentioned[43] brought back to
Segesta; it was returned there, and was restored to its
ancient seat, to the joy and grateful acclaim of the
citizens. It was raised on a lofty pedestal in the town,
with an inscription cut in large letters bearing the
name of Scipio Publius Africanus, "who had restored
this statue to its people after the capture of Carthage."
The statue was held in reverence by the citizens of
Segesta, and became the first point of call for visitors
to the town; when I went there, as quaestor, it was the
first thing they took me to see. It was a large and lofty
figure of the goddess in her stately gown; for all its
austere dignity and majestic size, however, the features
and array were those of a maiden. The arrows hung in
their quiver across the shoulder; the bow was in her
left hand, while her right brandished a blazing torch.

When Verres, archenemy of all things sacrosanct,
and official robber of religious treasures, saw the statue,
it was as if he had himself caught fire from that torch,
so ardently did he become inflamed with desire and
insane longing. He told the magistrates to have the
statue taken down and delivered to him, saying that
this would gratify him beyond imagining. They answered
that to do so would be sacrilege, that they were compelled to refrain, not only by their religious compunc-
tions, but also by the keenest respect for their laws and
courts. He, at first, phrased his request more diplomatically, then stormed and threatened, then held out
hopes, then renewed his terrorizing. By way of objection,
they brought up the name of Publius Africanus, saying
that jurisdiction over the statue lay with the Roman
people, and arguing that they, themselves, had no
power over an object which a renowned Roman general
had wished to serve as a trophy of the Roman people's
victory over an enemy city taken in war. As Verres
was unrelenting and every day pressed his demands
harder, the matter was referred to the Senate, only to

43 Cicero describes this Diana as a colossal figure, with the
characteristics of a young unmarried woman with long drapery,
not the short frock, as she was sometimes represented. The quiver
and arrows were suspended from her shoulder; in her left hand,
she held a bow, and in the right, the blazing torch. Diana is also
described this way by Sophocles in *Oedipus the King*, ll. 201 ff.
Sometimes, she was represented with a torch in each hand, and
the bow and quiver over her shoulder.

be sharply and unanimously shouted down. So, on the occasion of his first visit to Segesta, Verres was refused the statue. Afterward, when additional contributions could be demanded of any city in regard to levying sailors and oarsmen, or an allotment of grain, Verres exacted a greater toll from the Segestans than from any others, and often imposed a heavier burden than they could support. In addition, he used to summon their officials into his presence, or send for all their finest and foremost citizens, and rush them about with him from one forum to another in the province, where he presided over the courts of justice, and threaten them, each and every one individually, with ruin, and tell them all, collectively, that he intended to destroy their city completely. At last, having been gradually beaten down by the wrongs done them and by their mounting fears, the Segestans decided to comply with the praetor's command. As a great outcry of grief and pain engulfed the city, and amid the tears and lamentations of all the men and women, the contract for having the statue of Diana taken down was thrown open to bidders.

Please observe the religious compunction of these **35** people. Not a person could be found in Segesta, not one, gentlemen, free man or slave, citizen or foreign resident, who would dare touch that statue. Know that total strangers from Lilybaeum, barbarians, had to be brought in to do the work. As ignorant outsiders, they were quite unaware of the whole business, and the sacrilege it represented, and so, they contracted to remove the statue for a set fee, and did remove it. You can imagine the vast assemblage of women, as the image was being carried out of the town, and the weeping of the older men! Some of them could still recall the day when that same Diana had proclaimed the victory of the Roman people in person, as she was borne home again to Segesta from Carthage. But how different was this latter day from the former! Then, a general of the Roman people, a renowned person, was bringing back to the Segestans their ancestral gods, rescued from the enemy's city; now, a governor of the same people, a vile and detestable person, was stealing those very gods and committing an unspeakable sin. Nothing was more a matter of common knowledge throughout Sicily, than the massing of all the women who accompanied the goddess in her poignant recessional from the city to the very borders of their territory, anointing the image with oil, decking it out with garlands and bouquets of flowers, wreathing it in the fragrant smoke of incense and burning spice. If, Verres, you knew no fear when you were in command, because of your boundless greed and arrogance, do you not, even now, when you have placed your own future and that of your children in jeopardy, experience some slight anxiety? Who among men will ever stand at your side against the will of the gods, or what god will ever come to your aid, when you have trampled underfoot every vestige of honor and respect that is due them? And did not Diana herself, in her atmosphere of peace and quiet, transmit a single trace of good feeling to you? She had seen two cities, in which she had stood, captured in war and burnt; twice she had been rescued from the fire and sword, in two wars. At the time of the victory of the Carthaginians, she had changed her place, without losing a trace of her numinous power; then, owing to the valor of Publius Africanus, she had regained both her former, rightful place and her former, rightful worship.

Of course, when this foul act was committed, and the pedestal of the statue was left empty, except for the name of Publius Africanus carved in it, the unbearable grossness of the crime showed to all that Verres had not only violated the basis of religious decency but also had stolen a tribute to the glory of Publius Africanus, the most courageous of men, recording his accomplishments in war, a memorial to his character, a monument to his victory. When the situation of the pedestal and its inscription was reported to Verres, he thought that all would forget the matter completely, if he took away the pedestal also, which stood there, pointing to his crime. And the Segestans, by order of the praetor, let out a contract for the pedestal to be removed. The terms of that contract were read out to you earlier in the first part of this trial.

36   Now, I turn to you, Publius Scipio,[44] noble scion of

44 Publius Cornelius Scipio Nasica, a son of a father of the same name, who was praetor in 94 B.C. He was adopted by Quintus Metellus Pius, probably after the date of this oration. He was consul in 52 B.C., and the father of Cornelia, the last wife of Pompey the Great. Scipio was one of Verres' advocates.

a noble house, and confront you with the duty you owe your family name, and ask you to perform it. Why should you fight on the side of the very scoundrel who has cheated your family of the respect and honor it deserves? Why should you wish to defend him in this trial, while I protect your interests, while I uphold your honor; while Marcus Tullius demands reclamation of the monument of Publius Africanus, why should Publius Scipio join the defense of the man who perpetrated the theft? The custom of our ancestors has been for the descendants to protect the family's monuments zealously, not allowing these timeless memorials even to be graced by another man's name; and will you be of help to the villain, who has not merely impaired the view of Africanus' monuments, but done away with them and made off with them? By the immortal gods, who will then protect the memory of Publius Scipio now that he is dead, or defend the reminders and evidences of his valor, if you abandon and neglect them, and not only permit them to be trampled in the dust, but even come to the support of the one who has mocked and reviled them? Present here are the citizens of Segesta, your clients, allies and friends of the Roman people. They inform you that when Carthage was razed, Publius Africanus restored the image of Diana to their ancestors; that it was then set in place in the city of the Segestans, and dedicated in the name of that great general; and that Verres saw to it that the statue was taken down and carried off, and the name of Publius Scipio obliterated. They beg and beseech you to restore to them this object of their worship and rehabilitate the honor and respect due your family name. Then by your help they would recover from a pirate's den what they once recovered from an enemy's city, by the kind favor of Publius Africanus.

What can you in all fairness answer? Or what can *37* they do but appeal directly to your good faith? They are here and do so appeal. You can protect the honor of your family name, Scipio, you can do that. All the advantages that destiny or nature can bestow on a man are yours. I have no wish to overshadow you in the performance of your duty, and I seek no praise that rightly would belong to another. It does not harmonize with the modest bent of my character to step forward as the defender and advocate of the monuments com-

memorating Publius Scipio while Publius Scipio is
alive, young, and flourishing. If you assume the defense
of your family honor, it will behoove me to fall silent
regarding your memorials; indeed, to rejoice in the
good fortune of the dead Publius Africanus, whose
name will be kept honored by the members of his
immediate family, who has no need of outside help.
But if your friendship with Verres gives you pause, or
if you think that my request is not precisely a matter
of your duty—then I, in your stead, will succeed to that
office and pursue the work I have considered to be
not strictly mine to do. Let the haughty class of the
nobility cease complaining that the Roman people is
and has always been too ready to recognize the virtue
of new and hardworking men from outside their ranks.
In a city, which by its virtue governs all nations, this
is a groundless complaint. Let the figure of Publius
Africanus stand in the houses of other men, and let
heroes now dead be arrayed in virtue and fame. He
was a man deserving of honor among all the Roman
people, and deserving of the warm regard, not of any
one family, but of the entire state. I am, therefore,
partly involved in defending his honor with all my
strength, as a man of that city which he has made
mighty, famous, and splendid. This is so particularly,
because I exercise to the best of my ability those very
qualities for which Scipio was so distinguished: fair-
mindedness, application, self-control, the defense of the
disadvantaged, declared enmity to the dishonest. This
affinity of concern and action I share with him constitutes a relationship between us that is nearly as significant as the actual kinship of family and name to
which you lay such proud title.

38   I am now reclaiming from you, Verres, the monument that belongs to Publius Africanus; let me abandon
the defense of the Sicilians, and the case I agreed to
take—your trial for extortion. Never mind at present
the redress of grievances on behalf of the people of
Segesta. Only return the pedestal of Publius Scipio and
let that unconquered hero's name be again engraved on
it, and that gloriously beautiful image, recovered when
Carthage fell, be restored to its rightful place. It is not
I who make this claim, I, the defender of the Sicilians
and your prosecutor; it is not the Segestans. It is the
man who has assumed responsibility for the protection

of Publius Africanus' reputation and the preservation of his honor. I have no fears about justifying my performance of duty to the magistrate Servilius. He has done great deeds and lavished pains on having monuments erected to commemorate them;[45] he will, I feel sure, want such monuments safeguarded for the sake of his own descendants as well as that of all worthy men and loyal citizens, not handed over as loot to disreputable creatures. Nor am I worried about offending you, Quintus Catulus, invested with the privilege of restoring our Capitol, the finest and grandest monument in the world, when I insist that there be the maximum number of guardians for these monuments, and when I assert that all right-thinking men are under obligation to defend another's fame. I am sufficiently disturbed by Verres' other thefts and atrocities to think that they deserve rebuke. But I am so heartsick over this matter that nothing seems worse, nothing more intolerable. Is Verres to decorate his home with the monuments of Scipio Africanus, his disgraceful, indecent dwelling? Will Verres place monuments belonging to the most upright and self-controlled of men in that house, and an image of the maiden goddess, Diana, in the sexpit of pimps and whores?

But is this the only monument of Africanus you have *39* violated? What about the beautiful image of Mercury you stole from the people of Tyndaris, placed there by the kind office of the same Scipio? And the way you did it! Oh immortal gods, has there ever been so arrogant, lustful, and aggressive a move? Gentlemen of the jury, you have heard the deputies from Tyndaris say recently—and they were reliable and eminent spokesmen—that the Mercury they worshipped in all solemnity on religious holidays, a statue presented to them by Publius Africanus after he had taken Carthage, not only as a token of his victory, but as a symbol and sign of their loyalty to and cooperation with the Roman people, had been stolen by Verres by means of the illegal exercise of his powers. The moment he arrived in the town, as if it were mandatory—as if the Senate had ordered it and the Roman people ratified it—he commanded that they take down the statue and convey it to Messana. When this seemed unbelievably shocking to those who were present and heard it, Verres did not

45 Nothing is known of any monuments erected by him.

persist in the attempt on his first visit. But when he left, he instructed the chief magistrate, Sopater, whose statement you have heard, to have the statue taken down. When Sopater refused, Verres threatened him grimly, and promptly left the town. The magistrate referred the matter to the Senate, whose protest was loud and long. And, to conclude my story, quickly, Verres returned to the town soon afterward and inquired about the statue. Sopater's answer was that the Senate refused to allow it to be moved, and had proclaimed the death penalty for anyone who touched it without their permission; they had also emphasized the element of sacrilege involved. Verres said "What do you mean by talking about sacrilege to me? Or punishment? What's all this about your Senate? If you don't hand that statue over to me, you will be beaten to death." In tears, Sopater again reported the matter to the Senate, apprising them of Verres' greed and threats. The Senate had no answer for Sopater, but adjourned in confusion and distraction. Summoned by the praetor's messenger, Sopater informed Verres of the situation, pointing out that he was asking the impossible.

40   This last interview—I spare you no details of the man's outrageous behavior—was held out in the open in the assembly, with Verres loftily ensconced in his chair of office. It was the middle of winter, as you heard in Sopater's statement—and bitter cold weather, with the rain pouring down. Verres gave his lictors orders to heave Sopater headfirst off the portico where he was sitting and strip off his clothes. The order was no more issued than there lay Sopater, naked, the lictors towering over him. Everyone thought that the undeserving victim would now be scourged, but they were quite mistaken. Would Verres take the rod to a friend and ally of the Roman people, for no good reason? He is hardly so delinquent as all that; all the vices are not concentrated in this one man; on no occasion would you ever call the man cruel. And so, he handled the defendant gently and with great restraint.

In the center of the forum, as in other towns of Sicily, there are several equestrian statues of the Marcelli. Among these Verres chose the statue of Gaius Marcellus,[46] whose great public services to that city and

46 C. Marcellus, one of his descendants, who had become hereditary patrons of Sicily, was one of the *iudices* at this trial.

to the whole province were the most recent in men's
memory. He ordered that Sopater be set astride the
statue and bound to it—Sopater, one of the noblest
men of the city and at that time its chief magistrate!
How excruciating it was to be bound naked, skin
against bronze, in the lashing cold rain, is not hard to
picture. Even so, this insulting savagery did not come
to an end until the whole multitude of people passing
by, deeply affected by pity for the victim of so atrocious
a punishment, forced the Senate to promise Verres the
statue of Mercury. They cried out that the gods would
punish him, and that meanwhile an innocent victim
ought not be killed. The Senate came to Verres in a
body and promised him the statue. Sopater, stiff with
cold and more dead than alive, was finally taken down
from the statue.

I could not prosecute this man properly if I wanted   41
to. It calls not only for genius, but for a remarkable
range of abilities. For instance, this case of the Mercury of the Tyndaritans looks like one charge, and I
have presented it to you as a single accusation. But
here are many different specifications contained within
it, in such a way that I can hardly disentangle and distinguish them all. It is a case of extortion, for he deprived our allies of a statue worth a large sum of
money. It is a case of embezzlement, because Verres
appropriated a statue belonging to the Roman people,
from the place where it had been erected as a trophy
by a Roman general. It is a case of treason,[47] because
Verres took and stole monuments of our empire, of
our fame, of our achievements. It is sacrilege, for he
trespassed against the sacred principles of religion. It
is a case of assault, for he invented a new and original
method of torture and applied it to an innocent man,
a friend and ally of yours. I can find no name for it;
I am at a loss as to how to describe this case of the
statue of Gaius Marcellus. And what are the implications of this criminal deed? Marcellus was a patron of
the Sicilians, is that the point? And precisely what does
that have to do with the matter? Is that fact supposed

47 The law of *maiestas* is defined elsewhere by Cicero as, "the
offense of lessening the majesty of the people . . . impairing in any
way the dignity, consequence, or authority of the people. . . ."
Only by a stretch of the imagination could Verres' offense be
brought under this law, for which there was a special court at
Rome.

to be an advantage to him in giving help to, or meant to make him a cause of trouble for, his friends and clients? And were you, therefore, trying to show that patrons were no proof against your ferocious might? Who of us does not know that a bad man, if present, wields more authority than a good man who is absent? Or, do you merely wish to show by your behavior the reach of your high-handed, superb insolence? I suppose you thought, Verres, that you were somehow diminishing the stature of the Marcellus family. And so, the Marcelli are no longer the patrons of the Sicilians; Verres is instead. But what integrity or grace can you possibly lay claim to that would justify transferring to yourself so distinguished a body of clients as that province offers, and detaching them from their time-honored and absolutely reliable patrons? Can you, with your indolent, foolish, worthless ways, protect the interests of even one lowly Sicilian, let alone all of Sicily? Did you mean for the statue of Marcellus to serve as a gallows for the clients of the Marcelli? Were you looking for some way to make the horror done to him an instrument of punishment for the very persons who had held him in honor? Have you considered the further implications of your act? The Tyndaritans brought crashing down the statue of Verres, which he had ordered erected in his honor near those of the Marcelli, and on an even higher pedestal, the moment they heard that his successor had been appointed.

42   The destiny of the Sicilians has now accordingly given you Gaius Marcellus for your judge, so that we may hand you over to him shackled and bound, to the one to whose statue citizens were tied when you were their governor. First off, gentlemen of the jury, Verres said that the Tyndaritans had sold the statue of Mercury to M. Marcellus Aeserninus,[48] here present, and Verres hoped that M. Marcellus would speak on his behalf in the case. It seemed to me unlikely that a young man born of that high rank, and the patron of Sicily, would lend his name to such a man as a means of transferring the guilt. But I had, nevertheless, anticipated every eventuality, so that, if someone were found especially eager to assume the guilt for Verres' malfeasance, he would not be able to bring it off. I produced

48 Nothing is known of him beyond what is here stated. It appears he testified at the trial.

such witnesses and such documents in evidence that there could be no doubt whatsoever about his actions. Public documents exist that record the fact of the Mercury's being transported at public expense, and they state what the exact cost was. They show that a man named Poleas was officially put in charge of the business. Do you ask for anything more? What's that you say? Where is he? He is right here, as a witness, by order of Sopater, the chief magistrate. And who is Sopater? Oh, people, people! He is the person who was bound to the statue. What's that you're asking? Where is he, then? He is also a witness here. You've seen him and you have heard his testimony. Now, I say, Demetrius was the person in charge of the gymnastic school; as a strong man, he was appointed to look after the business of pulling down the statue. What is that you're asking me? Is it just I who say this? No, it isn't; Demetrius is present in court. Also, there has been given before you already the sworn statement by Zosippus and Ismenias, very eminent men and leading persons of the city, that Verres recently promised at Rome to restore the statue to the deputies, if the testimony against him were stricken, and he were assured that the Tyndaritans would not give evidence against him.

What have we now? Is there not at Agrigentum a 43 monument of this selfsame Publius Scipio, a most beautiful statue of Apollo, on the thigh of which the name of Myron was inscribed in small silver letters?[49] You stole that from the sacred shrine of Aesculapius, did you not? When he did that, secretly, employing as his accomplices some of the most disreputable people in that city to guide and help him, the whole city was extremely agitated. At one and the same time, the Agrigentines were trying to get back: the kind favor shown them by the object of their local worship, the city's showpiece, the evidence of their glory, the witness to their alliance with us. For Verres did not dare steal openly what they admired. (I imagine because of the great number of valorous men there and because Roman citizens, good and courageous people, live in this town on familiar terms with the Agrigentines and engage in business with them.)

Not far from the forum in Agrigentum is the temple

49 The name of Myron was put on the thigh of the statue in small letters of silver, let into the bronze.

of Hercules, a shrine they hold in the greatest awe. In it there was a bronze statue of Hercules, which I would call one of the most fetching I have ever seen (not that I am any real judge of these things, although I have seen a great many); its mouth and chin are worn down by the faithful, who bestow kisses on the image as well as prayers and expressions of thanksgiving. When Verres was at Agrigentum an attack was suddenly made against this temple at night, under the leadership of Timarchides, by a gang of armed slaves. The guards and watchmen at the shrine raised an outcry, but at first, they were badly mauled and cudgeled by the sticks and clubs of the intruders. The doors were torn off their hinges and smashed up, and the robbers started trying to pull down the statue and pry it off its base with levers. Meanwhile, the alarm had gone out through the whole city that their native gods were under attack, not from an unexpected invasion by the enemy or a commando raid by pirates, but from the praetorian guard at the governor's residence by a gang of runaway slaves armed and sent against the temple. There was no citizen of Agrigentum so advanced in years or weakened in strength as not to rise up that night in response to that warning, and seize whatever weapon chance placed in his path. Soon all were rushing to the shrine from every quarter of the town. For more than an hour the many invaders had been busily trying to get the statue down, but it refused to yield an inch all that time, no matter how some tried to pry it loose with crowbars, while others had looped ropes over all the projecting limbs and hauled away at them. Suddenly, the Agrigentines rushed in and began pelting the intruders with stones. The nocturnal troops of that great commander immediately took to their heels in flight. But not to return home to their sacker of shrines empty-handed, they stole two tiny statues. You know how the Sicilians can always find the presence of mind to make some clever remark, no matter how bad the situation is: on this occasion they observed that in the labors of Hercules the struggle with the Erymanthian Boar had been no worse than this difficulty with its equally boorish origins.

44   The people of Assorus copied the brave example of the Agrigentines, afterward, although their city is by no means so wealthy or high-ranking. The river

Chrysas flows through the lands of the Assorini, and by them the river is held to be a god and accordingly worshipped with solemn ritual. His shrine lies in the fields near the road leading from Assorus to Henna, and in it stands a famous marble statue of Chrysas. Verres didn't dare demand it of the Assorini because of the unusual reverence in which the shrine was held; so he assigned the job to Tlepolemus and Hiero. They came at night with an armed gang and broke in the temple doors. The temple custodians and guards immediately sounded the alarm signal by blowing the horn kept for this purpose, to alert all in the vicinity. Men came running from the farms, Tlepolemus was heaved out and chased away, and nothing was missing from the temple of Chrysas except one tiny bronze figurine.

Among the people of Enguina there is a shrine of the Magna Mater. (I must move along rapidly in mentioning these individual thefts, and even so, I will perforce omit a great number if I mean to come to the major and more famous exploits of Verres in the larceny line.) Here in the shrine were engraved bronze breastplates and helmets, and huge ewers, of Corinthian work, executed with the same masterly skill. Scipio, that man outstanding in so many ways, had deposited the objects in the temple, inscribed with his name. But, why now urge more against Verres, or complain of him? He took them all, gentlemen, and left nothing in the temple except the traces of its worship and the name of Scipio. After the famous names have been lost track of, these trophies taken from the enemy in war, these monuments of our commanders, the decorative and beautiful objects in these temples will be found among the household possessions and personal effects of Gaius Verres. And, of course, Verres, you alone are singularly endowed with the sensibility to appreciate the beauty of the Corinthian *hydria,* the temper of that bronze; you are an expert judge of the fine line represented in the work. Scipio, naturally, knew nothing of all this, a learned, cultivated man; whereas you, unskilled, uneducated, untalented, illiterate, ignorant, and insensitive, have just the feel for it! You might consider how Scipio surpasses you not only in self-control, but also in intelligence—you and other such self-appointed experts. It was because Scipio realized how invaluably

beautiful these objects were that he judged that they
should not be exploited as luxurious possessions, but
become a means of gracing cities and temples, thereby
ensuring the holy worth of our monuments for posterity.

45   How remarkable is the avarice of our hero, gentlemen, and his insolent, compulsive greed, not the least
in his ability to defame sacred things, which were forbidden to be touched by anyone; even forbidden to
think of touching. Among the people of Catina, there
is a sanctuary of Ceres, held in the same great reverence
as her shrines in Rome and elsewhere in the world. In
the inner sanctum of that temple there was a very
ancient statue of Ceres; what it was like exactly no
man knew; nor did any man actually know of its existence. For access to the inner sanctum was prohibited to
men. The sacred rites are traditionally conducted by
women and virgins. Verres' slaves spirited away this
statue by night from its holy and hallowed seat. The next
day the priestesses of Ceres and the attendants of the
sanctuary, older women of respected, noble families,
reported the matter to the magistrates. To all, it seemed
a repulsive, disgraceful, grievous offense. Verres, disturbed by the revulsion he had provoked, to divert suspicion from himself commissioned a certain friend of his
to find someone who could be blamed for it, and to see
that he was accused of the crime, so that Verres would
not be. The business went forward promptly. For, by the
time Verres had left Catina, the name of a certain
slave was reported to him. The man was arraigned and
false witnesses brought to testify against him. As is
their legal custom, the entire Senate of Catina sat in
judgment on the case. The priestesses were summoned
and given a private hearing in the Senate chambers,
where they were asked for their version of what had
taken place. They said that the praetor's slaves had
been seen in the precincts. By means of the testimony
of the priestesses, the matter, which had not been so
obscure anyway, became completely clear. When it
was put to the vote, the innocent slave was acquitted
unanimously. What is it you ask, Verres? What are
you waiting for, hoping for? Who among gods or men
do you expect to come to your assistance? Did you
actually dare unleash slaves as robbers of a temple in
which it was forbidden for free men to go, even for the
purpose of worship? Did you shrink from laying hands

on the very things the religious law forbid you to set eyes on? You were not impelled to commit this abominable and wicked crime, because your eye had been taken by any object.[50] You yearned lustfully after something you had never seen. You conceived so great a lust through your ears that no fear, no religious scruples, no power of the gods, no opinion of men could restrain you. I suppose you had heard of the statue from some eminent man, a reliable authority. But how could you have, in this case, when you could hear nothing at all from any man? So, you heard about it from a woman, since men were prohibited from seeing, even from knowing about, the image. Well, what sort of woman do you think that must have been, gentlemen of the jury, how modest in her conduct, to talk to Verres, how full of reverence, to show him a way to rob the temple? Or, is it the least remarkable that objects made sacred by vows of chastity on the part of men and women, had all the same been violated by his lust?

And so, what are we to make of this? Did he begin to desire only this statue, although he had never seen it? Oh, no, there were quite a number of others; but, among them all, I choose only the robbing of this noble, ancient shrine, which you have heard witnesses describe earlier in this trial. Therefore, I beg you now to listen carefully as you have so obligingly been doing, while I review some of the facts. There is an island called Malta, gentlemen, separated from Sicily by a broad expanse of treacherous sea; and a town there, of the same name, to which Verres had never been, but which served him as a source over a three-year period for the manufacture of women's garments.[51] On a promontory not far from the town, there is a shrine of Juno, an ancient site, one hallowed by such religious awe that, not only during the Punic Wars, wherein the clashing of great fleets around this region was a regular event, but also when the numerous bands of roving pirates were frequently in the region, the temple was

46

50 *Oculis captus:* i.e., it was not by the effect produced on his eyes that Verres fell in love with this statue, as Cicero explains. The expression usually describes one who is so affected in the eyes as to be blind.

51 Malta was very famous for its fine soft linen. The island was originally settled by the Phoenicians, who brought with them their arts and skills.

always left untouched, and its religious precincts never trespassed upon. We also remember very well the story that has been handed down relating how once, when the navy of King Masinissa[52] was driven ashore here, the king's prefect carried off some enormous ivory teeth from the shrine and brought them to Africa as a present for Masinissa. At first, the king was well pleased with the gift, but after he heard of its provenance, he immediately ordered that a quinquereme[53] be staffed with rowers to return the teeth to the temple. And he had a message written in Punic script saying that "King Masinissa had accepted these objects unknowingly, and when he found out where they had come from, had taken care to see that they were brought back and restored to their original location." In the temple there were also many other ivory ornaments, on many of them ivory statuettes of Victory carved with great traditional skill and artistic perfection. Not to linger over the details of my story, Verres took them one and all by the agency of one messenger, and in one stroke, delivered by the slaves of Venus he had sent to accomplish this mission.

47   By the immortal gods! What kind of man is this I am prosecuting, preferring charges here with due process on a court of law? Who is it your sentence will be passed upon? The official deputies from Malta say that the temple was robbed quite openly, that Verres left absolutely nothing in the sanctuary. Enemy fleets had often visited the place; pirates ships regularly hove to there for the winter; but what neither an enemy had ravaged nor a pirate touched was so thoroughly plundered by this one man as to leave absolutely nothing there. Is the person a defendant, am I a prosecutor, will this be called a court of justice? Is he obviously guilty of serious crimes, or is he brought here merely under suspicion? The gods will be found captured, shrines violated, cities left naked. And in every one of these things, I have clearly convicted him, witnesses corroborate the evidence; he is trapped by his own admissions, he is caught openly in the act; still, he sits

52 King of Numidia, he was an enemy of Rome at first, but he was won over by Scipio and became Rome's invaluable ally in Africa, provoking the Third Punic War for Rome's benefit.
53 He sent one of his largest warships (literally, *quinqueremis:* a ship having five banks of oars), so as to make a good impression.

there and in silence acknowledges them all, together
with me.

No doubt, I seem to be descanting too long on one
particular kind of offense. I realize, gentlemen, that
your minds and ears are probably saturated with the
evidence, and are even offering some resistance now.
Therefore, I will omit a host of particular items. But,
I do wish you to turn your attention most diligently
to what I am about to say further, and I beseech you
by the immortal gods, concerning whose worship we
have been speaking now for some time, to listen while
I recount one last crime of this sort he perpetrated,
which threw the whole province into a wild turmoil.
I must go far back to trace the origins of this matter,
and I hope you will bear with me as I discuss its religious antiquity. The significance of the episode does
not permit abbreviating the full extent of the horror he
produced.

There is a legendary belief, gentlemen, dating from   *48*
the oldest records and monuments of the Greeks, to
the effect that the whole island of Sicily was sacred to
Ceres and Libera.[54] Many other nations also believe
this, but it has been especially borne in on the Sicilians,
in such a way as to seem innately instilled in their
hearts forever. They believe that both these goddesses
were born on the island and the methods of agriculture
were first discovered there, that Libera was ravished
there—whom they call Proserpina—from the grove of
Henna, a region situated in the middle of the island
and called the navel of Sicily.[55] When Ceres desired
to search for Proserpina and inquire about her, she is
said to have kindled her torches from the flames erupt-
ing from Mt. Etna. These she carried before her on
her journey through all the lands of the earth. But
Henna, where the things I speak of are traditionally
celebrated, is in a lofty and commanding position: at
its summit there is a broad plateau, an unfailing supply of water, and a complete view in all directions of
every avenue of approach. Around it is a lake, and
the many glades blossoming with marvelous flowers at

54 The worship of Demeter was not native to Sicily, but was
imported from Greece. Cicero relates the Sicilian form of the
legend of the rape of Persephone. Libera was an old Italian goddess, afterward identified with Persephone (κόρη). For similar version of this myth, see Diodorus Siculus, 5, 2, 3.
55 Henna is one of the highest points in the center of the island.

Cicero

all seasons of the year seem to bear witness to the maiden's ravishment—as we know the story from our childhood years. Nearby there is a well-known cave of tremendous depth, where they say Father Pluto suddenly appeared to carry off the maiden; he rode away with her and then plunged again beneath the earth not far from Syracuse, where a lake materialized and where, even today, the Syracusans observe her annual festival, an event attended by vast throngs of men and women.

49   Because of the antiquity of the legend, and because in those places are to be found the traces and the cradles, virtually, of those gods, the cult of Hennian Ceres largely dominates all of Sicily in both public and private worship. Many portents frequently seem to demonstrate Ceres' power and holy presence. In the most difficult crises, she has often given sacred assistance to many. The result is the belief that she not only loves, but lives in and watches over the whole island. Many other peoples as well as the Sicilians ardently worship Hennian Ceres. The institution of her cult at Athens was based on a deep and mysterious spiritual passion; but, if Ceres came to the Athenians after her long wanderings and brought them the secrets of agriculture, how even more suitable is her worship by those among whom she was born and first made those arts known to man! So it was that among our fathers at a critical and troublous time in the republic, when Tiberius Gracchus had been murdered and there was widespread anxiety over the mysterious portents looming over us, during the consulship of Mucius and Calpurnius,[56] the Sibylline Books were consulted and we were instructed to placate the most ancient image of Ceres. Then the priests from the highest sacerdotal college of the Roman people set out on their journey to Henna—despite the fact that we could claim here in Rome a splendidly beautiful temple of the goddess. So great was the sacred reputation of her ancient seat of worship that in going there the priests felt that they were not so much going to a temple of Ceres as journeying to Ceres herself. I will not keep you waiting much longer, gentlemen, having been now for some time concerned that my oration would look much too

---

56 P. Mucius Scaevola and Lucius Calpurnius Piso were the consuls in 133 B.C.

different from the usual trial and the customary style of daily pleading. I simply say this, then: that this most ancient and hallowed Ceres, the foremost of all religious presences revered among all peoples and nations, was taken from her dwelling place and from her temple by Gaius Verres. Those of you who have been to Henna have seen the marble statue of Ceres and, in the other temple, that of Libera. They are very large and splendid, but not so old. And there was a certain bronze statue, moderately large and quite unique in its carving, holding the torches in its hand; this was by far the oldest of all the images in that sanctuary. He took that one too, and still he was not satisfied. In the broad open space at the front of the temple of Ceres there are two statues: one of Ceres, the other of Triptolemus, both of them large and extremely beautiful. Their beauty was their danger, their size their salvation; because taking them down and carrying them away looked to be practically impossible. In Ceres' right hand there was the seated figure of a beautifully fashioned Victory.[57] Verres made sure that this was ripped away from the statue and stolen.

What can be his state of mind now, as he recalls his crimes while I who recite them aloud, in the act of saying them, am affected not only in spirit but so, that my whole body trembles? Before my mind comes the vision of the shrine, its surroundings, the worship duly fulfilled there—all these things pass before my eyes. The day I came to Henna and the priests of Ceres stood before me, wearing their ceremonial headdress garlanded with verbena, there were heartbreaking sounds of weeping and mourning among the assembled throngs of people I addressed. The most bitter kind of sorrow seemed to have pervaded the city. They did not complain of the tenth-part taxes that were so diligently imposed on them, or of the seizure of their property or the injustice of the courts, or of Verres' loathsome lusts, or the overriding power thrust upon them, and the humiliating treatment they were exposed to. All they wanted accomplished by the punishment of that despicable and insolent creature was the atonement to the divinity of their Ceres, to the ancient reverence due their sacred rituals, to the hallowed worship of their temple.

50

---

[57] This statue of Ceres was probably in a sitting posture, with the hand outstretched, holding a small figure of Victory.

All the other wrongs done them they could endure, even disregard. So great was their tragic grief you would think that another King of Hell had come and carried away, not Proserpina this time, but Ceres herself. It was not so much a city as one entire sanctuary consecrated to Ceres. The citizens of Henna felt that Ceres dwelt in their midst; they seemed to me not so much like citizens as faithful devotees and guardians of the goddess. And Verres, you dared take the image of Ceres from Henna? You dared snatch Victory from Ceres' hand and thus wrench one goddess away from the other? No other person ever dared violate or even touch any of these objects, not one of those persons whose inclinations are toward wickedness rather than good. In the days of the consulship of Publius Popilius and Publius Rupilius,[58] the region was filled with runaway slaves, barbarians, and enemies. But those men were not so much slaves of their masters as you are the craven slave of your own lusts; they were not so much runaways from their masters as you are an outlaw and a fugitive from justice; they were neither so barbarous in language or nationality as you are in nature and in your habits; they were not such enemies to men as you are the sworn enemy of the immortal gods. And what possible excuse can be made for a man who outclasses slaves in his debasement, runaways in his boldness, barbarians in his wrongdoing, and enemies in his cruelty?

51   You have heard Theodorus and Numenius and Nicasio, the deputies from Henna, say in the name of their city that they had been ordered by their fellow citizens to go to Verres and demand from him the statues of Ceres and of Victory. If they succeeded, then, in accordance with the old custom of the Hennians, they would not testify against him in public, although he had harassed Sicily. If he did not return the statues, they would inform the judges of the wrongs he had done and make a special complaint concerning the sacrilege. Do not scorn their complaints, gentlemen of the jury, do not, by the immortal gods, overlook them or hold them in contempt. Grievous offenses against our allies are on trial here; the redress of those grievances is being put to the test of

[58] Consuls in 132 B.C. during the first Slave War in Sicily, a two-year-long revolt of slaves throughout the empire.

law; the good name of this jury and their sense of the
truth is at issue. All these are significant matters, but
the thing of greatest concern is this: the whole province
is so pervaded by religious fear, so dreadful a spiritual
fear has filled the minds of all because of what Verres
has done that, whatever mischance befalls them, publicly or privately, they trace its cause directly to that
sacrilegious crime. You have heard the representatives
from Centuripa, from Agyrium, from Catina, from
Etna, from Herbita, and many others, state under oath
that their fields are barren and ruined: the farmers have
abandoned their ploughs, all the land is desolated,
deserted, and uncultivated. What has caused this is indeed traceable to the many combined effects of Verres'
disastrous exercise of power, but this one crime carries
the most weight in the minds of the Sicilians, who are
firmly convinced that when Ceres was violated, all the
cultivated land and the potential harvest of her fields
perished. So, heal them of this sickness, gentlemen,
respect the religious beliefs of your allies, while
consistently observing your own. This is not a foreign
religion, nor a creed strange to you. Even if it were
not a belief you were inclined to accept, you, nevertheless, would have an obligation to indict the man
who has infringed upon its due rights. Now that a religion commonly shared by all people is assaulted in
this manner, and a sacred worship flouted which our
elders brought over and adopted from foreign nations
—holy customs which they called Greek, as indeed they
were—even if we wished to be unconcerned and insensitive to such matters, how could we be?

Now, gentlemen of the jury, let me remind you, if I *52*
may, of the plundering of Syracuse, foremost among
the beautiful and handsomely adorned cities of the
world. I will place the facts squarely before you and
thereby complete and conclude this whole section of
the case against Verres. There is none of you but
knows how Syracuse was once captured by Marcus
Marcellus, or who has not read of this episode in the
annals of our history.[59] I invite you to compare the

[59] Cicero's reference to the "Annals" of the conquest of Syracuse may refer to writers contemporary with these events. He
would probably not speak of the historical works of any of his
contemporaries as "*annales*." Elsewhere (*Actio Secunda*, Book 2,
Ch. 45), he speaks of L. Cornelius Sisenna, one of the friends of
Verres, as a writer of *historia*.

peace of Verres with the campaign of Marcellus in that phase of the Second Punic War, and to match the arrival in Syracuse of this our praetor with the victory there of the general appointed by our ancestors; and to contrast the corrupt cronies of Verres' clique with the invincible troops of Marcellus' disciplined army, and our provincial administrator's unbridled lusts with the correct, controlled conduct of the great commander.[60] Make the comparison and you will say Syracuse was founded anew by the man who captured it in war, but led into captivity by the man chosen to govern it under the flourishing conditions of peace. I will not add here to the many words I have already spoken on this subject and will resume elsewhere in the case, and I will omit any reference to such glaring facts as the following well-known points. The forum of Syracuse, decently protected from murderous violence when Marcellus entered the city, upon Verres' arrival soon overflowed with waves of blood, the blood of innocent Sicilians. The harbor of the Syracusans, at the earlier period closed to both our ships and the Carthaginians', was thrown open by Verres to a Cilician privateer and its crew of marauding pirates.[61] I decline to refer to the fact that freeborn citizens were violently attacked, and respectable women ravished when our praetor appeared, although such things did not take place when the city was originally captured—an invading enemy's fury and an army on rampage—or the customs of war and prerogatives of conquest might have been expected to prevail. I will not mention all the matters of this sort, the achievements of our distinguished governor over a period of three years. You well realize how closely connected they are to things I have already discussed.

You have often heard Syracuse called the largest and most beautiful of all Greek cities. And indeed, gentle-

---

[60] Livy (Book 25, Ch. 31) correcting Cicero's rhetorical exaggeration, relates that Syracuse was sacked in 212 B. C. by Roman soldiers, Marcellus reluctantly participating. The booty taken was nearly as great as at the sack of Carthage.

[61] Verres appointed a certain Cleomenes admiral of the fleet, whose duty it was to keep pirates from Sicilian waters. Upon hearing of the approach of pirates, Cleomenes hastily fled, leaving the other ships to follow him in confusion. The result was that the entire fleet ran ashore, and was burned by the pirates. Compounding the disaster, Verres spared Cleomenes, but had the other ships' captains executed.

men of the jury, it is what it is called. Admirably protected by its location, it commands a view of every approach by land or sea, and its harbor is virtually contained within the extent and structure of the city. Approaches to the residences and buildings can be made from several directions but they are joined together and closely linked by means of a common point of exit. At this juncture, the port section of the city, called the Insula, is united by a small bridge to the main city, over the narrow inlet that separates the Insula from the rest of the city.

The metropolis is so vast that it can be said to consist of four towns, one being the Insula, or Island, of Ortygia I have just mentioned, which projects out with one harbor on the ocean side and the other at the inlet. This is where the palace of King Hiero stands, now the place of residence for our governors. The Island also contains several temples, among them two that far surpass the others, one the temple of Diana,[62] the other that of Minerva, both noted, before the arrival of Verres, for their extraordinarily decorative works of art. At the Island's outer end lies the fresh water spring named Arethusa, affording a tremendous supply of water and abundantly stocked with fish, the famous spring that would be entirely engulfed by the ocean waves were it not for the stone breakwater that keeps out the sea.

The second town goes by the name of Achradina. Here are situated the extensive forum, fine porticoes, a lavishly decorated Magistrate's Hall, a capacious Senate house, and the superb temple of Olympian Jove. The other sections of this region are marked out by one broad street, with side streets leading into it separated by private residences. The third town is called "Fate," for it lies in the region where an ancient temple to Fortune was discovered. Containing a spacious gymnasium and several temples, this part of Syracuse is densely populated and always busy. The fourth part was the last to be constructed and is therefore called Neapolis or "New City."[63] On its highest elevation are a

---

62 Artemis Ortygia, the patroness of Syracuse.
63 Not to be confused with the mainland settlement called Neapolis, which still today exists under the same name, Napoli (Naples).

huge theatre and two fine temples, one of Ceres, the other of Libera, and the huge, magnificent statue of Apollo Temenites. If he had been able to move it, Verres would have not hesitated to carry it off.

54   I return to Marcellus now, to indicate why I reminded you of him and his era. When he took possession of so renowned a city by force of arms he thought it would not redound to the credit of the Roman people to disfigure and destroy its beauty, which, after all, posed no threat to him. He therefore took under his protection all the buildings, public and private, sacred and official, as if he had come to preserve, not assault them, with his army. With respect to the city's elegance, he showed regard for humanity as well as for victory: he found it within the prerogatives of victory to have brought to Rome many trophies that might enhance the city, but not in the definition of civilized conduct to strip bare a city he especially wanted to protect. In making a division of the city's art treasures, Marcellus' victory sought no more for the Roman people than it assured out of human instincts to the possession of the people of Syracuse. The objects he brought to Rome we see today enshrined in the temples of Honor and Virtue and in a few other public places. He placed none in his own home or park or in his country residence, thinking that if he did not appropriate the city's ornaments for his own house, his home would be all the more decorative to the city. Moreover, he left a quantity of excellent objects for the Syracusans; he did not lay hands on, or profane, a single one of their gods. Compare Verres with him, not as you would one man with another, for that would be to insult the dead, but as you would war with peace, violence with law and order, arms and iron with the forum and legal procedure. That will give you the comparison between the entry of the governor and his gang on their tour of duty, and the triumphant army of Marcellus.

55   I have referred to a temple of Minerva on the Insula: Marcellus did not touch it. He left it as it was, complete with its works of art. But this temple was so thoroughly ravaged and plundered by Verres as to appear to have been sacked, not by some enemy, who even in war would respect its traditional religious atmosphere, but by barbaric pirates. There was a hand-

somely painted picture of King Agathocles[64] in a cavalry engagement, a series of colorful panels that covered the interior walls of the temple. Nothing could be grander than this monumental piece; the Syracusans considered nothing more worth seeing. Despite the fact that his victory made Marcellus the possessor of all non-religious objects, he did not touch the painting because of his scrupulous regard for the sanctity of the place. Verres, who had come to preside over those sacred buildings and religious objects after a long period of peace and loyalty on the part of the Syracusan people, carried off every single one of those panels—he left the temple walls, whose handsome decoration had stood for so many decades and withstood so many wars, naked and disfigured. Marcellus, who had solemnly sworn to dedicate two new temples in Rome if he captured Syracuse, was, nevertheless, unwilling to embellish the buildings he planned to erect with loot like that. Verres, who habitually pledged his allegiance neither to Honor nor to Virtue, like Marcellus, but to Venus and Cupid, was the man to attempt the ravishment of the temple of Minerva. Marcellus refused to honor gods with objects looted from gods, but Verres transferred the jewels of the maiden Minerva to his own home, a hangout for prostitutes. In addition, he purloined twenty-seven exquisitely painted portraits of the kings and tyrants of Sicily, whose attraction lay not only in the skill of the artists' rendition, but also in the memorable likenesses of the famous men represented. You see how much more shockingly disgraceful a tyrant our governor was than any of his predecessors in power: they rendered the temple of the immortal gods beautiful, while he made off with the art treasures—even with the figures of the rulers themselves!

Might I now describe the doors of that same 56 temple? I am afraid that those of you who have not seen these doors in their entirety will think I am exaggerating and elaborating excessively on their magnificence. But none can suspect me of being so ambitious as to relish the prospect of many fine men sharing with me the guilt of wild and misleading overstatements, especially those in the ranks of the judges who have

---

64 Tyrant of Syracuse, 317–289 B.C.

visited Syracuse and seen these doors. I can roundly affirm, gentlemen, in all conscience, that nowhere were there to be found such great and splendid doors more superbly wrought of gold and ivory than those. An incredible number of Greek writers have left commentaries about the beauty of these doors. They have perhaps admired and celebrated them too effusively: be that as it may, it is much more to the credit of our republic, gentlemen, that what appeared to be beautiful objects to authorities on such matters our general left undisturbed in time of war, while our praetor made off with them in time of peace. There were mythological subjects painstakingly executed in ivory inlay. Verres took pains to see that every one of them was removed. He ripped off a breathtaking Gorgon's Head wound with snakes, and took it with him: yet, he revealed that he was motivated not merely by the artistic merits, but also by the market value, of the materials. He pried off the numerous heavily weighted gold bosses from both doors—here his pleasure clearly derived not from the work but from the weight of the objects. The result was that he left those temple doors, once notable primarily as a supreme artistic glory of the temple, looking as if they had been built only to be closed.

You even indulged your craving for ornamental bamboo spears, didn't you, Verres?[65] I noticed that the judges were somewhat startled when a witness introduced this item. Perfectly worthless pieces of wood, unremarkable in the way they were made, and singularly unattractive. Of course, they were huge—but most people would be satisfied with hearing about such freak objects, and would be positively bored to look at them more than once.

57 Of course, the Sappho stolen from the Magistrates Hall you might be excused for taking.[66] Perhaps we should overlook your theft of so exquisite an example of Silanion's[67] work, and admit that so

---

[65] Bamboo shafts often placed in the hand of statues of Athena, to serve as a spear.

[66] This statue, famous in antiquity, no longer exists even in copies. It is generally felt that this statue's existence in Sicily is proof that Sappho was at one time (c. 504–3) exiled from Lesbos, traveled to Sicily and lived there for some years.

[67] Silanion was a contemporary of Alexander the Great, but his statue is said to have been a replacement for an earlier one which was destroyed.

meticulously polished a piece hardly deserved to belong
to ordinary people once a connoisseur like Verres had
laid eyes on it. That is undeniable. Any of us, neither
as rich nor as sensitive as he, who might want to see
something this valuable can quite easily go to the temple
of Felicity,[68] the monument of Catulus,[69] or Metellus'
portico,[70] or can seek admission to the Tusculanum of
some one of those worthies;[71] or he can go to view the
decorations in the forum, if Verres has by chance
loaned some of his art works for display on a festive
occasion. Verres, of course, ought to have beautiful
objects in his own home, and have both a house and
a villa stuffed with the art treasures of shrines and
whole towns.

Would you like to hear further about how he puts
his taste for the beautiful into practice, gentlemen?
This, too, in a man so high-born and well-educated, one
so formed in body and in spirit as to appear more
appropriately made to carry statues than to steal them.
The stolen Sappho, incidentally, sends up a cry of
longing to be back in her original location that you
would hardly think possible. Not only was she sculpted
with singular genius, but also a very well-known epigram was engraved on the base, which would have
prevented stealing of the statue had our connoisseur and
Grecophile, who judged the work so perceptively, who
alone understood its priceless value, known a single
letter of Greek. As it is, the inscription on the empty
pedestal states what used to be there, thereby proclaim-
ing the fact that it is missing.

Verres, may I ask: did you not steal the statue of

---

68 See Chapter 2 of this oration. It is the temple wherein were
placed the priceless art treasures the "barbarian" Roman commander had carried off from Corinth. Mummius was rude and uncultivated, but he had innate sensibility, and took what he liked.
The works of Praxiteles in this temple perished in a fire in the
time of Claudius.

69 Not on the Capitol, but the temple of Fortuna which he had
vowed in the war against the Cimbri (101 B.C.).

70 That is, of Quintus Caecilius Metellus Macedonicus, in the
ninth region of the city (see Pliny, H.N. 34.14), built after his
triumph over Macedonia in 146 B.C. Pliny says that this *porticus*
contained the statue of Cornelia, the mother of the Gracchi.
Plutarch also mentions a statue of Cornelia (*Life of Gaius Gracchus*, Ch. 4).

71 A hit at Hortensius, who had a splendid villa at Tusculum.

Apollo the Healer,[72] a widely known work, from the
shrine of Aesculapius, a sculpture not only deservedly
famous, but awe-inspiring and venerable? People came
to admire its beauty and revere its spirit. And how
would you answer the charge that, by your express
order, the bust of Aristaeus was removed from the
shrine of Bacchus openly?[73] Or that you took the sanc-
tified and gorgeously wrought image of Jupiter Imperator from the temple of Jupiter, "God of the Favorable
Winds," as the Greeks call it? Or did you hesitate a
moment before lifting out of the temple of Libera
that charming little marble head we so often went to
look at? But the statue of Apollo the Healer was
held to be, together with Aesculapius, an object of
ritual worship among the Syracusans, who offered sacrifices and observed anniversaries there. Aristaeus, in
Greek legend the son of Bacchus and said to have
been the discoverer of the olive and its oil, was worshipped in the same temple along with his father
Bacchus.

58   And do you realize, gentlemen, how great was the
honor in which Jupiter Imperator was held in his own
temple? You can easily imagine if you care to recall
the tremendous religious significance attaching to a
sculpture of the same sort and style that Flaminius
captured in Macedonia and had placed in the Capitolium here at Rome.[74] As you know, there are said to be
three statues of Jupiter Imperator in the world made in
this one style, of a particularly beautiful design: one
being the specimen we can see in the Capitolium, the
second in the region of Pontus near the Bosporus, the
third owned by the Syracusans before the arrival of
Verres. Flaminius removed one from its original place
to establish it, as it were, in the domicile of Jove on

---

[72] Literally, the statue of "Paean," that is, Apollo in his aspect
as Healer, which would appropriately be in the temple of his son,
Aesculapius. Originally Paean was the physician of the Olympian
gods. His name was subsequently used in the general sense of
deliverer from evil, and was applied to Apollo. Our term "paean"
(from the epithet of Apollo as healer) describes the song to
Apollo, a "paean" as well as a battle song.

[73] The reference to him as "the son of Bacchus" is probably
an alternative parentage. Aristaeus was the son of Apollo and
Cyrene.

[74] This statue of Jupiter Imperator probably perished in the
burning of the Capitol in 84 B.C.

earth. The one at the Bosporus,[75] despite the many naval battles there, and the land wars in Pontus, still, to this day, stands intact and undamaged. The third, in the possession of the people of Syracuse, which Marcellus, triumphant in the panoply of victory, had seen and left with the Syracusans in due respect for its religious significance, which both citizens and resident aliens worshipped and visitors and tourists came to see and venerate, this masterpiece Gaius Verres took out of the temple of Jupiter. With reference again to Marcellus, gentlemen, please bear in mind the fact that at Verres' arrival, more gods were sought out and tracked down than were men at the time of Marcellus' conquest. Marcellus is reported to have asked for that man of great genius, Archimedes, and to have expressed deep sorrow on being told that Archimedes had been killed.[76] But everything Verres asked for, he inquired about not to preserve, but to take out of circulation.

Things of less significance, gentlemen, I will refrain from mentioning, such pieces as the tables of Delphic marble,[77] or those beautiful bronze bowls, or an enormous collection of Corinthian vases, that Verres lifted from all the temples in Syracuse. But the result, gentlemen, is that the "initiates,"[78] who guard the treasures and conduct visitors on tours to see these remarkable possessions, now have their powers of demonstration turned inside out. They formerly showed each object in its place; now they point out what was taken from where.

And what is the effect on the populace? Are they only mildly disturbed? Far from it, first, because most men are deeply affected by religious feeling, and hold that the native gods they have inherited from their ancestors should be zealously worshipped and securely

75 The statue belonged to a temple of Zeus Ourios ("God of the Favorable Winds") on the Bosporus on the Asiatic side, at the point where the channel opens to the Black Sea.

76 Archimedes was killed by a Roman soldier at the time of the capture of Syracuse by Marcellus in 212 B.C. In the *Tusculan Disputations*, Cicero said that he discovered the tomb of Archimedes when he was on his tour of duty as quaestor in Sicily (Book V, Ch. 23).

77 Three-legged console-tables, in imitation of the Delphic Tripod.

78 *Mystagogos*. In Greek it was the name for those who instructed the newly initiated in the ceremonial mysteries at Eleusis.

protected; secondly, fine works of art like these renowned masterpieces, outstanding examples of craftsmanship like these statues and paintings, exercise an
especially powerful appeal to the Greek mind. We,
therefore, see from the complaints lodged by the Syracusans, gentlemen, that the whole subject is to them a
serious, grievous matter, although we ourselves might
dismiss it as relatively unimportant.[79] Believe me,
gentlemen—while I realize that you yourselves have
heard the same—although our allies, and foreign nations too, have suffered many disasters and troubles
these many years, the Greeks have taken nothing so
hard as this sacking of their towns and looting of their
temples. Naturally, Verres can maintain that he bought
the works of art, as he usually pretends, but take my
word for it, gentlemen, no city-state in all of Greece
and Asia Minor ever, of its own free will, sold a single
one of its artistic possessions, not a statue, not a painting, not a piece of decorative work. Unless, of course,
you think that now, when the courts of justice have
relaxed their stringent measures, the Greeks have begun
a steady business in these things they refused to sell
when our courts of justice were vigilantly manned, and
even bought. Or, unless you think that Crassus, Scaevola, Claudius, men of great power and influence,
whose tenure of the office of aedile resulted in a great
deal of added beauty for the city of Rome, had no
traffic with the Greeks, but that later aediles, subsequent
to the era of laxity in the courts of justice, did do
business with them.

60   Rest assured that to the citizens of Syracuse that
pretense of buying was a most bitter pill to swallow,
more than if someone had covertly stolen or openly
laid hands on the objects and made off with them. They
think it reached the depths of depravity for their city
to be noted down on public records as having been
carried off, for a price, to contract for the sale to others
of the treasures handed down by ancestors. The Greeks
derive a very keen pleasure from these things, which we
might dismiss as inconsequential, and our ancestors
were more than willing to have them keep possession of
as many of their works of art as was feasible. As for
allies under our rule, the tradition has been to let them

79 An insight is given here into the apologetics necessary in
Cicero's Rome for displaying an interest in aesthetics.

continue wealthy in their artistic holdings. As for the countries our fathers conquered, and imposed tribute on or exacted taxes from, they were nevertheless left in possession of their art works, so that a subject nation would have the solace and pleasure that can be derived from the things it values so highly and we consider rather trivial.

What price do you think the people of Regium would take (and they are Roman citizens) to have their famous marble Venus taken away from them? Or the people of Tarentum, to lose forever their Europa on the bull, or the familiar Satyr in the temple of Vesta, or other things of the sort? How much would it be worth to the people of Thespiae in Boeotia to part with the statue of Cupid, the one reason strangers go there; to the Cnidians to lose their marble Venus,[80] or the Coans their painted one;[81] to the Ephesians to lose their Alexander; the Cyzicenes their Ajax or Medea;[82] the Rhodians the painting of their patron deity Ialysus; the Athenians their marble statue of Iacchus, their painting of Paralus,[83] or the bronze calf from the hand of Myron?[84] But it would be tedious as well as supererogatory for me to enumerate the sights to be seen in every city in Greece and Asia Minor. The reason I have reminded you of these things, and what I wish you to consider seriously, is the remarkable degree of sorrow they experience when works of art are taken out of their cities.

Gentlemen of the jury, I urge you to disregard the evidence of other nations and base your judgment on the conditions of the Syracusans. When I first went there I was under the impression, formed by listening to Verres' friends at Rome, that, thanks to the inheri-

[61]

---

[80] The people of Cnidos possessed a famous nude statue of Aphrodite by Praxiteles. The Medicean Venus has been thought to be a copy of it.

[81] The people of Cos possessed a draped statue of Venus, inferior to the nude figure just mentioned.

[82] Julius Caesar is said to have bought two pictures by Timomachus, a Medea and an Ajax, for eighty talents, to place in the temple of Venus Genetrix in his forum. Since Cicero here speaks of the pictures as being in the possession of the people of Cyzicus, Caesar apparently did not buy them from Timomachus.

[83] Works of Protogenes.

[84] One of the great works of representational sculpture, it was later removed from the Acropolis to the Temple of Pax at Rome.

tance of Heraclius,[85] the city of Syracuse was no less
favorably inclined toward Verres than the city of the
Mamertines was by virtue of its partnership in his loot
and thefts. Also, I was afraid that because of the
dominant influence of the beautiful women of the
nobility, at whose behest he had conducted the affairs
of his three-year praetorship, and the men they were
married to, I would be opposed by not only a distinct
feeling of tolerance, but a positively indulgent attitude
toward him, were I to search for evidence in the public
records of Syracuse. So, when I was first at Syracuse,
I frequented the company of Roman citizens for the
most part, looking into the wrongs done them, and making copies of their records. After having engaged in this
research for some time, I wished to rest and to turn
my mind away from the problem, and so had recourse
to the excellent documents of Carpinatius.[86] In that
investigation, helped by several of the finest men among
the Roman knights who were living in Syracuse, I
gradually worked out the case of the Verrutii, of whom
I spoke to you earlier; I expected no help, either public
or private, from the Syracusans, and had no intention
of asking for it. Then, while I was engaged in this
business there came to see me one Heraclius,[87] a Syracusan official, of noble birth, who had been the priest
of Jupiter, a position Syracusans hold in the highest
esteem. He asked my brother[88] and me if we would
be so good as to attend a meeting of the Senate at a
plenary session then in progress, saying that he was
making this request at the Senate's behest. At first, we

[85] This affair is described in the second oration of the *Actio
Secunda,* Chs. 15 ff. Heraclius the son of Hiero, a wealthy Syracusan noble, had received a legacy from a relation (also named
Heraclius) of some three million sesterces. Verres trumped up
charges against him in the praetorial court and he was condemned
in absentia. The inheritance as well as all his paternal property,
was given to the public gymnasium of Syracuse. Verres had meanwhile skimmed off 250,000 sesterces for himself.

[86] He is discussed in the second oration of the *Actio Secunda,*
Chs. 70 ff. Lucius Carpinatius was a tax-farmer, and later, usurer,
who became one of Verres' most helpful agents. Before he began
to work for Verres' interests, Carpinatius had written letters to
various men in the company of shareholders responsible for the
taxes, itemizing features of Verres' graft operations.

[87] A different person from the Syracusan deprived of his legacy.

[88] The text reads *cum fratre,* but the person meant is Lucius
Cicero, Cicero's cousin, as is specified in the reference in Ch. 65.

were not sure what to do, but upon reflection, we felt that we should not slight that body and its meeting place, and so we went to the Senate chamber.

As we entered, the Senators all rose in our honor; then, at the magistrate's bidding, we took seats, and Diodorus, the son of Timarchides, began a speech. He was the chief man of the Senate in influence and its oldest member; and, as it seemed to me, a man of marked political sagacity. His opening remarks were to the effect that the Senate and the people of Syracuse were deeply grieved and disturbed to find that, although in all the other cities of Sicily, I had notified the Senate and people of our concern for their interest and welfare, and had received from them all their commissions, their envoys, and their documents, I had not done the same for Syracuse. My answer was that representatives from Syracuse had not been in the group of Sicilians at Rome which had collectively solicited my help, nor in evidence when I had been entrusted with the cause of the whole province. I also said that I could hardly expect any resolution against Gaius Verres to be passed in a Senate chamber where I could plainly see a gilded statue of Verres. At the mention of the sight of that statue, so great a groan went up, that it looked as if it had been placed there as a monument to his wrongs rather than to his benefactions. Then, each Senator began offering his version of the matter, as fast as he could speak, reciting details of the things I have already discussed; how the city had been plundered and its shrines ransacked, about the legacy of Heraclius, partly shared with the men in charge of the gymnasium, but the bulk of it appropriated by Verres for himself— well, one would hardly expect sympathy for the staff of the gymnasium from the man who had stolen the statue of the patron saint of olive oil. About the statue in the Senate chamber, they said it had not been erected at public expense or by the government, but placed there by those who shared in some of the loot from Heraclius' legacy. And, they told me that the same men, his accomplices in wrongdoing, partners in crime, witnesses of his debaucheries, had been the ones appointed to be the representatives of Syracuse at Rome; that I should not be surprised if they failed to join the consensus in their resolution or failed to show interest in the welfare of Sicily.

63   When I realized that their distress, far from being
smaller than that of the other Sicilians, was even greater,
I explained my purposes to them and the general plan
and method of the whole investigation I had embarked
upon. I asked them to join wholeheartedly in the cause
of the common welfare, and to withdraw the panegyric
of Verres they had voted a few days earlier—under
pressure, according to what they said, of threats of
violence, and out of their general anxiety. Then, gentlemen, the citizens of Syracuse, Verres' clients and
friends, produced records, which they had carefully
stored away in the most sacred part of the Treasury,
and on these public documents were listed all the
things I have spoken of as having been stolen, and
many more than I have time to speak of. The language
specified "What was taken from the temple of Minerva;
what is absent from the temple of Jupiter; what is
absent from the temple of Liber . . . the following
pieces." Each individual responsible for the safekeeping
of the art treasures had kept his own accounts, and, in
surrendering them and turning over what had been
placed in his care, the custodians had asked to be excused for the missing objects. They had been absolved
of responsibility, and the whole matter kept secret. I
had all these documents sealed with the public seal and
brought away in my keeping.

    As for the panegyric, they explained to me that
when they had received letters from Verres a short time
before my arrival concerning this vote of thanks, they
had taken no action. Several of his friends urged them
to, but they were angrily shouted down. Then, later on,
as my arrival was imminent, the man who was at that
time the head of the government[89] had ordered that the
panegyric be passed as a resolution of the Senate. They
had done so, but in a way that did Verres more damage
than good. And this, gentlemen, is the truth of that
matter, which I pass on to you, just as I heard it from
them.

64   It is customary for the Syracusans to allow anyone
who wishes to state an opinion to do so, when a matter
is referred to the Senate. Although no one is called by
name, the man who holds precedence by virtue of age
and standing is usually the first to speak, a right
granted him by the other Senators. If all are silent,

89 That is, Lucius Metellus, Verres' successor as praetor of Sicily.

lots are drawn to determine the order in which each man must state his opinion. In these terms, then, the question of the panegyric for Verres was brought before the Senate. There being some delay, many Senators began speaking and interrupting one another. They cited the case of Sextus Peducaeus,[90] a person deserving of the highest recommendation in the city, indeed, in the whole province: when they wanted to pass a resolution of thanks to him for his many good deeds, on an earlier occasion, they had been prevented from doing so by Verres. They argued that it would be quite unjust, even though Peducaeus stood to gain nothing from their panegyric, not to pass that resolution first which they had formerly wished to express, before this one that was being forced upon them. The motion was unanimously affirmed and the question concerning Peducaeus was called for. Each Senator, in order of age and rank, gave his opinion in turn. You may learn from the decree of the Senate itself what their remarks were, for it is their custom to write down the opinions of the leading men. Will the clerk of the court please read the document aloud? [This is done.] So you see, those were the opinions expressed by the leaders of the Senate. Next, then, the question concerning Verres was called for. And in what form is that recorded? Will the clerk please read it aloud? [This is done.] Yes, now what comes after the heading? Oh, it reads, "No one rose to speak; no one wished to express an opinion on the question." And what follows? Oh, I see; the drawing of lots was made. Now, why was that done? Was there no one present who would volunteer to offer praise for your praetorship, to be of assistance to you at a time of crisis, especially, when by doing so, he would earn favor with the praetor? There was not a single person willing to do this. Your own dinner companions, your closest cronies and cooperators, did not dare utter a word. In the Senate chamber where your statue stood along with the nude statue of your son, no one in that whole province, which had also been stripped bare, felt any sympathy for you. They explained to me how they ended by passing a resolution

90 He was praetor in Sicily in 76 and 75 B.C.—in the latter year Cicero was quaestor under him. The praetor in 74 was Gaius Sacerdos. Then Verres' term came, in 73, 72, and 71. Now, in 70, Lucius Metellus was praetor.

which everyone could perceive was not a panegyric but a laughable damnation with faint praise for the disaster that his praetorship had been. They wrote, for example: "Because Verres scourged no one with rods . . . ," meaning that he had had the innocent and noble summarily beheaded; or, "Because Verres administered the affairs of the province by maintaining a constant watch over them . . . ," meaning that he was up until all hours of the night pursuing his powerful, perverse pleasures; or "Because Verres kept the pirates at bay and did not admit them to Sicily . . . ," meaning, of course, that he let them right into the harbor, the bay of Syracuse called the Insula. And, when I had received all this information from the Syracusan Senate, my brother and I withdrew from the Senate chamber, so that they might adopt what motions they wished without our being present. They immediately proceeded to decree, first, that my brother and I were to be considered guests of the government, he having shown the same good will toward them that I had always manifested. They not only recorded the motion in writing, but gave it to us engraved on a bronze tablet. So, Verres, you can see how much your Syracusans cherished you, the Syracusans you mention so often, who find justification in allying themselves with your prosecutor in the fact that he has come to develop a case against you and investigate your actions.

Their next motion, supported by a nearly unanimous expression of opinion, was that the panegyric of Verres be stricken from the record. Not only was a vote taken to this effect, but it was prepared in writing and put into the record; and, not until then, was an appeal made to the praetor. And who made the appeal? One of the public officials? No. A Senator? No, indeed. One of the Syracusans? Not at all. Well, who was it then, who appealed to the praetor? None other than the person who had been his quaestor, Publius Caesetius! So you see how absurd Verres' plight was—deserted, hopeless, abandoned by the officials of the Sicilian government! To keep the Sicilians from passing their resolution and from obtaining the rights that were legally and morally theirs, an appeal was made to the praetor, but not by some friend or associate, not, that is, by any Sicilian, but by his own quaestor. And, who was witness to this or heard it? The wise and just praetor, who immediately ordered the Senate to be adjourned. A great crowd of people came to me directly. The Senators loudly maintained that their rights and their freedom were being taken from them. The people praised the Senate and offered them their thanks. The group of Roman citizens stayed fast by my side. That day, in all the efforts I had made, none proved harder than to restrain them all from laying violent hands on the man who had originated the appeal. And then, when we appeared before the praetor's bench, he was obviously meditating profoundly on what decision to give: before I could say a word, he got to his feet and left. It being now nearly evening, we also left the forum.

Early in the morning the next day, I asked the praetor, Marcellus, for a copy of the Senate's decree which had been passed the previous day. He refused, saying, in the first place, that it was contemptible for me to have made a speech in a Greek Senate. As for speaking in Greek in the presence of Greeks, he found that quite intolerable. I answered the man as I could and wanted to and should have. Among other things, I remember having pointed out that it was easy to see the difference between him and the great Numidicus, the true and genuine Metellus;[91] for the latter had been unwilling to help his sister's husband, Lucius Lucullus, with whom he was on the friendliest terms, by passing a panegyric in his favor, whereas he was extorting panegyrics by pressure from cities for a man totally unrelated to himself. Then I learned that he had been influenced mainly by many messengers from Verres and by many letters, not of introduction, but of credit; and, at the advice of the Syracusans, I took formal possession of the records in which the Senate's resolutions had been transcribed. But now, some new quarrels and confusion developed: I don't mean for you to think that Verres was entirely without friends and associates at Syracuse or left completely stripped and

---

91 Quintus Caecilius Metellus Numidicus, consul in 109 B.C., the commander in the war against Jugurtha, the Numidian chieftain. His sister married Lucius Lucullus, the father of the Lucius Lucullus carrying on the war against Mithridates in 70 B.C. The father was prosecuted for embezzlement, and convicted. Metellus refused to make a laudatory speech or to testify as a character witness for his brother-in-law.

abandoned. A certain man by the name of Theomnastus
began to argue for the re-possession of the documents,
an absurd person, whose name the Syracusans changed
somewhat to read Theoractus, or "God-forsaken." He
is such a fool that children follow him around and
make fun of him every time he opens his mouth. His
insane antics, which others find laughable, I found
quite bothersome. Foaming at the mouth, his eyes starting out of his head, he was clamoring at the top of his
voice that I was assaulting him, as we arrived before
the praetor's bench. I began requesting that I be allowed to seal the records officially and carry them away
with me. He spoke in opposition to me, saying that
there should not be given into my possession a decree
of the Senate wherein was contained an appeal to the
praetor, on the argument that it was therefore not a
regular decree. I read aloud the words of the commission I had,[92] whereby all documents and records were
to be handed over to me upon request. Out of his
mind as he was, he stated that such commissions from
Rome did not apply to him. The judicious praetor decided that he was unwilling to have me take back to
Rome a copy of a Senate resolution which should
never have been ratified in the first place. But why go
on? If I had not threatened the man severely, if I had
not read him the commission and the penalties it imposed for its obstruction, I would never have been
allowed to impound the documents. And, mad as the
man was, who, on behalf of Verres, had so violently
denounced me, when he failed to win his point (and
thinking, I imagine, he could get on my good side), he
gave me a little book wherein were listed all of Verres'
Syracusan thefts. Of course, I had now been informed
of them by the Syracusans and had an accurate list.

67   And so,[93] then, most assuredly let the Mamertines
commend you, Verres, because they are the only ones
in this entire province who want you to go unpunished;
let them express their praise of you, provided only
that Heius is present to hear it, and provided only,
that they are themselves fully prepared to answer the
questions that will be put to them. I would not keep

---

[92] Cicero cited the provisions of the *lex Cornelia,* under the
authority of which he was collecting his evidence.
[93] This is not a real peroration, but a recapitulation of the case.

them in suspense as to the nature of these questions: were they or were they not obligated to supply a ship to the Roman people? They will admit that they were. Did they furnish such a vessel during the praetorship of Gaius Verres? They will admit that they did not. But, did they not commission a heavy draft freighter, which they turned over to Verres? That they will be unable to deny. Did Verres exact from them the tribute of grain due the Roman people, as his predecessors in office had done? They will admit that he did not. What allotment of soldiers and sailors did they supply during this three-year period? They will state that they did not supply a single man. They will be unable to deny that Messana was the repository for his stolen goods and loot. They will admit that vast quantities were shipped out of Messana and that the heavy draft freighter the Mamertines supplied to Verres sailed from Messana fully loaded when Verres sailed away from Sicily.

And so, Verres, you are perfectly welcome to any commendations the Mamertines may bestow on you. As for the city of Syracuse, on the other hand, we see that its attitude toward you is directly proportionate to the way you treated it. The city has now, for instance, done away with the foul "festival of Verres" you instituted there. It seemed quite out of keeping to pay god-like honors to a man who had stolen the very images of the gods. And, in fact, the actions of the Syracusans would come in for very sharp criticism, if they had removed from their list of holidays an originally solemn and festive occasion of rejoicing, because it became the day when Marcellus captured the city—and then, despite all this, had inaugurated a holiday in honor of Verres, of Verres who had stripped them of all that the earlier day of disaster had left them.

You see the man's insolence, gentlemen, his arrogance. He founded this absurd and tasteless "festival of Verres" with money taken from the legacy of Heraclius. He also ordered that the festival of Marcellus be promptly stricken from the annual list of holidays. What this meant was that the Syracusans would honor with sacrifices every year the man whose efforts had resulted in their going without their national gods and without the sacred rites they had always observed. They were invited to abandon the sacred days celebrated in the festival of Marcellus, in the name of the Roman family by whose efforts they had regained all their other religious festivals.

Against Catiline, I–IV

INTRODUCTION

The story of the conspiracy of Catiline is amply told in Cicero's four orations. The main facts in the sequence of events unfolded in these four speeches are also chronicled in the monograph written by the historian Sallust (86–c. 34 B.C.), whose *Bellum Catilinae* corroborates and completes Cicero's partial account of the crisis and its resolution.

Lucius Sergius Catilina (c. 108–62 B.C.) was the descendant of an ancient patrician family, now in reduced circumstances. He had been a partisan of Sulla in the civil wars between Marius and Sulla and had played an active part in Sulla's savage proscriptions. He was elected praetor of the province of Africa for two years in 68 and, on his return to Rome, made his first canvass for the consulship. Disqualified from standing for this office because of an indictment for extortion, Catiline joined forces with the consuls-elect for 65, who had also been disqualified by having been prosecuted and condemned for bribery, Autronius and Publius Cornelius Sulla. These three and Gnaius Calpurnius Piso, a young patrician, formed a plan to murder the new consuls, Cotta and Torquatus, on January 1 at the inaugural ceremonies. This action, sometimes called the First Catilinarian Conspiracy, was postponed until February 5. It miscarried because Catiline gave the signal to attack before his accomplices were ready.

By the summer of 64, Catiline had widened his circle of adherents and by bribery had gained an acquittal in his extortion trial. He became a candidate for the consulship, among

six others, including Cicero and Gaius Antonius Hybrida.
Antonius aligned himself with Catiline against Cicero, but
Cicero was elected despite their opposition, chiefly because
of the strong support of the equestrian order; he and Antonius took office on January 1, 63. Cicero immediately
offered Antonius the lucrative province of Macedonia for his
post-consular year, thereby winning his alliance, or at least
neutrality, in the conflict with Catiline. Cicero then made a
valuable contact with Fulvia, the mistress of Quintus Curius,
one of Catiline's accomplices.

By bribing Fulvia to tell him everything Curius told
her, Cicero was able to obtain detailed information about
Catiline's secret plans and his political "program." The latter
exerted a strong appeal to marginal men of various ranks
and classes by its assurance of *tabulae novae*, or a cancellation of debts, and promised speedy action by its schemes
for the forcible seizure of power and the murder of the
presiding consul. And so, when Catiline again became a
candidate for the consulship for 62, Cicero persuaded the
Senate to postpone the date of the elections and to hold an
assembly prior to this time to consider the case against
Catiline. At the meeting, which Catiline attended, Cicero
presented a detailed revelation of Catiline's secret plans, and
Catiline, when called upon to reply to the charges, made his
famous speech describing the government.

It consisted, he said of two bodies, one weak with a
weak head, the other strong, but lacking a head: but as long
as he lived, the other body would not be without a head.
Having defiantly declared his position in these words, Catiline
walked out of the meeting; still the Senate took no direct
action. On the day of the deferred election, Cicero appeared
in the Campus Martius wearing a cuirass beneath his toga
and protected by a bodyguard. At the sight of the presiding
consul's determined stance, Catiline's mob, which had also
come to the Campus, armed and ready to coerce the elector-
ate, dispersed without interfering with the elections. The
candidates chosen as consuls for 62 were Silanus and Murena.

It was undoubtedly this third defeat which caused
Catiline to set in motion the desperate course of action of
the "Second," far more deadly conspiracy. For the planned
coup d'état, he organized a mob of needy and desperate
citizens in Rome and collected a number of sympathizers in
the municipalities and the country, including bands of gladiators; Piso was on the alert in Spain, and Sittius in Maure-
tania. At least four hundred assassins in Rome were assigned

the task of murdering the leading citizens and officials of the government. Catiline raised sums of money by borrowing on his credit, to supply his forces with weapons, equipment, and pay. The main force he could count on was assembling at Faesulae under the direction of Manlius. The plot called for Manlius to raise the standard of revolt at the headquarters in Faesulae on October 27, with the uprising in Rome to begin the following day. When he learned of the plan, Cicero called a meeting of the Senate on October 21, and, after two days of discussion, the Senate issued the *consultum ultimum,* conferring dictatorial powers on the consuls, "to take all measures necessary for safeguarding the security of the state." A state of war was declared in Italy and martial law in Rome, field commanders dispatched to levy and deploy troops against the conspirators' army. Antonius was to conduct the operations against the enemy in the field, Cicero to direct the security of the city. Meanwhile, Catiline, informed that he would be prosecuted by Lucius Aemilius Paullus, a young patrician, for breaking the peace (under the *lex Plautia de vi*), volunteered to place himself in custody at the homes of several eminent citizens in Rome, all of whom refused the responsibility. His design was to brazen out the situation in Rome and then get away to lead his revolutionary army against the city before it could prepare itself to meet the attack. The final touch given to his plot was the planning meeting held at the house of Marcus Laeca on the night of November 7. Manlius had begun operations as scheduled, and now Catiline made the final distribution of assignments, naming the men to stay behind in Rome and those to accompany him to the army, allotting the twelve different sections of the city which were to be the targets of simultaneous conflagrations synchronized with the general massacre. As a coup de grâce, Catiline now called for the murder of Cicero, and two knights, Cornelius and Vargunteius, volunteered to murder the consul in his home the next morning. Having been informed of all these preparations, however, Cicero secured himself against attack, and Cornelius and Vargunteius were turned away at the door when they appeared among the throng of morning callers. Cicero increased the security guards throughout the city and convened the Senate at an emergency meeting in the temple of Jupiter Stator the next day, November 8.

Catiline, who seems to have devoted much of his time to meetings, appeared with the rest of the Senate at this session. He was cold-shouldered by all, who moved away from the section of the meeting chamber where he took his seat, and was treated to the fiery invective of Cicero's First Oration with its unmistakable counsel that he anticipate the punishment inevitably coming to him by going into voluntary exile. After Cicero's speech, Catiline attempted a placating reply, asking the Senators not to form hasty opinions about his intentions, and reminding them how unlikely it was that he, a patrician of aristocratic origins and eminent family connections, should cast in his lot with those who aimed at the destruction of the city, and Cicero, a mere upstart of no distinguished origins, in fact, an "immigrant" (*inquilinus*) to Rome, should be the savior of Rome. He had gone no farther than this in his speech when he was drowned out by cries of "enemy" and "traitor," and he rushed from the temple. That night, Catiline left Rome for the camp of Manlius, never to return.

The next day, November 9, Cicero delivered his Second Oration against Catiline to the people in the forum. Its purpose was to inform them of the situation and enable them to assess the action, to counter the alarm and panic that might arise through ignorance and fear. Cicero also wanted to show the conspirators in Rome that the government had the crisis under control. So, the speech is both a defense of the consul's action and a challenge to the remaining conspirators. The latter nevertheless continued with their plots and plans inside the city, while Catiline and Manlius built up the field forces, which would soon number 10,000 recruits. The regular Roman army, it should be said, was in Asia under the command of Pompey the Great and could not be gotten back to Rome in time to deal with the revolt.

At this juncture, Cicero was distracted from his pursuit of clinching evidence of the conspirators' maneuvers by the accusation of bribery brought in as an indictment against Murena, one of the consuls designated for 62. The puritanical Cato, great-grandson of the doughty Censor, had chosen this moment to press charges against Murena for bribery and corrupt practices during the recent electoral contest. In spite of the confusion and disturbance the issue created, Cicero consented to act as Murena's defense counsel at the ensuing trial—and delivered the masterful speech *Pro Murena*, which follows next in this volume of translations. Late in November of 63, therefore, in the midst of the strenuous activities required by his investigations of the conspiracy, Cicero produced the searching, persuasive, colorful, witty, and effective oration which secured the acquittal of Murena. Appearing in the sequence of events between the Second Oration against Catiline and the Third Oration, the speech in defense of Murena illustrates Cicero's capacity as statesman and spokesman to meet a variety of challenges. As he listened to Cicero's summation from the prosecutor's bench, Cato was heard to remark, "What an amusing consul we have!"

The break in the case against the conspirators came from an unexpected quarter. The story itself is narrated in Cicero's Third Oration against Catiline and need not be repeated at length. While Lentulus and Cethegus were waiting for Catiline and his army, and formulating their final plans for massacre and conflagration within the city, they made contact with envoys of the Gallic tribe of the Allobroges. The latter had happened to come to Rome at that time to protest to the Senate over injustices being done to their transalpine people and to plead for relief, especially from the heavy debts Roman money lenders had burdened them with. One of the conspirators, Gabinius, seized on the idea of involving the discontented Allobroges in the plans of the conspiracy and of obtaining from them cavalry units for use in Catiline's army. At first, the Gauls showed some interest in the scheme, but they soon decided that they had more to gain from helping the government. After consultation with Fabius Sanga, the patron of their tribe, they became double agents, pretending to cooperate with the conspirators, and obtaining written documents describing their intentions. The Third Oration dramatically portrays the incidents leading up to the capture of the conspirators, who had inadvertently taken their last treacherous step. The ambush which trapped the returning party of the Allobroges, accompanied by one of the conspirators, Volturcius, at the Milvian Bridge on the night of December 2, resulted in the arrest of four other leaders of the conspiracy and the seizure of overt evidence in the incriminating documents which Cicero laid before the Senate at a meeting on the morning of December 3. After this meeting, Cicero delivered his Third Oration against Catiline before the people in the forum, reviewing the events of the crucial action.

With five leading members of the conspiracy under arrest and factual proof now made undeniably plain to all, it remained to be decided how to punish the guilty. At a meeting of the Senate held in the temple of Concord on December 5, Cicero delivered his fourth and final formal speech on the subject of the Catilinarian conspiracy. Silanus, consuldesignate, had spoken first and offered the motion that the death penalty be inflicted on Lentulus, Cethegus, Statilius, Gabinius, and Caeparius, the five prisoners then in custody. Julius Caesar, the praetor-elect, after Murena and the other Senators had spoken in support of Silanus' motion, spoke against it and proposed a motion for life imprisonment. Cicero then took the floor to argue in his Fourth Oration for the death penalty. Even so, the Senate was not impelled to vote the death penalty until, at last, Cato spoke strongly in support of the original motion. Then, by an overwhelming majority, the Senators decreed the execution of the conspirators.

On the evening of the same day, December 5, Cicero carried out the orders of the state. The five conspirators were led to the underground vault of the old prison, the Tullianum, and were strangled. Cicero supervised the performance of this last scene in the drama of the Catilinarian conspiracy at Rome and after it was over, addressed a one-word curtain speech to the people assembled in the forum: *vixerunt;* "they have lived their lives." On the Nones of December, 63, Rome could breathe again. Exactly one month later, on the Nones of January, 62, Catiline's army, now dwindled to 3,000 men, was confronted by a larger force from Antonius' army at Pistoria, twenty miles from Faesulae, under the command of Petreius. The army of the conspirators was totally destroyed, and Catiline fell at the head of the fighting.

The First Oration Against Catiline

1   How long, Catiline, how long, I say, will you keep wearing down our patience? How long will that raving madness of yours baffle us? How long will that wild arrogance you glory in last? Is it nothing to you that the Palatine[1] is now guarded at night, nothing that the city is protected by patrols, nothing that the people are panic-stricken, nothing that loyal citizens have formed

---

[1] The Palatine Hill was the site of the original city of Rome. In case of danger it would be occupied as an important military point. Cicero and Catiline both had houses on this hill, as Augustus did later; the emperors after him built more lavish residences there. The *Palatium*, or *mons Palatinus*, as a place name gave rise to our word "palace."

a solid front against you, nothing that this very meeting place of the Senate[2] is strongly fortified? Do you take no notice whatsoever of the looks on the faces of all these men? Do you not realize that all your plans have been exposed? Can you not see that your conspiracy is now held in check by the simple fact that all the Senators met here have accurate knowledge of it? What one of us, do you think, is not fully aware of what you did last night, and the night before last, of where you were, of who was with you, of what plans you laid?

Oh, modern times! Oh, this contemporary conduct![3] The Senate has knowledge of these matters, the consul sees them, and yet he lives. Lives? Walks into the Senate to take part in the public discussion of them, and of course, to make a mental note as his eye glances on each one of us he will list in his murder book. But, as for us heroes, we find our duty to the state well done if we manage to avoid his anger and his daggers.

You should have been long since led to your death, Catiline, by order of the consul, and the destruction you devised for us trained on you. In former days, Scipio Nasica[4] put to death Tiberius Gracchus, when the security of the state was slightly threatened. As pontifex, Scipio was a private citizen, not a public officer. And shall we, men of consular rank, put up with a Catiline bent on destroying the whole world by fire and slaughter? Precedents of a more distant origin I do not cite: for instance, the action of Ahala in slay-

---

2 That is, the temple of Jupiter Stator, near the *sacra via*, on the northern slope of the Palatine. Usually, only the temples of the forum and the Capitol were used as meeting places of the Senate, which could convene only in a *templum*, that is, on consecrated ground. Its regular council chamber was the Curia Hostilia on the north side of the Comitium (Assembly Ground) in the forum. For this meeting the temple of Jupiter Stator was chosen because the *mons Palatinus*, at the lower slopes of which it stood, was occupied by guard troops; perhaps also, because it was near Cicero's house, and he did not want to run unnecessary risks.

3 Cicero's famous utterance, *O tempora, O mores!*, was first voiced in his fourth oration against Verres, then here, then later in two other orations.

4 Consul in 138 B.C. When Gracchus stood for re-election in 132 to carry through the reform measures he had begun as Tribune in 133, he was assailed and killed by a mob of Senators headed by Scipio.

ing with his own hands Maelius,[5] when the latter was
encouraging revolt. In the past, there was clear and
present in this state so courageous a sense of duty that
brave men checked a traitorous citizen with harsher
punishment than that dealt to the worst enemy. We have
a decree of the Senate[6] now in effect against you,
Catiline, weighty and severe in its powers. The government has the support and the authority of the Senators
behind it. It is only we—and I say it frankly—we, the
consuls, who are delinquent in our duty.

2   On an occasion in the past, the Senate directed a
consul, Lucius Opimius, to "see to it that the republic
suffer no wrong." Not one night intervened before
Gaius Gracchus[7] was killed on slight suspicion of
treason, Gracchus the descendant of a famous father[8]
and grandfather[9] and famous ancestors. Marcus Fulvius,[10] a consular, was killed together with his children.
By a similar decree of the Senate, the republic was
entrusted to Marius[11] and Valerius, the consuls. Did
death, the penalty exacted by the republic, wait one day
longer to descend on Saturninus the tribune and Servilius the praetor? But here we are, now letting the
twentieth day go by, dulling the edge of our senatorial
authority. For we have a decree of the Senate of the

---

5 In 439 B.C. Servilius Ahala, master of the horse under the
Dictator Cincinnatus, was sent to arrest Spurius Maelius, suspected
of aiming at regal power. Maelius refused to accept the summons
of the Dictator and was killed on the spot.

6 The *decretum ultimum*, passed on October 21, conferred dictatorial powers on the consuls "for the safety of the republic."
Whether it sanctioned capital punishment of a Roman citizen is,
however, an open question.

7 In 121 B.C. Opimius the consul had been invested with dictatorial powers "for the safety of the state." In the riot that broke
out, Gaius Gracchus, the brother of Tiberius, was killed.

8 Tiberius Sempronius Gracchus, twice consul (177 and 163
B.C.) and twice honored with a triumph (178 B.C. over the
Celtiberians, 175 B.C. over the Sardinians).

9 His mother's father, Publius Cornelius Scipio Africanus Maior,
the conqueror of Hannibal.

10 Marcus Fulvius Flaccus, an adherent of Gaius Gracchus, and
consul in 125 B.C. He and his two sons were put to death by order
of the consul Opimius.

11 On the occasion of the consular elections in 100 B.C., the
agents of Saturninus and Servilius tried to force the election of
Servilius by assassinating his rival, Gaius Memmius. Marius had
to intervene against his former democratic ally, Lucius Appuleius
Saturninus, when his followers, to carry the election of Gaius
Servilius Glaucia, had beaten Memmius to death on the Campus
Martius.

same sort, but it is confined to the record, like a sword sheathed in its scabbard; a decree of the Senate by which you, Catiline, ought to have been summarily executed. Yet you live, and live on not to lay aside your boldness, but to harden it in practice. Fathers of the state,[12] I want to be merciful; at so dangerous a juncture in the affairs of the republic, I do not wish to seem remiss. But as it is, I now find myself guilty of negligence and inaction.

An armed camp hostile to the Roman people has been set up in Italy, in the mountain passes of Etruria;[13] the number of the enemy increases from day to day; you see the commander-in-chief of that headquarters, the general of hostile forces, inside our walls, here in the Senate, daily devising some new subversive plot against the republic. If, Catiline, I order you to be seized and put to death, my main fear, I suppose, will be whether my eminent fellow citizens may say that I acted too savagely rather than too late. But I am not yet persuaded of the unequivocal sentiment behind this action which ought to have been taken long since. I will decide on the death penalty when no one as conscienceless and desperate, as alike you, can be found to say that the penalty was not justly enforced. As long as there is anyone left who dares defend you, you will survive as you now live on, hedged in by the many strong guards I have posted to keep you from attacking the republic. The eyes and ears of many men will have you under observation, unknown to you; they will keep you under surveillance as they have so far been doing.

What more is there to wait for, Catiline, if neither night with its lurking shadows can cloak your criminal clandestine meetings, nor a private residence confine within its walls the voices of your whispering subversion? If everything you do breaks out of hiding and is brought to light? Change your mind! Take my advice: forget the murder and arson you are bent on. You are

3

---

12 *Patres Conscripti.* The Senators were originally called *patres,* fathers, then later *patres conscripti,* conscript fathers, that is, fathers enrolled on the lists of the Senate.

13 The camp of Manlius was at Faesulae (modern Fiesole) just north of Florence. The choice of this headquarters provided easy contact with Cisalpine Gaul, and a location in one of the colonies occupied by the veterans of Sulla's campaigns who favored Catiline's schemes. Gaius Manlius, the commander at Faesulae, had been a centurion in Sulla's army.

hemmed in on all sides; your schemes are clearer than daylight to us; as with a little prodding from me, even you may now recognize. You remember my saying on the twenty-first of October in the Senate that Manlius, the satellite and chief henchman of your insolent enterprise, would be up in arms on a certain day, namely the twenty-seventh of October? Was I deceived, not only as to the momentous and dastardly, incredible facts of the situation, but even as to the very day, which is still more remarkable?

And I also announced in the Senate that you had postponed the slaughter of the influential citizens to the twenty-eighth of October: although by that time a number of our chief citizens had left Rome; not so much for the sake of saving their skins as to thwart your design. Can you deny that, on that very day, you were unable to move against the republic, because you were restricted by the forethought I displayed in establishing guard patrols, and then asserted that you were well-satisfied at the prospect of murdering us who had remained in the city? And what do you say to the following: When you believed that you would take Palestrina in a night attack on November first, were you aware that the municipality had been reinforced at my order by guard troops, roving patrols and sentries? You take no steps, make no moves, plan no tactics I not only hear of but see and clearly assess.

4   Review with me now the events of the night before last, and you will quickly realize how much more I am on guard for the city's safety, than you are ready for its ruin. I state that the night before last you came to the Street of the Scythe-makers—I will not be vague—and entered the home of Marcus Laeca; that a large number of your like-minded colleagues also came there, their thoughts bent on the same mad criminal intent as yours. Dare you deny this? Why so silent? If you deny my statement, I will prove it easily by the presence of those I see here in the Senate who were with you.

Immortal gods! Where in the world are we? What city is this? What republic do we claim to govern? Here, here among our very number, fathers of the state, in this the most sacred and somber assembly on earth, are those who devise the destruction, not only of us all, but indeed of this city, and in fact even of the world. These men I see with my eyes, I, the consul, and ask their opinion in affairs of state; men who should have been put to the sword I will not yet wound with my voice by naming. Catiline, you were at Laeca's home that night; you divided up the regions of Italy; you decided where each of your accomplices should go; you chose whom you would leave at Rome and whom you would lead off in your train; you assigned the regions of the city to the men who would burn them; you said you were delayed by the fact that I was alive. As for that anxiety, two Roman knights were found willing to relieve you of it by offering to kill me in my bedroom the same night just before dawn. I obtained all this intelligence practically before your meeting adjourned. I increased the guard at my home and armed it heavily. I refused to admit those whom you had sent to pay their morning call, for those very men came precisely at the time I had predicted to many eminent people.

Since this is the way things stand, Catiline, continue on your way; go, at last, out of the city. The gates are wide open: get under way. The camp you share with Manlius has been awaiting you, its long overdue commander. And take your helpers with you, if not all of them, at least as many as you can accommodate; purge the city. You will free me of a considerable fear when a wall intervenes between you and me. You can toy with us no longer: I will not bear it, I will not tolerate it, I will not allow it. Heartfelt thanks must be accorded to the immortal gods, to Jupiter Stator himself, most hallowed guardian of this city, because we have already so many times escaped the clutches of so foul, loathsome, and dangerous a curse. The ultimate safety of the state should not be in peril from one man too often. As long as you plotted against me, Catiline, when I was consul-designate, I defended myself, not by a public guard, but by private precautions. When, at the last election for consul, you wished to kill me and your competitors in the Campus, I thwarted your attempts by a bodyguard composed of my friends, and no public outcry was made. Finally, as many times as you tried to attack me, I resisted you by my own devices, although I realized that my undoing would be followed by catastrophe for the republic. Now, you are openly attacking the state as a whole, the temples of the immortal gods, the dwellings of the city,

the life of all our citizens—you summon all Italy to
death and destruction.

Therefore, since what is first in order and most in
keeping with the power of this state and habitual dis
cipline of our ancestors I dare not yet perform, I will
do what is more qualified in its severity, but more
useful to the public safety. For if I order you killed
there will remain in the republic the rest of your gang
of conspirators; but, if you, as I have been urging upon
you long since, go into exile, the foul dregs of your
group, gross and pestilential, will be drained off from
the republic. What is it, Catiline? Why do you hesitate
to do what you were intending to do of your own accord
when I bid you do it? The consul orders the public
enemy to withdraw from the city. Do you ask if I mean
exile? Officially I do not so order, but if you consult the
consul, he strongly advises it.

6   Really, what can possibly afford you any pleasure
in the city now, where no one outside your dreary pack
of conspirators can be found who does not fear and
detest you? What brand of disgusting conduct has your
family not been marked with? What lustful craving is
foreign to your eyes, what crime unfamiliar to your
hands, what indecency not known to your body? Is
there a single young man, trapped in the seductive
pleasures you offer, whom you have not equipped with
a sword for his violence or a torch to light him to his
lusts? And, what now? Recently, when you created
room in your home for a new set of marriage rites by
the convenient death of your former wife, did you not
go even farther and heap another incredible crime[1]
on top of that one? I forgo mention of it, so that so
foul a deed may seem either not to have occurred in
this country of ours or, at least, not to have gone un
punished. I omit all mention of the bankruptcy you are
heading straight toward, which you will feel in its full
force on the next Ides when the payments on your
loans fall due. I proceed to those matters that pertain
not to the personal indecency your vices have led you
into, not to your private difficulties and unsavory
behavior, but rather to the ultimate interests of the
state and to the lives and safety of us all.

Can the very light of day, Catiline, or the breath

14 Catiline was rumored to have murdered his son, as well as his
wife.

of air you draw under this sky, be a source of pleasure to you, when you know that there is none here present ignorant of the fact that, on the last day of December in the consulship of Lepidus and Tullus,[15] you stood armed[16] in the square before the Senate house and organized a band of men for the express purpose of slaying the consuls and chief citizens? That no design or fear on your part stayed your crime and your madness, but only the good fortune of the Roman people? I forgo further mention of these outrages—they are far from unfamiliar, and they have been succeeded by others since then equally well known—and I have lost count of the number of times you tried to kill me when I was consul-designate, and then when I was consul. How many times I avoided your apparently unavoidable dagger thrusts, by a slight swerve, a "body-feint," as they call it in dueling! You get nowhere, attain no success, but you do not stop trying and wanting to dispatch me. How often that dagger was twisted loose from your hands! How often by chance it slipped out and fell! Still you cannot do without it for a single day. I cannot imagine how many holy vows and sacred rites you may have re-enacted because you thought it imperative to plunge that point into the body of a consul.

And now, in truth, what does your life amount to? 7 I will speak to you for a moment in such a way as to seem not motivated by the hatred I ought to feel toward you, but by the sympathy of which you are not the least bit deserving. A short while ago you entered the Senate chamber. Who in the vast throng, who of your friends and kinsmen extended you a greeting? If this has happened to no man else within living memory, do you expect the disgrace of an articulate rebuke, when you have been crushed by the weighty verdict of silence? What of the fact that at your entering the seats near you were vacated, and that all the consulars whom you had often marked out for murder left that section of seats bare and empty as soon as you had taken your place? In what spirit do you react to this? By Hercules, if any of my slaves feared me the way your fellow citizens shrink from you, I would consider that I ought to leave

15 In 66 B.C.
16 It was unlawful for citizens to carry weapons within the city. Catiline's plan had been to assassinate the consuls-designate for 65 B.C., Cotta and Torquatus.

my home; don't you think you ought to leave the city? And, if I saw that I was seriously suspected, even though unjustly, by my fellow citizens, and detested as a harmful force, I would prefer being out of the sight of my fellow citizens to meeting the eyes of all, hatefully trained on me. Since you, by the consciousness of your crimes, acknowledge that the hatred of all toward you is just and long overdue, do you hesitate to avoid the sight and presence of those whose minds and feelings you are injuring? If your parents feared and hated you, and you could not appease them in any manner, I imagine you would withdraw somewhere out of their sight. Now your country, the common parent of us all, hates and fears you and is convinced that you have been thinking for a long time of nothing but her destruction. Do you not revere her authority, not acquiesce in her judgment, not fear her power?

Silent as she is, I am sure she is talking the matter over with you somewhat as follows:

These many years no crime has come to pass except by your help, no disgraceful deeds have been done without your connivance; you alone have murdered many citizens, have plundered and exploited[17] our many citizens, have gone free and unpunished in experimenting with murder, blackmail, and extortion on your fellow citizens; you have managed successfully not only to disregard the laws and judicial investigations but to resist and destroy them. These previous provocations I put up with to the best of my ability; but, it can no longer be tolerated, Catiline, that I should stand trembling in total fear before the single one of you, that whenever a noise is heard we nervously think "Catiline's coming!", and that I can undertake no course of counteraction which may be at variance with your criminal schemes. Therefore, go; and take with you and from me this fear; so that if it is justified, I may not be crushed by it, if it is baseless, at last, I may now cease to live in dread.

8   If our country should address you with words of the sort I have just spoken, do you not think she ought to gain her point, even though she cannot bring force to bear? What of the fact that you have handed yourself over into custody, that for the sake of avoiding

---

[17] Cicero is referring to Catiline's extortions while propraetor in Africa in 67 B.C.

suspicion you said you were willing to go into house arrest[18] at the residence of Manius Lepidus? When he refused your request, you had the nerve to come to me and ask for asylum with me. When you had my answer to the effect that I could hardly feel at all safe within the same house walls as you, for I sensed the critical danger of being within the same city walls, you went to Q. Metellus, the praetor.[19] Rejected by him, you gravitated toward your close friend Marcus Metellus,[20] a ferociously fine fellow, whom you surely thought of as best trained to guard you closely, prone to suspect others, and most aggressive in your defense. But how far off is it really from actual prison and fetters for a man who deems himself worth watching? And, this being the case, Catiline, do you still hesitate, since you cannot face the prospect of death with an unruffled mind, to go somewhere far away from here and to entrust the life you have saved from the many just penalties it has long deserved to flight and to solitude?

You say "Refer the question to the Senate"; you request that and, if it be the Senate's pleasure to decree your exile, you will be only too ready to comply. But I will not take such a course of action which is quite the contrary of the consistent attitude I have maintained in this whole matter. I think I can make you realize, however, what the sentiments of this council toward you are. Leave our city, Catiline, and release our country from fear; depart for your place of exile, if this is the word you are waiting for. And what now, Catiline? Do you hear any objections being raised? Do you grasp the total silence? They consent, they are silent. Why do you wait for their spoken word, they whose will you can immediately apprehend from their silence? Now, if I had said the same things to the very fine young man, Publius Sestius,[21] or to the excellent and forth-

18 Persons suspected of treason might volunteer to be taken into custody in the home of some eminent citizen, until their innocence or guilt could be established. Catiline had had the effrontery to apply successively to Lepidus, an ex-consul, Cicero, the consul, and Metellus, the praetor.

19 Quintus Metellus Celer, who later took an active part in the military operations against Catiline.

20 A friend of Catiline. The reading is uncertain; the reference may be to Quintus Metellus Nepos.

21 The quaestor, later very active in securing Cicero's recall from exile.

right Marcus Marcellus,[22] the Senate would have already
laid strong hands on me, the consul himself, here in
this hallowed place, and most deservedly. But, since
they are perfectly quiet in regard to you, Catiline, they
confirm what I urge—indeed, they sanction it—they
themselves decree it; their very silence is a deafening
roar of approval. Not only they, whose authority is no
doubt considered as significant by you as their very
life and existence is considered cheap as dirt, but the
Roman knights as well, upright men and the finest sort
of men confirm it; not to mention the rest of our manly
citizens massed outside our meeting place, whose throng
you saw, whose desire you understood, whose voices
you heard a few moments ago. For some time now,
I have barely been able to restrain them from laying
hands and weapons on you. But I will easily persuade
them to accompany you cheerfully to the city gates, if
and when you decide to drop the plans for our destruction you have so long been busy devising.

9   To what purpose, really, do I speak? As if anything
could budge you, as if you could ever collect your wits,
as if you had ever considered the idea of flight, or ever
thought of exile! Would that the immortal gods might
grace you with such a turn of mind! Indeed, I see what
a storm of popular hatred may be brewing for me—if
not at present, while the memory of your nefarious
conduct is still fresh, then later on—if, cowed by my
commanding tones, you were induced to go into exile.
But, it is well worth it to me if your disaster is a private
affair and is detached from dangers to the state. Still,
to think that you might be talked out of your vices,
or show concern for the penalties of the laws or yield
to the exigencies of the state is not a sensible expectation. You, Catiline, are not one to be recalled from
depravity by shame, from danger by fear, or from madness by reason.

So, as I have often said already, leave; but, if you
want to arouse unpopularity against me as your enemy,
as you keep insisting, do go directly into exile. I will
probably be unable to face people's talk if you do; if
you go into exile under order of the consul, I shall come
close to crumpling under the weight of people's ill

22 Consul in 51 B.C., a determined opponent of Caesar, by
whom he was pardoned in 46 B.C. after Cicero's oration on his
behalf, *Pro Marcello*.

feeling. Or, if you would prefer to add to the praise and
honor that might accrue to me, take your pick-up gang
of thugs with you and go straight to Manlius; inspire
your desperate crew; segregate yourself from the good
citizens; bring war on your own country; revel in your
role as renegade robber. Then it will appear that you
have not been shoved off by me on foreigners, but have
responded to an invitation to be with others of your
own kind.

But why do I politely request this of you, a man
who has already dispatched armed accomplices to a
rendezvous point at Forum Aurelium[23] and is soon to
meet them there? So my information tells me, and it
also tells me a convenient day has been picked and
agreed on between this great leader and his henchman
Manlius. I also learn that the leader has sent ahead
to the rendezvous the silver eagle[24] battle standard—may
this be a lethal augury for you and all your gang—the
very eagle which an evil shrine had been built to harbor
in your home. Can your heart no longer bear being
separated from this, so often the object of your worship,
as you went out to do murder and before whose altar
you have often raised your ghastly sword arm, vowed
to the butchery of citizens?

In the end, of course, you will go where your
unhinged and rabid lust for power has long since been
rushing you. For this whole agitation causes you no
pain, but gives you a remarkable thrill of pleasure. Not
only have you never lusted after peace, but not even
after war, unless it were a criminal war. You have
acquired a gang of thugs swept up from the leavings
of fortune and deserted by everything but desperation.
With these congenial cohorts what pleasure you will
taste, what joys you will rejoice in, what self-indulgence
you will carouse in when you realize that in the entire
company not a single upright and reliable Roman is to
be seen. Your Herculean efforts to train for a life like
this will be well put to the test: sleeping on the soil to
lay siege to the object of your lust, or committing a

10

23 A small market town on the Aurelian Way about fifty miles
northwest of Rome on the route Catiline would take toward
Manlius' camp outside Florence.

24 A silver battle standard, said to have once belonged to Marius.
In camp, the standard of the legion was kept in the *praetorium*
near the tent of the commander. Here, the eagle standard was
kept by Catiline in a private chapel in his own house.

crime; going without sleep to keep nervous husbands awake, or to keep honest citizens on edge for fear of robbery. You now have the chance to demonstrate that famous ability of yours to endure hunger, cold, and deprivation. And shortly, you will find out that these powers have been your undoing. What I have succeeded in accomplishing, in keeping you out of the consulship, is to have you attack the republic as an exile rather than as its consul, and to have your dastardly undertaking fall under the heading of criminal assault, not war.

11   And now, fathers of the state, if I am to avert by protest and plea the well-taken criticism our country might see fit to make of me, mark my words carefully and commit them to your minds and hearts. Suppose our land, dearer to me than life itself, suppose all Italy, suppose the whole state, were to address me as follows:

> Marcus Tullius, what is this you are doing? Will you allow a man you have found to be a public enemy to go into exile, a man you see will be their leader in war, one you well know is eagerly awaited in the enemy's camp as their commander-in-chief, the author of the crime, the head of the conspiracy, the agitator of slaves and confused citizens? Will you let him trail off into exile and appear one you have not sent out of the city but set on it?

> Will you not issue orders to have this man clapped into chains and hustled off to his death? Will you not inflict the supreme penalty on him? What keeps you from it? The tradition of our ancestors? But, on occasion, even private citizens have inflicted death on traitorous citizens in this republic. Or is it the laws that have been enacted[25] regarding the punishment of Roman citizens? But, in this city, those who have defected from the state have never retained their rights as citizens. Or are you fearful that this may make you unpopular with posterity? Indeed, that is returning fine thanks to the Roman people who have raised you, a man become famous through your own efforts, not through the recommendation of aristocratic forebears,

25 Such laws as the Valerian (509 B.C.), the Porcian, and the Sempronian, forbade a Roman citizen's being put to death without the sanction of the people. These are the laws Saint Paul invoked to prevent his being scourged (*Acts* XXII, 25–29). The right of appeal, and the alternative granted accused persons of going into exile instead of standing trial, made capital punishment uncommon in Rome.

so rapidly to the highest office through all the ranks of office[26]—a fine return for this, if because of fear of unpopularity or some other danger you should neglect the safety of your citizens. And indeed, if there is any fear of unpopularity you ought to be watchful of, it is of arousing resentment because of temporizing or being reluctant, rather than because of being too strict and bold. When Italy is being torn apart by war, its cities being ransacked, its dwellings going up in flames, do you think you will not burn, too, with the scorching fire of the unpopular will?

I would answer frankly these austere words of the state, and the thoughts of those who share these sentiments. If, fathers of the state, I thought that the best course was to put Catiline to death, I would not have allowed that gladiator one more hour of life. If great leaders and chief citizens in the past have not only kept from soiling themselves, but have even purified themselves by demanding the blood of Saturninus, and the Gracchi, and Flaccus, and other ancients, I obviously have no cause to fear any resentment's lashing back on me for having killed this self-appointed assassin of our citizens. Weighing the matter as carefully as I can, now, as always, I would consider the unpopularity earned by valorous conduct glory, not unpopularity.

Nevertheless, there are some members of the senatorial order who either fail to see the menace or pretend not to see it. They have nourished Catiline's hope by the timid opinions they have expressed, and strengthened the embryonic conspiracy by refusing to acknowledge its existence. Had I moved against him many—not only the irresponsible but also the ignorant —would say, persuaded by the influence of these men, that I had acted ruthlessly and tyrannically. I now know perfectly well that, if Catiline arrives at Manlius' camp where he is headed, no one can be so dumb as not to see that a conspiracy has been formed, nor so irresponsible as not to admit it. With this one man executed, however, I also know perfectly well that this disease in the republic can only be temporarily contained, not permanently rooted out. If he casts himself out and

12

26 Cicero was quaestor in 75 B.C., aedile in 69, praetor in 66, consul in 63 (at the age of 42, the earliest age at which a citizen was eligible for the consulship).

takes his forces with him and herds all the rest of his crew of castaways together in the same place, not only this fully grown disease in the body politic, but also the root and seed of all future evil will be stamped out and done away with.

13   For a long time, fathers of the state, we have lived in the midst of the dangers and snares of a conspiracy; for some reason or other, it has only flared forth in the full development of its accumulated viciousness, its seething hatred and raving compulsion, in the year of my consulship. If that one culprit were taken out of the pack of robbers, we should enjoy a brief respite from our fear and anxiety. But the danger would still lodge deep in the veins and the vitals of the body politic. Just as, often, men racked by disease and by the searing heat of a fever, when given cold water to drink, seem at first to be getting better; but then are attacked all the more severely and agonizingly; so if this disease in the body of our state is lightened by the punishment of that one villain, it will descend again all the more heavily because the rest have been left alive.

Therefore, let the wicked depart, and segregate themselves from the good, and gather in one place; and, as I have so often said, let them be separated from us by a wall. Let them cease from their plotting against the consul in his own home, from surrounding the tribunal of the city magistrate with their threatening gangs, from lying in wait at the Senate house, armed with swords, from storing up their ammunition of incendiary darts and torches to use in setting fire to the city. And finally, let every man's intention toward the state be engraved on his forehead. I can promise you this, fathers of the state: so great will be your consuls' diligence, so mighty your own influence and authority, so valorous the determination of the knights, so unanimous the resolve of all good citizens, that when Catiline has gone his way, you will see all these matters made clear, brought to light, overwhelmed, and punished.

And so, Catiline, in the light of these omens, and to the complete deliverance of the state, go: set forth on your unholy course of war, and take your pestilence and your plague with you; the day of reckoning is also at hand for those who have joined themselves to you in every kind of crime and parental murder. But you,

Jupiter Stator,[27] our bulwark and defender, whose worship Romulus established under the very auspices by which he founded this city, and whom we have rightly named the establisher and protector of this city and of its dominion, you will surely keep this man and this man's confederates from your temples and from the temples of the other gods, from the houses and walls of our city, from the lives and fortunes of our citizens. And you will harrow with everlasting punishment, alive and dead, these men who have become the personal enemies of loyal citizens, the public enemies of the state, the robbers of Italy, an abominable brotherhood for sedition and crime.

The Second Oration Against Catiline

Now, at last, my fellow citizens, we have driven Catiline from the city, a Catiline raving in his arrogance, exhaling crime, foully devising the destruction of his fatherland, menacing you and this city with sword and flame. Or, perhaps, we did not so much drive him out as usher him to the city gates, when he decided to leave, our parting words still ringing in his ears. He has gone, departed, made off, disappeared. So now, no disaster will be aimed at these very walls from within the walls by that fantastic fiend. We have triumphed over the supreme commander of the civil war: there can be no question about that. The dagger will no longer play about our ribs, we no longer need fear him on the Campus Martius, in the forum, in the Senate house, nor within the walls of our own homes. He has been thrown off balance by being forced out of the city, and we can now wage a proper war openly, unhampered by any secret enemy. We have thoroughly ruined the man and won a splendid victory, by flushing him out of concealment and exposing him for the outlaw he is. What thoughts are running through his mind now that he has

1

27 This oration was delivered in the temple of Jupiter Stator and these closing words were undoubtedly addressed to the statue itself. The epithet Stator, "the Stayer," was given to Jupiter, according to Livy, because of an incident in the fight between the Romans under Romulus and the Sabines. When Romulus' men started to run away, Jupiter stopped them from running.

been prevented from raising the bloody tip of his
sword in the air wet with my blood, his most cherished
desire, and has left Rome with me still alive? Now that
we have wrested the iron from his hands, and he has
been made to withdraw from the city, while its citizens
are still unharmed and the city still stands? Can you
not imagine the sorrow and pain that assault him? He
now lies prostrate, my fellow citizens, knowing full
well he has been struck down and cast out: surely he
keeps glaring back at the city with baleful eyes, grieving
to sense that it has been snatched from his jaws. But
the city, I imagine, rejoices greatly, because it has
spewed forth so vile a traitor and cast him out of its
teeth.

2   Should there be someone among you who thinks,
as all right-minded men ought to, that I am to blame
for not apprehending so dangerous a public enemy
rather than allowing him to leave the city—even in this
oration wherein I declare our joy and gladness, I say
to you, my fellow citizens, that the fault is not mine,
but that of the times in which we live. Catiline should
have long since been put to death after being visited
with the most drastic sentence in our law. I should
have followed that course, according to the dictates of
tradition, the emergency authority of the powers conferred on me by special decree of the Senate, and the
republic itself. But how many were there among you
who refused to believe the facts I reported, who even
defended Catiline! Yet, had I come to the conclusion
that with Catiline out of the way, all danger to you
would be past, I would have done away with him long
ago, whatever the cost, not merely to my popularity,
but even to my life. When I saw, however, that, as the
fact of the conspiracy was, even then, not taken as
proved by all of you, if I took his life as he deserved,
I would be kept by the resentment it provoked from
following up after his accomplices, I brought the matter
around to this position in order that you might fight
openly against an enemy you clearly saw.

And, my fellow citizens, how seriously I felt this
enemy was to be feared outside the city, you will judge
from the fact that I am quite uneasy about the very
small number of adherents who left town with him. I
wish he had taken all his troops, but I see that he only
took along Tongilius, whom he has liked ever since he

was but a boy, and Publicius and Minucius,[1] whose unpaid bills in cheap restaurants and dives would not turn them into revolutionaries against the state. But he left behind quite a few bold allies, many men desperately in debt or bankrupt, and many influential members of good families!

In comparison with our Cisalpine legions, and the levy of troops Quintus Metellus[2] has made in Umbria and on the plains of Picenum, I have nothing but scorn for the mob Catiline has glued together, composed of some superannuated veterans of Sulla's armies, a motley crew of country wastrels, a group of bankrupt peasants, and some suspicious characters who rather would jump bail than desert the ragged ranks of Catiline. They will promptly fall to pieces if they see, not even our army in battle order, but an order of the day issued by the praetor. I would much rather he had led out of the city in his train, to be soldiers in his ranks, those I still notice in evidence hereabouts, flitting about in the forum, or standing around near the Senate house, or entering the Senate, sleeked down with pomade, sporting togas with broad purple-striped borders. If they stay in the city, mark my words, it is not Catiline's field army we need guard against, but these deserters from his army. Especially alarming, I find, is the way they realize perfectly well that I know what they are plotting, but are not the least upset. I can see the man who has been awarded the province of Apulia as his share of the victory spoils, the man who will take over Etruria, the one who will have the region of Picenum, the one who gets Cisalpine Gaul, the one who has pre-empted for himself the treacherous scheme for murdering citizens of Rome here within the walls and for setting fire to the city. They know that all their secret plans, made the night before last, have been duly communicated to me: I revealed them in the Senate yesterday. Catiline took fright and took flight—so what are these minions waiting for? If they hope that my originally lenient attitude will last any longer, they are utterly mistaken.

---

[1] These men are known to us only by the reference to them here.
[2] Quintus Metellus Celer, the husband of the Clodia Cicero takes to task in the oration *In Defense of Caelius*. In 63 B.C., he was the *praetor urbanus*. Subsequently, he was the governor of Cisalpine Gaul; and in 60 B.C., he was consul.

4   The thing I have been waiting for I have at last
accomplished, that you might see clearly how a conspiracy has been formed against the republic—unless,
of course, someone thinks that the people who are like
Catiline do not think the way he does. There is no place
for clemency now, the affair calls for the most stringent
measures. But, even so, I would make one concession:
let these conspirators also depart and go their way, let
them not suffer poor Catiline to languish with desire
for his own sort. I will point out the road: he took the
Via Aurelia; if they are willing to hurry along they can
overtake him by nightfall. Blessed be the republic, if it
can rid the city of its refuse! By Hercules, with only
Catiline gone, the city already seems to me much relieved and much better. For was there a variety of evil
or a manner of crime he could not plan or invent? Is
there anything wicked he failed to think of? Was there
in all of Italy a murderer, a parricide, a thug, a
poisoner, a robber, a forger of wills, a defrauder, a
glutton or spendthrift, an adulterer, a shameless
woman, a corrupter of youth, a ruined and desperate
man, who does not admit to having been on the closest
of terms with Catiline? What killings have been perpetrated these past years without his having something
to do with them, what frightful indecency, but that he
has stage-managed it? And, has any man's power to entice
young men ever been so great as Catiline's? Some of
his followers he made passionate love to, others he
generously helped find satisfaction elsewhere, others he
promised a plentiful harvest of lust to, to still others
he promised their parents' death, urging them on to it,
helping them out with it. And so, how suddenly he
collected a huge group of ruined men, from the countryside as well as from the city! He did not overlook a
single man, not merely in Rome, but even in every
corner of Italy, who was crushed by debts, as a likely
candidate for membership in this criminal conspiracy.

5   Looking at the various interests he displayed and
the different relationships he developed, you will see
that there is not a gladiator with a developed taste for
crime but admits freely to having been a close friend of
Catiline, not a flighty foolish actor but boasts of being
a close comrade of Catiline. And this man, Catiline,
habituated to the indulgence of crime and debauchery,
was proclaimed by his coarse companions to be im-

pervious to cold, hunger, thirst, and grueling hours on guard, even though he was wasting the substance of his energy in the gratification of lust, and applying the means of valor to the end of braggadocio.

Indeed, if these comrades-in-arms had followed him, if these infamous flocks of desperate men had made their way out of the city, how happy we would be, how blessed the republic, how great the glory attaching to my consular year! Their passionate lusts are not average but extreme, their arrogance not understandably natural or limited in extent: they take thought for nothing but murder, arson, robbery, rape. They have recklessly spent their inheritance and mortgaged all their possessions. Cash has long since been lacking to them, and their credit is running out. But the same voracious lust, which they always had in ample supply, continues undiminished. Of course, if they were merely after women and drinking companions for their bouts with the bottle and dice, they would be hopeless cases, but pitiably tolerable. But, who can abide this: that lazy louts should plot against courageous citizens, fools against sensible men, sots against the sober, sleepers against the vigilant? Look at them, curled up on the couch at dinner with an arm draped around their all-too-willing woman's waist, thick-headed with wine and bloated with food, wreaths askew on their brows, reeking of pomade and oil, sapped and drained by sexual feats! And they dare belch out their sour talk of revolution and murder, and foreseeing the city in flames!

I am morally certain that some inescapable punishment, some inevitable fate long since overdue their wicked, sterile, criminal debauchery, either actually threatens this mob now, or is approaching them remorselessly. If my consulship, being unable to heal, has endured men of this stripe, it has only thereby continued for some short space the long life of our republic. There is now no nation we stand in fear of, no king exists capable of waging war against the Roman people. Abroad, all is peaceful on land and sea, thanks to the commanding leadership of one man, Pompey the Great. But civil war lies in waiting, treachery within our walls, a clear and present danger is enclosed in the city, and the enemy is within. We must do battle with extremists whose violence will stop at nothing. To you, my fellow citizens, I volunteer my services as leader in this war; I assume the burden of incurring the hatred of the foul villains with whom we are infested. If the disease can be cured in any way, I will treat it by every means possible. But, what calls for surgery I refuse to allow to continue in existence as a virulent source of infection for the state. So, let them leave, or dissolve. Should they persist in the city and in their attitude, let their diseased souls expect what they deserve.

6   There are, nevertheless, among us, my fellow citizens, some who assert that Catiline has been driven into exile by me. Could I accomplish such a feat, I would expel those who make these claims. Naturally a nervous and self-effacing sort of person, Catiline could not endure the consul's scolding, and, as soon as he was ordered to decamp, he went obediently on his way into exile!

The day before yesterday, when I came close to being murdered in my own home, I convoked the Senate at the temple of Jupiter Stator and reported the entire affair to our assembled leaders. When Catiline entered the Senate, what Senator hailed him, greeted him, or, in fact, even looked at him as if he were a ruined citizen rather than a savage enemy? Indeed, the chief Senators rose and left the section of seats he was approaching empty and bare. And I, the irate consul who can hurl citizens into exile with one word, inquired of Catiline whether he had attended the meeting at the house of Marcus Laeca or not. This model of effrontery, conscious of being caught, fell silent, and I laid bare the rest of the plan: what action had been taken that night and decided upon for the following night, how he had mapped out the tactics for the whole assault; I explained it all to the Senate. When Catiline wavered and was covered with confusion, I asked why he hesitated to march off where he had long been preparing to go, and where, as I knew perfectly well, the axes and rods, the trumpets and ensigns, the splendid silver eagle, for which he had had a private shrine made in his own house, had all been sent on in advance. I exiled him? A man I could see had already set out on a course of war? Or, was I, perhaps, meant to suppose that the centurion Manlius, with a camp pitched in the fields near Faesulae, had declared war against the Roman people in his own name, that the army camp was not now awaiting the arrival of its rightful leader, but that Catiline expelled in disgrace was heading toward Massilia, as some people said,[3] and not hurrying to his army in the field?

That would be a sad situation for managing, as well as for safeguarding, the republic, if Catiline, hemmed in by the plans, perils, and perspiration I produced at such cost to myself, should have suddenly taken alarm and felt his strength ebbing away. And then, of course, changed his mind, deserted his troops, veered off the course of crime and counteroffensive, to ride out on the road to exile. Then, not stripped of his weapons by me, stunned, terror-stricken by my energetic initiative, beaten down from his hope and effort without having had sentence passed upon him, he would be called an innocent victim forced into exile by the threat of violence from the consul. If he did this, there would surely be people who thought of him not as wicked, but as unfortunate, and of me not as a completely conscientious consul, but as a terrorizing tyrant. Still, my fellow citizens, it would be well worth it for me to face such a storm of mistaken and false resentment, provided the dire dangers of the foul and beastly war were kept from you.

And so, let it be said that he was driven away by me, provided only that he does end up in exile. However, you may take my word for it, that is not his destination. I would never ask it of the immortal gods, my fellow citizens, in order to reduce my own unpopularity, that you should hear of Catiline leading an enemy host and rushing about under arms; but, in three days' time, that is precisely what you will be hearing. I am much more concerned that I will eventually be reproached for having allowed him to leave without interference, instead of having had him ejected from the city. Since there are some to insist that, when he left of his own accord, he was in fact thrown out, what would they say if he had been put to death?

Actually, the people who keep saying that Catiline has gone to Massilia are not protesting; they are worried. None of them is so compassionate as to wish he had gone to the Massilians, not the Manlians. But, even if Catiline had done something of this sort which

[3] Catiline and his friends circulated the rumor that he was going into voluntary exile in Marseilles.

he had not contemplated before, he would still prefer being killed as an active outlaw to living in exile. Now, since nothing has ever so far happened to him contrary to his own wishes and thoughts, except, possibly, for the fact that he left Rome, and I was still alive, we could afford to wish that he had gone into exile, rather than complain of it.

8   But why discuss one enemy at such length, an avowed adversary, and one I have no fear of, now, that, as I have always wished, the city wall stands between us? Have we nothing to say of those who still lurk in hiding among us here in Rome? Them I would willingly cure of their disease in any way possible— I am not simply bent on exacting revenge—and if they listen to me, I do not see why this cannot be achieved. Let me explain to you, my fellow citizens, what kinds of men comprise the forces of Catiline; I can apply the advice conveyed by my oration as medicine, for what it is worth, to each kind in turn.

The first type consists of men with extensive holdings in real estate, which they have borrowed heavily to acquire, and which they are so fond of that they cannot bear to take any action to diminish their debts. These men make a decent enough appearance, being, after all, very wealthy. But, their inclinations, like the cause they have attached themselves to, are unspeakably shameless. You, there, with your land, you with your buildings, you with your slaves, you with your silver: loaded and well stocked with all kind of valuables, you still hesitate to reduce your holdings and increase your credit by settling some of your debts? What are you waiting for, my man? A war? And what then? In the general ransacking and looting, you think that your possessions will be sacrosanct? Or, are you expecting the cancellation of debts and establishment of new accounts?[4] Those who expect this of Catiline are much mistaken. I will do you the kindness of having new accounts established, but they will be the ledgers of the auction at which your property has been offered at public sale. There is no other way by which those who do have some assets can be rendered some-

---

4 *Tabulae novae:* new account books. From time to time, laws were enacted reducing all debts in a uniform ratio. Such a sweeping alteration in favor of the debtors had been promised to his followers by Catiline.

what solvent. By committing themselves to the losing struggle to pay the interest on their debts with the produce of their estates, they let slip the chance to sell their property to pay off their debts: if only they had done this in time, we should now find them to be better, as well as wealthier citizens. The men of this first class, however, do not worry me greatly, because either they can be made to change their minds, or, if they persist, look to me more like men praying against the republic than armed men preying upon her.

The second class consists of men who, although 9 hard pressed by debts, are, nevertheless, waiting for the overthrow of the government by force, and who want to get into power, but cannot hope for this so long as the state continues under law and order; they estimate that their chances are greatly increased at a time of crisis and confusion. The best thing for them to learn is something that I believe also applies to the others: there is no basis for their hope. First of all, I stand here, on guard constantly, watching over the interests of the republic; secondly, there is the great courage of our loyal citizens, the unity that welds them together, the ample forces at their disposal; thirdly, at our side stand the immortal gods, ready to come to the aid of this indomitable Roman people, this magnificent empire, this incomparably beautiful city, against the concerted efforts of this criminal assault. And, supposing, even then, that the enemy succeeded in what their depravity desires to attain, could they hope to assume consular, or dictatorial powers, or even to rule as kings over the ashes of the city and the blood of the citizens, the end result of their crooked, conspiratorial ambitions? Can they not see that they want a form of power which, once gained, waits only to be yielded to the next fugitive slave or gladiator?

The third class consists of older men, soldiers still in good training, like the Manlius Catiline has gone to link up with. They come from the ranks of the veterans Sulla settled in colonies in central Italy after his campaigns. Brave men and true are they all, I well realize, but they are veterans who lived too extravagantly and conspicuously when the unexpected windfall suddenly made them rich. Although they put up buildings like magnates and savor their choice estates, their throngs of retainers, their sumptuous feasts, they have fallen so deeply into debt that the only way to free them from it would be to summon up Sulla from the grave. They have also driven many needy displaced peasants to the same hope for a return of the former days of plunder by proscription. My advice to both of these types, as members of the same gang of looters and sackers, is to cool down and drop their ideas of purges and dictatorships. So painful to the state is the mere recollection of those days that it is hard to believe that brutes, much less men, would have tolerated such reigns of violence.

10   The fourth group is a hodgepodge of dynamic confusion, consisting of people who have always been in debt and never gotten out of it, some of them because of sheer shiftlessness, others of sheer ignorance of how to do business, others staggering under the load of long-standing indebtedness because of their lavish expenses. They are said to be repairing to Catiline's camp from the city streets and the country lanes to escape being hauled into court and sued, to avoid being jailed, and forced to sell their property. I think of them as experienced shirkers, rather than as willing military workers. Well, if such heroes cannot collect their wits, let them fall to ruin, but in such a manner as may fail to affect not even their nearest neighbors, let alone the state itself. I, for one, cannot imagine why, if they are incapable of living respectably, they should choose to die disgracefully, or why they consider it less painful to die in the thick of a rebel army than to perish alone.

The fifth class is made up of murderers, parricides, and every imaginable sort of criminal. I distinctly refrain from asking these men to leave Catiline. Since they cannot be torn from his side, anyway, they are perfectly welcome to forfeit their lives staging some holdup. And besides, there are too many of them to fit into our one prison.

The sixth and final class is the dearest and nearest to Catiline, hand-picked in quantity and quality as the most sympathetic sharers in his way of life. You see them around everywhere, their hair sleeked down and oiled, either smooth-faced or barbarously bearded, wearing long-sleeved tunics that flow down to their ankles; gowned, really, not clad in the toga. The sum of their watchfulness in the night hours is expended on banquets that last until dawn. In these hordes are

featured the majority of the gambling set, batches of
nimble adulterers and polished perverts. The lads have
learned other lessons as well, how to administer poison,
how to brandish and drive home a knife-blade, in addition to their cultivation of seductive techniques, and
compliance with sexual advances. Unless they leave
us and die off, even though Catiline has been destroyed,
you may rest assured that they will be for the republic
the cubs of future Catilines. What in the world do such
sorry specimens want for themselves? To take away
with them their winsome whores *de combat* to the army
in the field? How, in fact, have they gotten through
the last few nights, especially, without them? And
could such manly types survive the Apennines, the
frost and snow? Perhaps, they think they will endure
the winter weather all the better for having learned to
dance in the nude at their all-night parties?

Oh, how our hearts are terror-stricken at the pros- **11**
pect of the war Catiline is about to conduct, with
that praetorian cohort of prostitutes under his command! Against these splendid troops under Catiline,
I say to you, sons of Romulus, marshal your forces
and man your defenses. First, confront this commanding gladiator, weakened by the wound I have already
delivered him; face him with your consuls and commanders. Then, lead out the flower and strength of all
Italy against that stranded, helpless crew of castaways.
Then, too, the cities of our colonies and municipalities
will meet the challenge of a Catiline lurking on the
wooded heights of the countryside. I will not need to
bring any other resources, equipment, or defenses of
yours into play against those helpless, harassed rene-
gades of that highway robber.

But, let us leave out of consideration all the advantages we are so well supplied with, and he is so
much in need of: the Senate, the Roman knights, the
city and its treasury, its income from taxes, all of Italy,
all our provinces and allied nations. If we disregard all
this and only wish to match the causes in conflict, we
can see at once, from the comparison, how prostrate
they lie. On our side contends self-respect, on theirs
discontent; on ours honorable conduct, on theirs shameless indecency; on ours trust, on theirs deceit; on ours
wholesome faith, on theirs abject guilt; on ours honor,
on theirs dishonor; on ours self-control, on theirs self-

indulgence. Finally, justice, temperance, courage, wisdom, the entire range of virtues, is ranged against injustice, sensual indulgence, violence, indolence, and the entire range of vice. Lastly, abundance contests with deprivation, wise public policy with foolish measures, sanity with madness: and, finally, sound convictions and hope with total despair. In an engagement and battle of this nature, would not the immortal gods, should man's powers somehow fail, ensure that monstrous vices were overcome by splendid virtues?

12   In view of the situation, then, my fellow citizens, protect your homes—as I advised earlier—by mounting guards and establishing guard posts. I have taken measures and made provision for the sufficient defense of the city, without your affairs having to be unduly disrupted. All your farm population and your municipal authorities I have informed of Catiline's journey out of the city last night; they will readily take the necessary steps to defend their cities and territories. The gladiatorial troops he was so certain of having in his ranks (but are, in fact, better disposed toward us than some of the aristocracy) will submit to our control. Quintus Metellus, whom I have dispatched as an advance agent on reconnaissance in Cisalpine Gaul and on the plains of Picenum will either bring the enemy to heel or harass his every maneuver and attempted sally. The question of determining further measures and of proceeding to enforce them I shall soon refer to the Senate, which you see, even now, being called together.

And now, as for the persons who have remained in the city, purposely left here by Catiline to threaten the security of the city and of all of you, although they are enemies, they are still citizens, and I want them to be clearly warned. My attitude may have appeared, so far, lenient and pliable: the reason was that I was waiting for these elements to break out. As of now, I cannot forget that this is my country, that I am the consul of its citizens, and it is my part to live or die with them. No guard stands at the gate, no agent in ambush lurks at the side of the road. If these subversive citizens now decide to take their departure, I can close my eyes to it; but, if any one of them makes a move within the city, and I seize him in the act, or even the intention and plan, of an attempt against the state, he will discover that in this city there are alert consuls, exemplary magistrates, a courageous Senate; we have the weapons, and the prison, our ancestors intended for our use against declared enemies and criminals.

All this will be carried through, my fellow citizens, in such a way that the maximum results will be gained with the minimum confusion, the most severe dangers met without disorder; an internal war of sedition, that men will remember as our most ruthless and dangerous one, will end with me, still clad in the civilian garb of the toga, your sole commander. I will manage the business, my fellow citizens, so that, if there is any possible way of doing so, not even one of the guilty culprits will suffer the consequences of his crime in this city. If the force of open aggression, or the fact of a clear and present danger menacing our country perforce deprives me of the luxury of lenience, I will perform my duty, I firmly believe, so as to achieve the results devoutly to be wished for in so great, so treacherous a war: not a single loyal citizen will lose his life; all of you will be saved by the penalty exacted of a few.

And I promise you this, my fellow citizens, relying not on my own foresight nor on human advice and consent, but on the many unmistakable intimations of the immortal gods, the commanders in whose service I have entered upon these very hopes and convictions. They are now protecting their country not, as in time past, against a foreign enemy far afield, but the temples and homes of their city, by their immanent presence and ready support. It is to the gods that your prayers are to be directed, my fellow citizens. Worship them, and implore them that, inasmuch as they have ever desired our city to be beautiful and prosperous above all others, they may guard the city they have protected against all the assaults of its enemies, on land and sea, from treachery and subversion by disloyal citizens.

The Third Oration Against Catiline

1   You see, my fellow citizens, that the republic has been saved, all your lives, your possessions and property, your wives and children, this distinguished seat of empire, this resplendently beautiful city spared. Thanks to the immortal gods and to my steady affection for you, my ceaseless work and planning, my willingness to encounter danger, you see your city rescued from sword and flames, virtually snatched from the jaws of fate and restored to you intact and entire. If these days are as great a cause for rejoicing and glory, days during which we have seen our salvation, as the day of our birth, the truth is that today's happiness we can consciously appreciate, unlike the precarious condition of our birth. We are born quite unaware of that; today, we experience the conscious joy of being born again. It is my opinion that inasmuch as we have raised Romulus to the heavenly ranks of the gods,[1] because of the good will and fame he earned by founding our city, the man should also be held forever hereafter in honor among you and your descendants who ensured the city's continued existence. This same city, born many years ago, we have preserved, quenching the fires threatening to encircle its temples, shrines, houses, and walls. And I, one and the same person, have blunted the edge of the swords unsheathed against our state and beaten aside the tips of the blades poised at your throats. Now that I have brought these matters to light and disclosed them amply and clearly in the Senate, I will report briefly to you. Then, you, who are as yet uninformed and are eagerly waiting to know, may learn how important and undeniably clear the things we have discovered are, and the means by which we investigated and gained control over them.

First, then, when Catiline stormed out of the city a few days ago, I maintained a close watch here, because he had left behind in Rome his companions in

---

[1] Romulus was deified under the name of Quirinus. His legendary assumption into the ranks of the immortal gods was observed in the holiday of the Quirinalia, on February 17.

crime, among them, the most impetuous ringleaders in this abominable war against the state. I kept a sharp lookout, and I searched out the ways in which we might be best protected against the huge trap being set for us in secret.

At the time when I was in the act of exiling Catiline—and I no longer fear the unpopularity of the term, his having left here alive being, now, a much greater cause for concern—I wanted him banished because I thought that, then, either the rest of his gang of conspirators would depart in his train, or that those who had stayed behind would be weak and powerless without him. As soon as I saw that the remnants in Rome were the very men most on fire for violence and malefaction, I spent all my days and nights observing and evaluating their moves and strategy. Imparting the knowledge of this to you publicly in an oration would win less credence in view of the enormity of the intended assault; if I could catch them in the act, you would take thought for your security, when you saw with your own eyes the evil at work. Therefore, when I found out that envoys from the Allobroges had been approached by Lentulus[2] with the proposition that they incite unrest and revolt in Transalpine Gaul, and that, after they had been sent with letters and instructions to their fellow citizens in Gaul, they were, on the same return journey, to go to Catiline, and, that Titus Volturcius[3] was accompanying them with a letter to Catiline, I felt that the opportunity was now before me to bring the whole affair unmistakably to your attention and to make known, not only to myself, but also to the Senate and to you, yourselves, the problem that had so far proved intractable, and the solution of which I had constantly prayed that the gods would send me.

Therefore, the day before yesterday, I summoned the praetors Lucius Flaccus and Gaius Pomptinus, courageous and public-spirited men, laid the matter before them, and outlined what I wished them to do. They accepted the commission unhesitatingly and un-

[2] At this time, Publius Lentulus was a praetor. In 71 B.C., he had held the consulship. Subsequently expelled from the Senate in disgrace, he was now once more a candidate for the higher offices, as a means of winning back his eligibility for the Senate.
[3] An errand boy for Lentulus.

questioningly, for they entertain the finest and best
sentiments toward the republic; it was drawing near
evening and they proceeded unobserved to the Milvian
bridge where they divided their forces into two groups
and stationed them in two farmhouses on either side
of the bridge and the Tiber. Without arousing suspicion, they had marched to this same location a large
complement of hardened troops, and I had dispatched
an elite group of young men under arms from the
prefecture[4] of Reate,[5] a resource I frequently employ
in defense of the state. Meanwhile, the third morning
watch was nearly over, and, as the envoys of the Allobroges were starting across the Milvian bridge with
their numerous train that included Volturcius, we
launched our attack; both sides drew swords; the cause
of the attack was known only to the praetors and not
to any of the others involved.

3   Pomptinus and Flaccus intervened to quell the fight
that had begun. All letters of whatever kind in the
possession of those in the retinue of the Allobroges were
handed over with their seals intact to the praetors. The
troops were taken prisoner and brought to me, just as
daylight appeared. I at once summoned Gabinius
Cimber, the shameless contriver of this whole nefarious
scheme; next, Lucius Statilius and, after him, Gaius
Cethegus. Trailing far behind the others, Lentulus
finally arrived: I suppose he had stayed up later than
usual that night writing letters. To the principal men of
the state who had gathered at my side early in the
morning, when they heard of the incident, it seemed
advisable that I break open the letters before reporting
the matter to the Senate, so that, if they were found
to contain nothing of interest, I would not appear to
have alarmed the state unnecessarily; but I reminded
them I could only refer this whole matter concerning
the public safety to the public council. For, even if what
had been reported to me was not found in the letters,
I did not think, my fellow citizens, that, at such a
serious crisis, I could exercise too much caution. As
you saw, I convened the Senate quickly. And meanwhile, acting on the advice of the Allobroges, I immediately sent the praetor Gaius Sulpicius to seize any
weapons there might be at the residence of Cethegus.

4 A city of the Roman allies governed by a Roman prefect.
5 A Sabine town about forty miles from Rome.

There he appropriated a large cache of swords and daggers.

I had Volturcius brought in without the Gauls and placed under public protection by command of the Senate. I urged him not to be afraid to tell what he knew, and, barely having recovered from his fright, he said that he had been carrying a letter and instructions from Publius Lentulus to Catiline, instructing Catiline to take a guard of slaves and hurry to the city with his army as quickly as possible. This move was to be synchronized with the general strategy, so that, when they had set fire to the city in the different regions allotted in the manner agreed upon, and had completed their large-scale massacre of the citizens, Catiline might be at hand to intercept the fugitives and link up with the leaders of the conspiracy in the city. The Gauls were then brought in and stated that they had been put on their oaths, that they had been given letters to their people from Lentulus, Cethegus, and Statilius, and instructed by these men and by Lucius Cassius to send a cavalry detachment to Italy as soon as possible, for which supporting infantry troops would be supplied. Lentulus, they testified, had sworn that, according to the Sibylline prophecies and the prognostications of seers, he was that third member of the Cornelius family,[6] upon whom the rule of this city and its empire was fated to devolve. He had said that this same year was the very one fated for the fall of the city and its empire, being the tenth after the acquittal of the Vestal Virgins and the twentieth after the burning of the Capitol. They also reported that there had been disagreement between Cethegus and the other ring-leaders: the idea of Lentulus and the others was to fix the Saturnalia as the date for the massacre and the burning of the city; to Cethegus that seemed to be too long to wait.

To be brief, my fellow citizens, I ordered the

4

5

---

6 The three famous Sibylline books said to have been purchased by King Tarquin had been destroyed twenty years before, at the time of the burning of the Capitol. Other alleged Sibylline prophetic books were still in circulation, and among them, was the prediction interpreted as meaning that three members of the Cornelian gens should rule at Rome. Lentulus maintained that the three Cornelii were Publius Coren Cornelius Cinna, notorious for his tyranny and cruelty, Lucius Cornelius Sulla, the dictator, and himself, Publius Cornelius Lentulus.

letters[7] said to have been given them by each leader
brought in. First, I showed his to Cethegus, who
recognized the seal. We cut the string and read the
contents. He had written, by his own hand,[8] to the
Senate and people of the Allobroges that he would do
what he had assured their envoys he would; he, in
turn, firmly hoped that they would do what they had
promised him. Thereupon, Cethegus, who, a few moments earlier, had made some sort of answer to the
question about the swords and daggers seized at his
house, to the effect that he had always been a connoisseur of good iron weapons, visibly shaken by the
reading aloud of this letter, lapsed into conscience-
stricken silence.

Statilius was brought in next and recognized both
the seal and the handwriting as his own; his letter in
much the same vein as the preceding was read aloud;
he confessed to it. I then showed his letter to Lentulus
and asked whether he recognized the seal. He nodded.
"As a matter of fact," I said, "it is a very familiar seal,
bearing the likeness of your famous grandfather,[9] a
man uniquely devoted to his country and his fellow
citizens. That image, speechless as it is, should have
made you recoil from so dastardly a deed."

His letter in the same vein to the Senate and people
of the Allobroges was read aloud, and I gave Lentulus
permission to make a statement about them if he so
wished. At first, he said he did not, but, subsequent to
the whole revelation and recording of the evidence, he
rose to his feet demanding to know of the Gauls why
they had come to his house, and what they had to do
with him; he made similar demands of Volturcius.
After they had answered briefly and consistently, saying
who had been the intermediary and how often they had
visited him, and, in turn, asked him whether he had said
nothing to them concerning the Sibylline prophecies,
Lentulus, driven mad by his crime, suddenly showed
what the power of conscience can be. He could have

7 *Tabellae* (tablets) were shallow trays, not unlike the modern
slate, filled with wax on which writing was done with a sharp-
pointed stylus. Two of these closed face to face, tied together with
a string, and sealed with wax and the impression of a signet ring,
were the equivalent of a modern letter in an envelope.

8 Emphatic, because letters were often written by an amanu-
ensis, usually a slave, to whom the letter was dictated.

9 Publius Cornelius Lentulus, consul in 162 B.C.

denied the accusations, but, contrary to what everyone expected, suddenly, he confessed. So, his very intelligence and the masterful skill in speaking, in which he had always been dominant, failed him, as did the shameless assurance which he had shown to a much higher degree than the others, in the face of being caught in the act and being clearly guilty of the crime.

But, Volturcius suddenly ordered the letter produced and opened, which he said had been given to him by Lentulus to give to Catiline; Lentulus, violently disturbed though he was, recognized the seal and the handwriting. The letter, which bore no name, ran somewhat as follows: "From him whom I send you, you will know who I am. Be heroic; consider the position you are now in. Look to your needs and make use of all the help available, including slaves." Next, Gabinius was brought in; he began by answering arrogantly, but ended by denying none of the charges the Gauls made against him. And the incriminating proof of guilt seems to me, my fellow citizens, to have been clearly established: the letters, the seals, and the handwriting identifying each one; each man's confession; but, perhaps even more convincing were the color, eyes, countenance, and silence of each conspirator. They were so dumbfounded, looking at the ground, yet furtively casting sidelong glances at one another, as to seem to be convicting themselves, rather than being convicted by others.

When the evidence had been duly revealed and recorded, my fellow citizens, I consulted the Senate as to the course of action that would best serve the interests of the state. Tough, firm opinions were expressed by the senatorial leaders and adopted by the Senate without a dissenting voice. But, since the decree of the Senate has not yet been formally promulgated, I will report the terms to you as I remember them. First, a resounding vote of thanks was extended to me for the valor, intelligence, and foresight I had shown in freeing the state from the gravest peril. Next, justly deserved commendation of Lucius Flaccus and Gaius Pomptinus was recorded, the praetors whose stouthearted energy and loyalty I had called into play. A word of praise was also voiced for my colleague Gaius Antonius for having removed from his councils and from the official councils of the state the persons implicated in the conspiracy. They voted as follows: Publius Lentulus was to resign his office of praetor and, subsequent to that, would be taken into custody; Gaius Cethegus, Lucius Statilius, Publius Gabinius likewise, all being present, were to be taken into custody directly. The same measures were to be adopted against Lucius Cassius, who had arrogated to himself the special privilege of burning the city; against Marcus Ceparius, identified as the person to whom Apulia had been allotted for the purpose of inciting the shepherds to revolt; against Publius Furius, one of Sulla's veterans who had been re-settled in Faesulae, and against Quintus Annius Chilo, who had engaged with Furius in the active subversion of the Allobroges; and against Publius Umbrenus, the freedman, shown to be the one who first conducted the Gauls to Gabinius. In passing sentence on the persons present and absent, the Senate observed this restraint with the thought that, if from this vast conspiracy and its host of enemies, nine of the worst offenders could be punished, the minds of the rest might be cured of their sickness.

Furthermore, a thanksgiving to the immortal gods was decreed, in my honor, expressing gratitude for their strong support in this crisis—the honor thereby conferred on me being so accorded to a civilian for the first time—formulated in these terms: "Inasmuch as I liberated the city from conflagration, the citizens from massacre, Italy from war." If this proclamation is compared with others, the difference is, that the others have come as expressions of gratitude for good administration of state affairs, this one for saving the state.

Then, the thing that needed to be done first, was accomplished correctly and completely. Publius Lentulus, although by undeniable evidence and by his own confession, had, in the judgment of the Senate, forfeited his rights, not only as praetor, but as citizen, nevertheless, now, formally resigned his office as praetor, that the scruples which had not prevented the great Marius from killing the praetor Gaius Glaucia[10] (who had not been indicted by name) might not obstruct us in meting out the punishment to Lentulus the private citizen.

10 Glaucia is the Gaius Servilius Glaucia referred to in the First Oration, Ch. 2. He was being held in custody in the Senate house awaiting trial when a mob broke in and killed him.

And, now that the nefarious ringleaders of this most perilous war have been apprehended and are held prisoner, you are free to think, my fellow citizens, that all Catiline's forces, all his hopes, and all the help he was promised have collapsed, for the danger within has been averted. When I drove Catiline out, I thought to myself that thenceforth sleepy Lentulus, fat Cassius, stark, raving Cethegus would give me little cause for worry. Catiline was the main one to be feared, but only so long as he was within our city's walls. He knew everything and the approach to everyone: he could and dared to summon, tempt, cajole. His mind was made for crime, and his hand and tongue were suited to its service well. Moreover, he had picked the right men and assigned them to the right jobs. He did not think of something as done, simply because he had ordered it done, and there was nothing too small for him to attend to, involve himself directly with, spend wakeful hours over, or work at. He could withstand the rigors of cold, hunger, and thirst. Had I not forced him out—and I mean what I say—forced him out of hiding and off into his thieves' lair in the fields, I could not have so readily relieved you of this great weight of evil. Catiline was bold, energetic, well prepared, shrewd, alert to the opportunities for crime, and busily bent on making the most of them. He would never have chosen as late a date as the Saturnalia, nor have announced so long in advance the day fixed for the fatal destruction of the republic, nor have allowed his seal and his letters to be captured to become witnesses to his crime. But, in his absence, it has turned out that no theft in a private dwelling has ever been so clearly discovered as this monstrous conspiracy within the republic has been detected and seized. Had Catiline remained within the city—even though, while he was here, I managed to interfere with and obstruct his plans—still, to put it in the mildest language, this struggle would have had to be hammered out between him and me. With an enemy of that stripe in the city, I would never have liberated the state from its dreadful danger in so peaceful, controlled, and quiet a manner.

All the results I have gained I believe I have planned and carried through in accordance with the will and purpose of the immortal gods. This can be inferred from the fact that the management of such mighty

8

affairs scarcely seems to lie within the reach of human wisdom; rather, in bringing us resources to help us during these days, the gods have made known their presence and virtually appeared to our eyes. Not to mention the torches and fiery glow in the western sky at night, the crash of thunderbolts, the succession of earth tremors, and other phenomena manifested so often in such quantity in my consulship that it looked as if the immortal gods were predicting the events now taking place; yet, what I do want to say must neither be omitted nor unintentionally overlooked. Surely you remember how, in the consulship of Cotta and Torquatus,[11] many things in the Capitol[12] were struck by lightning: the statues of the gods were toppled, statues of ancient heroes overturned, the bronze tablets of the law liquefied; and even our founder Romulus was wounded, as you recall the wound shows in the scar on the golden statue on the Capitoline of the infant drinking at the wolf's teats. At that time, when soothsayers from all Etruria had gathered here, they declared that massacre, conflagration, the extinction of law and order, civil war, revolt, the fall of the entire city and its imperial authority, were drawing near, unless the immortal gods were placated in every way possible, and so, averted by their own will, the fates nearly at an immovable juncture.

Because of their pronouncements, a ten-day festival period was proclaimed, and nothing was overlooked that might serve to conciliate the gods. The soothsayers also ordered that a large statue of Jove be made and set up in a high place facing east, in the opposite direction from the previous statue. The hope they voiced was that this statue, which you can see here today, by looking out over the sunrise and the forum and the Senate house, would bring to light the secret plans being formed to undermine the security of the city and its imperial authority, and would make them visible to the Senate and the Roman people. Those consuls contracted for the setting up of the statue, but the work progressed so slowly that the statue was not put into place by our predecessors in the consulship, nor by us ourselves, until the day before yesterday.

11 In the year 65 B.C.
12 That is, in the temple of Jupiter on the Capitoline Hill. It was burned in 83 B.C. and subsequently rebuilt.

Who can be so blind to the truth or so heedless of it, so perverse, as to deny that this whole wide world which we see, and above all, this city, is governed by the will and the power of the immortal gods? For, after this prediction of the soothsayers that massacre, fire, and destruction awaited the republic, prepared for it by its own citizens, which seemed to some men at the time incredible, simply because of the enormity of such evil, did you not in fact become aware of its being, not only planned by abominably disloyal citizens, but also being carried out by them? Is not what follows so plainly providential as to appear to be the will of Jupiter Greatest and Best? Early yesterday morning, as by my order, the conspirators were being taken to the Temple of Concord, at precisely the same time the statue of Jove was put into place. When it was in position facing toward you and the Senate, you beheld all the plans made against the security of all clearly brought into view.

Worthy of all the greater hatred and punishment, then, are those who attempted to fasten their ill-fated destructive fire, not only on your houses and homes, but also on the temples and sacred shrines of the gods. Were I to say I held them off, I would be unendurably presumptuous. It was he, that Jupiter, who held them off: he wanted the Capitol, these our temples, this our city, and all of you kept safe and sound. With the immortal gods as my guides, my fellow citizens, I framed my purpose deliberately and gained this incontrovertible proof.

Indeed, such important materials would not have been so insanely handled by Lentulus and the other enemies in our midst, the letters never entrusted to strangers and foreigners, unless this desperate gang had been deprived of their senses by the immortal gods. And is not this also implied? A group of men from a region of Gaul, from a state hardly subdued, the one people remaining who seemed able to wage war against the Roman people and were not unwilling to attempt it —were they likely to overlook the hope for power and all its advantages proffered voluntarily by members of our nobility? Would they be expected to place your welfare ahead of their own advantage? Do you suppose such a thing happened without divine intervention, especially, to people who might have overcome us, not by fighting at all, but merely by keeping their mouths closed?

10   Therefore, my fellow citizens, because a feast of thanksgiving for all our blessings has been decreed, make these days of rejoicing with your wives and children. Many due and deserved honors have been paid to the gods, but, in my opinion, never were there any more justified than these. You have been rescued from the horrible and merciless powers of destruction, without murder or bloodshed, without an army, without combat; you, citizens clad in the toga, have won the day under my leadership as your sole general and commander, a civilian also clad in the toga. You remember, my fellow citizens, all our civil disruptions,[13] not only those you have heard about, but also those you have witnessed. Lucius Sulla crushed Publius Sulpicius; Gaius Marius, the keeper of this city, and some of his adherents, Sulla exiled, others he executed. Gnaius Octavius, when consul, drove his colleague from the city by force of arms; and this whole place we are in overflowed with mounds of bodies and the blood of citizens. Afterward, Cinna regained power with Marius; but all that time, many bright luminaries[14] of the state were being extinguished. Then, Sulla gained his revenge with savage success. I need not say what those proscriptions cost by way of the loss of citizens' lives and general disaster to the state. Lepidus quarreled with his colleague, the eminent and noble Quintus Catulus, but Lepidus' death brought less grief to the republic than that of the others involved.

11   All those conflicts were of the sort intended to change, rather than destroy the state. The leaders wanted, not that there be no republic, but only that they be in charge of it. Not to burn the city, but to thrive in it. Nevertheless, all those struggles, none of which had the destruction of the republic as its design, were of a sort to be settled not by the restoration of concord, but by the mutual slaughter of citizens. In this, without exception, the most savage war in the

[13] Cicero reviews some of the events in the wars between Marius and Sulla, 88–78 B.C.

[14] Among them, Marcus Antonius Orator, born in 143 and put to death by Marius and Cinna in 87 B.C. His grandson, Mark Antony, was born about 83 B.C.

memory of man, on the other hand, such a war as no
barbarian nation ever found itself in, the rule was
adopted by Lentulus, Catiline, Cethegus, and Cassius
that all who were safe in the city were to be considered
as in the ranks of the enemy. But, I conducted myself,
my fellow citizens, so that you all were saved, even
though your enemies had thought that there would
remain only as many citizens as might have survived
the indiscriminate massacre, and only as much of the
city as had not gone down in flames. I preserved its
citizens safe and unhurt.

In return for these great services, my fellow
citizens, I ask of you no reward for my valor, no medal
of honor or monument to my glory, but the everlasting
memory of this day. It is in your minds and hearts that
I wish my triumphs enshrined, my emblems of glory and
memorials of fame to be engraved. Nothing mute,
nothing silent can give me pleasure, and nothing of the
sort that less-deserving persons may attain. But, in your
memory, my fellow citizens, my deeds will be kept
alive, in your discussions of them they will grow, in
the words written about them they will mature and be
fully confirmed. I am certain that the same duration
(an everlasting one, I hope) has been granted both to
the preservation of the city and to the memory of my
consulship, that at one time, two citizens existed in this
republic, one of whom (Pompey the Great) extended
the limit of your authority to the boundaries, not of
earth, but of heaven, while the other protected the
home and center of this empire.

Inasmuch as what I have accomplished has not the   12
same destiny and character as the achievements of men
who have fought foreign foes afield, and I must live
among those I have overwhelmed and conquered,
whereas military leaders leave their enemies behind
them slain or crushed, it is your duty, my fellow citizens—if others rightly benefit from their deeds—to take
care that my deeds do not injure me. I saw to it that
the criminal and wicked designs of the most unscrupulous men could not harm you; it is your part to see
that they do me no harm. And yet, my fellow citizens,
I can suffer no harm from them. My ultimate security
lies safe with loyal citizens, from this time forward.
The great sense of duty inherent in this republic will

always silently protect me; the mighty power of conscience will incriminate any who dare disregard it by trespassing against me.

I am of a mind resolved, my fellow citizens, not only to yield to no man's aggression, but to take the initiative in harrying all who would do wrong to me. And, if every assault of the enemies in our midst has been deflected from you, only to be trained on me, you, my fellow citizens, must look to the status of those hereafter who, for your welfare, have exposed themselves to smoldering hostility and to every form of danger. For me, myself, what can possibly be added to my life's harvest, especially, since I now stand at the highest point attainable in your esteem and in acknowledgment of my merit? I will continue, my fellow citizens, I firmly believe, as a private citizen to watch over and bring honor to these events carried through in my consulship, so that, if hostile resentment develops because of my having protected the republic, it may not only injure men of ill will, but reinforce my fame. Finally, I will so conduct myself in the republic as to be always mindful of what I have done, and ensure that these were the achievements of virtue, not the happenings of chance. And now, my fellow citizens, as night draws nigh, depart to your homes after paying your due respects to great Jupiter, yours and the city's good guardian. Look to your own security, even though the danger has been driven off, just as you did last night, by posting guards and keeping watch. I will see to it that you need not do this much longer and that you shall live in uninterrupted peace.

The Fourth Oration Against Catiline

1   I see, gentlemen of the Senate, that all your eyes and all your faces are turned on me. I see that you are deeply concerned over the danger to the state and to yourselves, but further, with this danger averted, over what may still be in store for me. I find your good will a joy in trouble, a solace in pain; but do now lay it aside and take thought for your children. If the circumstance of my consulship has meant my bearing

the brunt of widespread calamity, distress, and anguish, I accept the result, not merely with resignation, but with elation; provided, that through my labors the Roman people have been assured of their due authority and safety. I have been the consul, Senators, for whom the forum, where all matters of justice are dealt with, the Campus Martius, consecrated by the auspices[1] taken before the consular elections, the Senate house, the ultimate refuge of all peoples and nations, have never once been free of the threat of treachery and death; the consul, whose home, the common shelter of men, whose bed, ordinarily dedicated only to rest, or even this curule chair of office, have not been free from these threats. Many details I have kept to myself; I have endured a great deal, I have made many concessions, and remedied many matters at some pain to myself in your time of apprehension. Now, if the immortal gods will that my consulship end by having rescued you and the Roman people from lamentable massacre, your wives and children, and the Vestal Virgins, from foulest outrage, the temples and sanctuaries of the gods, this beautiful land that belongs to us all, from the foul fury of fire, all Italy from war and devastation, let whatever destiny may await me alone be endured. For if Lentulus could be beguiled by a soothsayer into thinking that his name would be decisive for the destruction of the state, why should I not rejoice in the fact that my consulship has emerged as virtually guided by the fates to effect the salvation of the Roman people?

Therefore, gentlemen of the Senate, look to your own immediate needs and those of your country, take thought for your wives and children and for your lot. Protect the name and the security of the Roman people and have no further concern for me or the consequences to me of the decisions before you. First, I must hope that all the gods who safeguard this city will recompense me in accordance with my deserts. Next, should something happen to me, I will be ready to meet death with equanimity. Death is no disgrace for a brave man; it is not untimely for a man who has held the consulship; it is not a source of sorrow for a wise man. Still, I am not so iron-hearted as to be unaffected by the grief

2

[1] The consular elections were held in the Campus Martius and ritual auspices observed prior to the event.

written on the countenance of my dear and much-
loved brother here present, and by the tears in the eyes
of all whom you see around me here. My wife, on the
verge of collapse, not infrequently calls my mind back
to thoughts of home, as does my daughter, prostrate
with fear, and my small son,[2] whom the state seems to
embrace as a kind of hostage of my consulship, and my
son-in-law,[3] standing over there within my sight awaiting the results of today's decisions. I am moved by all
these circumstances, but so as to make me wish them
all safe in your hands, should some force destroy me,
rather than that they and we should perish alike in one
general disaster.

Therefore, gentlemen of the Senate, bend to the
oars, for the safety of the ship of state. Keep a weather
eye out for the storms that may fall on you if you do
not look ahead. It is no Tiberius Gracchus standing
imperilled before your stern tribunal, who wished to be
re-elected for a second year to the office of Tribune;
no Gaius Gracchus, who agitated strenuously among
the supporters of the agrarian laws; no Saturninus,
brought to answer for having slain Memmius. We have
under arrest men who stayed behind for the express
purpose of setting fire to the city, of butchering you, and
of welcoming Catiline to Rome. We have their letters,
their personal seals, their handwriting, and now the
confession of each one. The Allobroges are asked to
turn traitor, the slave population is being incited to
revolt, Catiline is being summoned. A plan of action
has been embarked upon that will leave, when we have
all been killed, no one to mourn the name of the
Roman people or grieve over the disaster that descended
on a mighty empire.

3   Informers have reported the facts to us, the defendants have admitted them, and you have virtually
arrived at your verdict by the many decisions you have
already taken. First, you offered thanks to me in most
remarkable terms with the resolution that, by my
courageous stand and tireless efforts, a conspiracy of
desperate men was exposed. Secondly, you compelled
Lentulus to resign his praetorship. Thirdly, you decided

---

[2] Cicero's son Marcus was then two years old.
[3] Gaius Calpurnius Piso, then engaged to Tullia, present on
this occasion as a spectator.

that he and the others over whom you had deliberated should be placed under arrest. Especially, you have decreed that they must undergo punishment, and this, in my name, an honor that has befallen no civilian leader wearing the toga before me. Finally, you yesterday rewarded the envoys of the Allobroges and Titus Volturcius very generously. Everything points to the fact that the men specifically remanded to custody unquestionably appear to have been found guilty by you.

I am, nevertheless, resolved to refer the whole question to you anew, to judge with regard to the facts of their guilt and to set the terms of the punishment for it. But, let me first state the consul's views. I have long since been aware of subversive passions rife in the state, of the rebellious spirit of hatred that was being exploited, but I never believed this large-scale, murderous conspiracy could be the work of our citizens. Whatever the case may now be, in whatever direction your judgment inclines, whatever form your recommendations take, you must decide the matter before nightfall. You see the huge extent of the crime that has been reported to you. If you think there are but a few concerned in it, you are gravely mistaken. This dirty business has reached the ears of many. It has not only coursed through Italy, but climbed the Alps and wound its way secretly into many of our provinces. In no manner can it be crushed by being put up with, or put off; and whatever means you decide to adopt, you must deal with it swiftly.

I see that two proposals have been made, one that of Silanus,[4] whose opinion is, that they who have tried to destroy all of us should pay the death penalty themselves; the other proposal is that of Gaius Caesar,[5] who would reject the death penalty, but accept all the rigorous provisions of the other penalties proposed. Each speaker insists on the utmost severity, as befits his authority and the crucial importance of the matter before us. The latter speaker does not consider that they who attempted to take the lives of us all, to destroy the

4 As consul-designate for the following year, Decimus Silanus was the first man invited to speak on the question of the penalty.
5 Gaius Julius Caesar, at this time praetor-designate for the following year.

authority and blot out the name of the Roman people,
ought to enjoy another moment of life and draw one
more breath in common with their fellow men. He
remembers this type of punishment as one frequently
invoked against seditious citizens. The former speaker
appreciates the fact that death was not given us by
the gods as a form of punishment, but rather is either
a necessity or a peaceful rest from labor and sorrow.
Therefore, the wise have never met it unwillingly, the
brave often joyfully. But imprisonment, and life imprisonment at that, have assuredly been discovered as
the uniquely appropriate penalty for revolting wickedness! And so, he orders them remanded to different
municipalities for incarceration. But such a plan as that,
Caesar, would seem to involve injustice, if you command
it; to invite reluctance, if you request it. Should it so
please the Senate, nevertheless, it ought to be decreed.
I will undertake and hope to find persons who will not
consider it inconsistent with their dignity to refuse what
you have decreed in the interests of the common welfare. Caesar further enjoins a severe penalty on the
municipality in question, should one of the culprits
escape. He stipulates that a guard force of brutes be
set over them, who know how to handle criminals
of this stripe. And he deprives them of all hope, the
one thing that usually serves to comfort men in their
misery. He orders as well that all their property and
possessions be disposed of at public auction. The one
thing he leaves to these abominable creatures is life.
For had he deprived them of that, his argument runs,
he would have removed, along with life, their painful
suffering in mind and body, and the whole penalty for
their crimes. In ancient times, men insisted that some
such punishment as this had been arranged for the
wicked in the lower world in order to instill some fear
in the depraved in this life, our ancestors realizing
full well that, without such threats, death itself was
nothing to fear.

5   But now, gentlemen of the Senate, I see clearly
what is to my advantage. If you adopt the recommendation of Gaius Caesar, since his political course in the
state is aligned with that of the people's party, I will
need to be much less on guard against attacks from that
quarter, with him as the author and advocate of this
resolution. If the other resolution prevails, I rather

believe more trouble may come my way. Nevertheless, the interest of the state must win out over consideration of the risks I may have to run. What we have from Caesar, as is quite in keeping with his own status and his impressive array of ancestors, is a recommendation that creates a permanent pledge of the government's intentions. It was perceived that he drew a clear distinction between the fickle passions of the mob in an assembly and the genuinely popular spirit of regard for the security of our people.

I observe that, of the men who wish to be thought of as favoring the people's interests, several are conspicuously absent, to avoid being associated with a sentence of death[6] affecting Roman citizens. But, the day before yesterday, one of these absent officials placed Roman citizens in custody and proclaimed a thanksgiving in my honor, and yesterday, rewarded the state's witnesses with very generous payments. In view of this, there can be no doubt in anyone's mind as to what verdict has been reached concerning the whole case at issue by one who has placed the defendant in custody: he decreed thanksgiving in honor of the investigating officer and a reward for the person who provided the evidence.

Caesar, on the other hand, knows full well that the Sempronian Law[7] is in effect to safeguard Roman citizens against being sentenced to death without the consent of the Roman people. But a public enemy cannot be legitimately considered any longer a citizen. And we are reminded that Gaius Sempronius Gracchus, the very author of this law, paid the death penalty without the consent of the people. And Caesar, again, does not consider Lentulus himself, lavish and prodigal though he may be, to deserve the name of the people's friend, when he has schemed so cruelly and bitterly to bring about the destruction of the Roman people and the downfall of this city. Therefore, a man of lenient and forgiving temperament has no hesitation in relegating Lentulus to the gloom of perpetual confinement;

---

6 Only the *comitia centuriata* could pass judgment on capital punishment. The Senate had no legal right to condemn the conspirators to death.

7 The law of Gaius Sempronius Gracchus provided that no citizen could be put to death, except by vote of the people: *ne de capite civium Romanorum iniussu populi iudicaretur.*

and he enjoins anyone against boasting in the future that he has mitigated the punishment, and thereby possibly won favor with the popular wing in politics by plotting the destruction of the Roman people. Caesar insists, in addition, upon the confiscation and sale of their goods, so that every imaginable torment of body and mind, including poverty and want, may attend them the rest of their days.

6   Therefore, should you decide to accept Caesar's proposal, you would confer on me a pleasant ally in the public assembly. If you prefer to adopt the resolution offered by Silanus, I will readily clear both myself and you of being charged by the Roman people with extraordinary cruelty, and prove that the death sentence was, if anything, too mild. But, gentlemen of the Senate, could punishment be called cruelty in the light of the monstrous malefaction before us? I weigh it in terms of my own sense of the matter. Sharing with you in the salvation of the state, I am not motivated by cruelty in this case, in which I am so passionately involved—for am I not the mildest sort of man?—but by a distinct feeling of human sympathy and kindness. In my mind's eye, I see this city, the light of the world and the fortress of all nations, suddenly collapsing in one great unheralded conflagration; I envisage our fatherland in flames, ghastly heaps of unburied bodies, the bodies of our citizens, and across my vision prances the figure of Cethegus reveling insanely in your slaughter. And when, in fact, I thought to myself of Lentulus ruling Rome, as he confessed he hoped the fates had decreed, and of Gabinius with him, robed in royal purple, and of Catiline arrived with his army, I shuddered at the prospect of the mothers' sorrowful laments, the panic of maidens and boys, the violation of the Vestal Virgins. Because all this seemed to me deeply pathetic and pitiable, so I present a passionately severe self to those who dared try to bring it to pass. Indeed, I ask: if some father of a family, with his children murdered by a slave, his wife struck down, his home burned, did not exact as dire a penalty from the slave, would he appear to be merciful and mild, or barbarically cruel and inhuman? To me, a man is barren of all human consideration and is iron, not flesh and blood, who does not assuage his own torment and grief by returning grief and torment to his wrongdoer. So should we be passion-

ately strong against the men who intended to butcher us and our wives and children, and bring down the houses of each and every one of us, as well as the whole dwelling place of this government, and would have installed the Allobroges in the ruins, on the ashes of our burnt-out empire. Then we will be thought of as merciful to men. Were we remiss, we must deservedly earn the infamy attaching to us for utter cruelty in the face of the destruction of our country and of our fellow citizens. Of course, unless Lucius Caesar[8] seemed too cruel, that most courageous and patriotic man, when he said three days ago that the husband of his excellent sister should be deprived of life (and Lentulus was present to hear it), or when he said that his grandfather[9] had been put to death by order of the consul, and the grandfather's son[10] thrown into prison and executed when still a mere youth, and while representing his father as an envoy to the government. But what act of these men was in any way similar to the conspirators'? Was it an attempt to overthrow the government? A spirit of winning favor by bribery was rampant at the time in the state, as was a definite rivalry among parties. At this time also, the grandfather of this very Lentulus, a renowned personage, joined in the forceful assault on Gaius Gracchus. He even received a serious wound, that the highest public welfare might suffer no damage; but here is his own grandson summoning the Gauls to overthrow the foundations of the government, arousing the slave population, calling in Catiline, handing us over to Cethegus to be carved up and the rest of the citizens to Gabinius to be murdered, the city to Cassius to be wrapped in flames, and all of Italy to

8 Lucius Julius Caesar Strabo, consul in the preceding year, 64 B.C. Lentulus had married Lucius Caesar's sister, Julia, after the death of her first husband, Marcus Antonius Creticus, by whom she had three sons, among them Mark Antony.

9 On the mother's side: Marcus Fulvius Flaccus was the consul in 125 B.C. whom Opimius killed as an adherent of Gaius Gracchus.

10 The younger son of Fulvius, then eighteen years of age, sent by his father with a herald's wand to Opimius to prevent bloodshed by proposing terms of reconciliation. In the "Life of Gaius Gracchus," Plutarch describes the incident that concluded with Fulvius and his elder son being discovered in a bathing house where they had hidden, being taken, and killed. Subsequently, the forces of the Senate and Opimius murdered the younger Fulvius.

Catiline to be ravaged and plundered. You apparently fear seeming to have made too trenchant a decision in this matter that involves so monstrous and execrable a crime; it ought to be more concern for fear that we seem harsh to our country by mitigating the punishment than too passionately strong against our worst enemies by the stringency of the penalty we invoke.

7   But I cannot pretend, gentlemen of the Senate, not to hear the words you are saying to one another. Voices reach my ears from those who seem to fear that I may not have enough power at my disposal to carry out the decisions taken yesterday. All has been anticipated, arranged for, prepared, gentlemen, carefully and diligently for my part, but, chiefly, thanks to the greater determination of the Roman people to keep control of its august authority and safeguard the public welfare. All our people are present, of all ranks and classes and ages; the forum is full, as are the temples about the forum; all the approaches to the temple of Concord where we are met today are thronged. For this trial is the first since the founding of the city in which we all share one and the same thought—except, of course, for those who, seeing that they were lost, wanted everyone else to perish with them, rather than to lose out alone. These men I except and gladly segregate, for I think they should be considered among the ranks, not of unworthy citizens, but of utterly ruthless enemies.

As to the rest of our people, O immortal gods, in what noble and strong determination are they concerted, resolved to protect the safety and good of the whole state! Why should I single out the order of Roman knights for special mention, who yield the highest place in rank and authority to the Senate, yet rival you in the manifestation of their love for their country? After the difference of many years' standing between your senatorial order and the equestrian order, yesterday's crisis has restored harmony and joined together the two in fellowship and concord. If we retain forever hereafter this union of parties as an enduring achievement of my consulship, I assure you that no civil discord, no internal dissension will henceforth arise in any group within the state. I see gathered here and impelled by an equal fervor those forthright men, the tribunes of the treasury;[11] and likewise the scribes[12] who, by chance,[13] on this date, when their assignments were to be drawn by lot, have assembled in force at the Treasury,[14] but are directed away from that business to the problem of our common security. The whole class of freedmen, even the humblest, are, also, at hand. For who is there to whom these temples, the sight of our city, the possession of liberty, and this very sunlight, and this native soil we share in common, is not only dear, but sweet and pleasant?

It is well worth while, gentlemen of the Senate, to realize how heartfelt is the zeal of our freedmen, who, having gained by their own merits the advantage of this citizenship, truly consider this to be their veritable native land, the country which certain others, born here and born to high station, have adjudged to be, not their native city, but the city of their enemies. But why do I compliment these persons and these classes of men whom private possessions, the government they share in common, and liberty, the sweetest thing there is, have aroused to the defense of their native land and its security? There is not one slave—provided, only, that the condition of his bondage is tolerable—who is not aghast at the effrontery of citizens, who does not want to preserve the status, who does not dare with might and main to do his part for the common welfare. You have, no doubt, been intrigued by the story that is making the rounds of how a certain operator in the pay of Lentulus went dashing about to the various shops here in the forum. He hoped he could subvert, for a price, the souls of needy and unskilled laborers, and started on the project by approaching many of them. But he found no takers for his offer, either among men who were hard-pressed or among men who had

---

11 Originally, financial officers of the tribes, whose current duties as paymasters we do not have definite information about. By the Aurelian Law, they had recently been raised to the rank of a distinct order in the state.

12 The public clerks, employed as registrars and secretaries in various departments of the government. They too formed a distinct order. The poet Horace was a *scriba* in his early career.

13 On December Fifth, the Nones, the quaestors and clerks drew lots for their provinces and clerkships and entered upon their duties.

14 In the temple of Saturn, near the temple of Concord where the Senate was meeting.

discarded their sense of loyalty. There was not a single one who did not prefer the security of the very work-bench he occupied, of the place where he earned his daily wage for work done, of his own tiny bedroom and cot, and the peaceful pace of his own life. The majority of these workers—in fact, I should rather say the whole class—are universally addicted to peace. Every means of earning an income and drawing a daily wage is supported by the number of citizens who can go out and buy things, and thrives on peace. If their income can be curtailed by closing the shops, what would become of it when the shops were burned to the ground?

9   And so, gentlemen of the Senate, the facts indicate that the Roman people are solidly behind you with all the support at their command. You, in turn, must see that you do not seem to fail the Roman people. You have a consul who has been vouchsafed to you, amid the many dangerous traps set for him, and his narrow escape from death, not for the sake of his own life, but for the sake of your salvation. All parties are unanimously resolved to defend the government with mind, body, energy, courage, and voice. Set upon by the firebrands and weapons of this accursed conspiracy, your fatherland holds out its hands to you in prayer and entrusts to your keeping the life of all its citizens, the Citadel and Capitol, the altars of its household gods, the eternal light of the flame of Vesta, the temples and sanctuaries of the gods, the very walls and houses of this, its city. And, on this very day, you must reach the decision that affects your life, the breath of life in your wives and children, the destiny of all, your hearths and homes.

You have a leader mindful of you and forgetful of himself, an advantage that does not always obtain in such situations. You have all the ranks and classes of your society, all the individual members of those ranks, and the whole body of the Roman people united in one and the same feeling, an event that is happening on this very day for the first time in the case of a political and, therefore, civilian crisis. Think of what mighty work went into the founding of this empire, of the valorous accomplishments whereby liberty has developed as a stable and dependable element in our life, of the prosperity won and increased, thanks to the compassion of the gods, which one single night has nearly swept away! We must make sure, on this very day, that such is hereafter, not only not performed, but not even contemplated by Roman citizens. I have spoken as I have, not to urge you on further, for you nearly outstrip me in your eagerness, but only in order that the foremost voice in the commonwealth may appear to have lived up to the demands of its consular duty.

And now, before resuming as your presiding officer to canvass your opinions, I will say a few words concerning myself. As great as is this gang of conspirators and their cronies—and you see that large numbers are involved—so great is the multitude of enemies I see that I have acquired. I find them, as a group, despicable and spineless, the lowest of the low. Should this crowd of crooks at some point, worked up by the compulsive hatred of one of their number, prevail over your authority and the state's, I will nevertheless never regret, gentlemen of the Senate, the planning I have done and the action I have taken. For death, which they no doubt mean to use to terrorize me, is stored up well in advance for every man. But the accolade for my life you have honored me with in your official proclamations no one has ever gained. You have passed resolutions voicing thanks to others for their military successes, but to me alone for having saved the state.

Let Scipio[15] be acclaimed for having bravely planned the action that forced Hannibal to abandon Italy and fall back on Africa. Let the younger Africanus[16] wear his adornment of praise for having brought to the ground the two cities most hostile to our empire, Carthage and Numantia.[17] Lucius Aemilius Paulus is entitled to fame as the great and glorious leader before whose chariot walked in captivity the once mighty and majestic king, Perses. Everlasting honor is due the memory of Marius, who twice liberated Italy from aggression and the fear of being en-

10

[15] Publius Cornelius Scipio Africanus Maior, who ended the Second Punic War by defeating the forces of Hannibal at Zama in 202 B.C.
[16] Son of Lucius Aemilius Paulus, an adopted grandson of the elder Africanus. He ended the Third Punic War by razing Carthage in 146 B.C. His father Paulus conquered Perses, king of Macedonia at Pydna in 168 B.C.
[17] Scipio subjugated Numantia in Spain in 133 B.C.

slaved. Pompey the Great must rank above all men:
the fame of his accomplishments fills the world, described by the same boundaries and limits as the sun
observes in its course through the heavens. I believe
that, among the glories accruing to these men, there
will still be some place for my fame, unless it is somehow more significant to open up provinces we might
repair to, than that those who exert themselves afar
have a place to return to in triumph.

In one respect, of course, an external victory is
better than a domestic success: foreign enemies are
either conquered and become subservient to us or
admitted into our friendship and feel themselves placed
under obligation by this favor. But, once citizens have
started turning into enemies of their fatherland, and
you have kept them from bringing calamity on the
state, you cannot force them into submission by being
generous. This is why I can see that I have become
engaged in a continual warfare against all disloyal citizens. I am, all the same, completely confident that I
and mine can readily fend off the enemy, with the aid
of yourselves and of all responsible citizens, and by
virtue of the memory of the crucial dangers we have
been through, a memory that will abide, not only in the
minds of our own people, but in the speech and consciousness of all people of all nations. And no force
of aggression will ever be found—I am convinced of it
—capable of weakening the bonds of concord between
your order and the Roman equestrian order, or of shat-
tering the great good and true "conspiracy"[18] of honorable men that we have formed.

11   These, then, gentlemen, are the facts. And what
do I ask in return for my services to you and to the
state, for the strenuous efforts you see I have made to
ensure the defense of the government? You are aware
that I have refused the command of a province for my
proconsular year and the eventual triumph I would
thereby enjoy. It is an appointment which brings the
governor clientships and guest friendships among
prominent persons in provincial society, and, that I
prize such contacts can be seen from my consistent
efforts to form and retain these relationships by my

[18] Cicero often uses the word *conspiratio* in a favorable sense,
meaning concerted agreement, resolve, etc. He refers to the conspiracy of Catiline always as a *coniuratio,* a sworn pact.

influence here in the city. But I want nothing from you in exchange. I only ask that you remember this period we have been through together, and my whole consular year. If that is lodged firmly in your minds, I will think myself admirably encompassed by the safest wall in the world. Should violent attack from some disreputable quarter deceive my hopes and crush them, I commend to your care my small son, who will have— I am convinced—as a guarantee, not only of his life, but also of his position, the fact that you will remember that he is the son of the man who preserved all these things at his own peril.

Therefore, attend to your chief concerns with energy and courage, as you have begun to do. See to it that the ultimate safety of yourselves and of the Roman people is maintained. Devote your continual care to your wives and children, your altars and hearths, your sanctuaries and temples, the buildings and dwellings of the whole city, your empire, your freedom, the welfare of Italy and the state as a whole. You have a consul who will not hesitate to enforce the decisions you take and the resolutions you adopt, who will himself be your protection and your shield so long as he lives and can do so.

In Defense of Murena

Murena and Silanus were elected consuls for the year 62 B.C., defeating Sulpicius and Catiline. When the election results were announced in the fall of 63, Catiline began putting into action his plans for overthrowing the government by force and subversion. After Cicero had taken the countermeasures described in the first and second orations against Catiline, Sulpicius brought charges against Murena for *ambitus* (illegal canvassing for an office), hoping thereby to win back the consulship he had lost in the voting booths. The case for the prosecution was presented by Sulpicius, Cato, another person also named Servius Sulpicius, and Gaius Postumus. The counsel for the defense consisted of Cicero, Hortensius, and Crassus.

It is remarkable that Cicero found the time and energy to apply to this harassing lawsuit in the middle of his difficulties with Catiline. The speech he delivered in late November of 63 summing up the case for the defense of Murena is sufficient evidence of the fact that he did. *Ambitus,* from which our word "ambition" derives, originally meant going around the forum and Campus Martius soliciting votes, but it soon came to signify bribery, in the main, or any illegal means of winning office. Several laws had been enacted against it; Cicero himself had, in 63, sponsored a severe law regarding it, named after him, the *lex Tullia.* Like cases of extortion, embezzlement and treason, cases of *ambitus* were heard before standing courts of inquiry, presided over by a praetor. The trial was conducted openly in the forum in the presence of a large jury composed of *iudices* drawn largely from the senatorial and equestrian orders, and of any and all interested listeners who cared to witness the proceedings.

Making the last speech for the defense, Cicero had left various detailed points of argument to Hortensius and Crassus. This left him free to impress upon the jury of "judges" the importance of Murena's acquittal. He could well afford to emphasize the political crisis engendered by Catiline's attack upon the state as a reason to ensure that the duly elected consuls assume office on January 1: emergency elections could not safely be held during those disturbed days. Murena may have been culpable on some counts in his election campaign. But Cicero argued primarily for Murena's fitness for the office to which he had been elected. Murena was acquitted and served as consul in 62.

The main quality of Cicero's speech is its restoration of good sense and good humor to the political scene. He used the occasion as an advantageous time-out from the rough, vicious contest with Catiline the state found itself facing. In a way, he almost seems to dismiss the case by refusing to take it as seriously as the prosecution might want. Casually and devastatingly, Cicero examines the unbending Stoicism of his good friend and distinguished opponent, Cato. He reminds his respected colleague Sulpicius that lawsuits can become matters of quibbling over technicalities, and suggests that the law itself is, perhaps, somewhat overrated.

A strong state owes its security to the vigilant exercise of its military power, Cicero says—and incidentally, Murena had won laurels in the field, while Sulpicius was accumulating his share of legal prestige in the forum. Were it not for our men of power we would have little freedom to press even such charges as these, puny and irrefutable as they are, that have descended on Murena.

Cicero clearly enjoyed the unexpected weekend in the war with Catiline provided by the harassment of Murena. His more than forty pages on the subject leave little doubt as to who was at that moment in command of the situation at Rome. It was a good-natured consul, well qualified for his office, who, in the midst of many urgent obligations, could find time to handle the problems of a fellow citizen sympathetically and resolve them in a spirit of gay and confident understanding.

In Defense of Murena

Gentlemen of the jury,[1] just as I prayed to the immortal gods on that day when, in the traditional manner of our ancestors, I took the auspices[2] and declared to the assembled citizens that Lucius Murena had been duly elected consul;[3] and prayed that the event might turn out well and happily for me, for my honor and high office,[4] for the Roman people, and the plebs;[5] so, do I pray for the same thing from the same immortal gods on behalf of the same man's obtaining the consulship without jeopardy,[6] and that your thoughts and your verdict here will coincide with the expressed wishes and votes of the Roman people, and that this agreement may bring to you and to the Roman people peace, tranquillity, rest, and concord. But if that prayer, traditionally offered at elections and consecrated by the consular auspices has as great and awe-inspiring a force

1

---

1 This speech is called *Oratio pro L. Murena ad Iudices,* and dealing with a public issue, bribery (*ambitus*), was heard by one of the standing courts of inquiry, or *quaestiones perpetuae.* In Cicero's time, there were eight such permanent courts under the supervision of the praetor or his representative, the president of each being called the *quaesitor.* The hundred judges (*iudices*) whom Cicero addresses by title as *iudices* and I call, "gentlemen of the jury," were originally drawn from the ranks of Senators, but, by this time, were equally distributed among Senators, knights and tribunes of the treasury (well-to-do plebeians).

2 On the morning the assembly (*comitia*) was to be held for voting at the elections, the auspices were taken on the Campus Martius, and the *comitia* held or postponed, in accordance with whether or not the auspices were favorable.

3 *Renuntiavi:* the formal word used by the presiding magistrate in making the official announcement of the result of an election, which was preceded by a proclamation of the herald.

4 Cicero deliberately uses terms from the old established formulae employed on such occasions.

5 *Populo plebique Romano:* these words are evocative of the time when the patricians alone formed the *populus,* or body-politic of Rome, as distinct from the *plebs* (masses), who were originally excluded from political privileges.

6 In other words, that Murena be acquitted of the charge of bribery, which would destroy his civil status by depriving him of his civic rights.

in it as the public dignity demands, I also prayed that the event might turn out favorably, fortunately, prosperously for those men to whom the consulate had been awarded by my official request when I presided at the elections. This being so, gentlemen of the jury, and the fact that the power of all the immortal gods has either been transferred to you or shared with you, the same person who previously commended the consul to the immortal gods now commends him to your care, so that, both declared consul and defended by the same voice, he may watch over the office conferred on him by the Roman people, with your welfare in mind and that of all our citizens.

But, because my readiness to do this service for Murena, not only to defend, but even to undertake this case, has drawn the criticism of the prosecuting attorneys, before I begin to speak in his defense, I will say a few words on behalf of myself, not because, indeed, at this point my position as consul is more important than his acquittal, but so that, with my course of action made acceptable to you, I may proceed with increased authority to repel his enemies' attacks against this man's high position, his reputation and all his possessions.

2   First, let me answer Cato with regard to my action, Marcus Cato, who rules his own life according to the sure standard of the Stoic philosophy and who most scrupulously weighs the relative importance of each of our various duties. Cato says that it was not right for me, a consul and the author of a law[7] against bribery, and one whose consulship has been so severely administered, to defend Murena. His reproach deeply impels me to justify my action, not only to you, gentlemen of the jury, to whom I am immediately obligated, but also to Cato himself, a thoroughly committed and perfectly upright man. After all, Marcus Cato, who is in a better position to defend a consul than a consul? Who can or ought to be more closely linked to me, than the very man to whom I will turn over public affairs to be carried forward and upheld, as they have been upheld at my peril by my own efforts? But if, in

---

[7] During the year of his consulship, 63 B.C., Cicero sponsored a law against bribery, limiting the amount of money a candidate might spend on gladiatorial games and other popular entertainments. It was named, after him, the *lex Tullia de ambitu*.

suing for the recovery of goods sold at a formal sale, it is the duty of one who has bound himself by a contractual obligation[8] to stand the risk of a decision, with still more justice, surely, in the trial of a consul-designate, that man, before all others, who has declared him consul will be bound to become the guarantor of the title conferred by the Roman people and be the man to repel attacks against it. And if, as is the custom in some city-states, a public advocate were appointed for this case, the best choice would be one who had held the highest office and could bring to bear as much authority and eloquence, by virtue of having been distinguished by the same honor. But, if those who are returning back into harbor from a voyage on the deep are exceptionally interested in informing those who are about to weigh anchor concerning the weather, the pirates, the tricky and dangerous reefs and shoals (because nature tells us to help those who are embarking upon the same dangers which we have just passed through), with how great a concern should I not be filled now, seeing the land after my stormy year as consul, for him whom I see must undergo tempestuous trials in affairs of state? And so, if it is the role of a good consul, not only to see what is going on, but to foresee what will happen, I shall indicate at a later point how important[9] it is for the common welfare that there be two consuls in office January first. If that is so, then, it is not the sense of duty that calls on me to support the situation of a man who is my friend, but the republic calling on the consul to protect the public interest. That I had a law against bribery passed is certainly a fact, but I did not thereby abrogate a law I had long since taken seriously, a law to defend citizens from danger. Indeed, if I admitted that bribery had been committed, and offered as a defense that this was justifiable, I would be acting improperly, even

9

---

[8] Cicero refers to a typical Roman procedure respecting the rights of contract sale, and compares himself, a person bound to make good Murena's title to the consulship, to the original seller of possessions passing from one owner to the next, and compares Murena to the buyer, in this transfer of the "property" of the consulship.

[9] At this writing, in late November, 63 B.C., Lentulus and Catiline's other accomplices had not yet been punished, and Cicero anticipates the troubles that may still await the new consuls in January.

though someone else may have proposed the law, but, since I maintain that the law has not been broken, how does my having proposed the law interfere with my right to defend the accused?

Cato argues that I am not being as severe when I speak in behalf of Lucius Murena as I was when I was driving from the city by threats, and virtually by force, a Catiline who was menacing our city with destruction within its very walls. But I have always gladly shown the restraint and forgiveness which nature herself has taught me; I have not been eager to wear the mask of dead seriousness and hardness, but I wore it willingly when the crisis of state and the solemn requirements of my office demanded. If, then, when the republic wanted force and uncompromising severity, I overcame my nature to become as ruthless as I was forced into being, not as I wished, may I not now respond to the sympathetic and humane qualities which all the motives in this case prompt in me and accord them my usual degree of natural energy and enthusiasm? At a later point in this speech, I will, perhaps, see fit to discuss further my obligations to the defense and your criticism of it.

Gentlemen of the jury, I am as much disturbed by the complaint of Servius Sulpicius, a most learned and gifted man, as I am by the accusation of Cato. Sulpicius objects most seriously and forcefully that I forget the close familiarity that exists between him and me and our long friendship when I undertake to defend Murena's case against him. I want to satisfy him on this score by proposing that you, gentlemen of the jury, decide between us. And, as it is a serious matter to be accused of betraying a friendship, to have been falsely accused is not something to be overlooked. Servius Sulpicius, I myself am the first to admit, that in your claim to the consulship, I ought to have shown you every consideration and service in view of our close friendship, and, I think, I did so. When you were canvassing for the office of consul, you lacked nothing in the way of support from me that was yours to be asked for from a friend, or a man of influence, or a consul. That time is now over and the position of things is changed. I therefore think, and I am utterly convinced, that, just as I was under obligation to you to whatever extent you saw fit to require then, now I am

under absolutely no obligation to you when you attack
the good name and welfare of Murena. Even if, when   *4*
you were seeking the consular office, I was of service
to you, when you now prosecute Murena, I ought not
to be your ally in the same way. This is not only not
to be praised, it is not to be acquiesced in, that, when
our friends are the accusers, we may not defend even
total strangers. Gentlemen of the jury, there is between
Murena and me an old and well-tested bond of friendship which in this suit Servius brings against Murena's
civil status,[10] will not be submerged even though it was
overwhelmed when he competed for the consulship
against Servius, and I supported Servius. If the problem
had not come up, still, the man's dignity or the grandeur of the high office he has attained would have
branded me with the reproach of pride and cruelty,
had I refused a case in which so much is at stake for
a person of such significance, both in his own attain-
ments and in the distinctions conferred on him by the
Roman people. It is not allowed me, nor is the possibility open to me that I should not communicate my
willingness to work toward relieving men in danger.
Because greater rewards have been bestowed on me
for my efforts than on any other man before my time,
I think it would be cunning and ungrateful to discontinue the efforts after one has gained the rewards, and
would imply that the efforts had been based on self-
interest, that he who once made them had conveniently
forgotten about all those who assisted him in achieving
his ends. If it is permissible to discontinue, if I can do
that on your assurance that I would be beyond reproach, if no fault of laziness, pride, or disregard of my
fellow man attaches to me, indeed, I am content to
desist. But if, avoiding effort convicts me of sloth, the
rejection of suppliants of pride, the neglect of friends
of disloyalty, no wonder the present trial is of such a
sort that no one who is sympathetic and loyal can re-
linquish it. This interpretation of the matter, Servius,
you will most readily grasp by considering your own
profession. For, if you think that it is necessary to give
legal advice to opponents of your friends who consult
you about points of law, and consider it disgraceful, if
the very person by whom you have been consulted

10 The *lex Tullia de ambitu* carried as a penalty degradation
from the Senate and banishment for ten years.

loses his case when you oppose him in court, do not be so unfair as to think that, when your fluent resources of legal advice lie open to even your opponents, ours ought to be closed to our friends. If my intimate association with you had induced me to decline this case and similarly had affected Quintus Hortensius[11] and Marcus Crassus,[12] those outstanding men, if the same effect were produced on others by whom, I imagine, grateful obligations to you are strongly felt, it would have happened that, in this state, a consul-designate would not have a defense attorney: something our ancestors wished no citizen to lack, of however low a degree. I, indeed, gentlemen of the jury, think I would be quite the villain if I neglected a friend, and a heartless beast to disregard a person in need, an arrogant creature to refuse help to a consul. Therefore, what ought to be accorded to friendship will be freely granted to me: to contest with you, Servius, as if you were my own brother, nearest and dearest to me, sitting on the benches provided for the prosecution. As to what should rightly be bestowed on duty, honor, and piety, I will so apply myself as to remember that I am pleading for a friend in distress against the efforts of another friend who is eager to secure his conviction.

5   I understand, gentlemen of the jury, that there have been three separate sections of the indictment, one an accusation of Murena's personal conduct, another

11 Quintus Hortensius Ortalus (114–50 B.C.) was the most famous orator and statesman in Rome until Cicero, who first scored against him in the trial of Verres. Until 63 B.C., Hortensius usually supported the nobles, but from then on, he and Cicero are often found, as here, on the same side.

12 Marcus Licinius Crassus (c. 112–53 B.C.). His surname, Dives (literally: wealth), signifies how enormously wealthy he became (by educating slaves and selling them at high prices). He was also awarded large donations by Sulla of confiscated property. His wealth made him useful to Julius Caesar, and he, Pompey, and Caesar formed the "First Triumvirate." After serving as consul twice with Pompey (in 70 and 55 B.C.), Crassus was appointed, by arrangement with Caesar, to the province of Syria, and set out before the end of his consular year on an expedition against the Parthians (attracted by their wealth). In this campaign, Crassus was eventually led into an ambush and killed, together with his son, at Carrhae on the Euphrates. The memorable defeat and loss of the Roman battle standards in this engagement became a point of honor for the emperor Augustus, who ultimately avenged the incident by a triumph over the Parthians.

a prejudicial comparison of the respective merits of the candidates, the third the charge of bribery. Of these three, the first, which ought to be the most serious, was so weak and empty as to force the prosecution to fall back on the legal habit of impugning the defendant's character, for lack of any real grounds on which to attack his personal life. The mere fact that he had been in Asia,[13] a province notorious for its liability to corruption, was thrown in his face. But his appointment there was not sought out of a desire for pleasure or luxurious self-aggrandizement, but as a field mission in military service. If, as a young man, he had refused to serve under his father, the general, he would have seemed to be either shrinking from the enemy or from his father's commission, or being repudiated by his father and barred from accompanying him. But when underage sons are permitted to ride on the trace-horses that pull their father's chariot in the procession, was he to have avoided embellishing his father's triumph with military trophies showing that he had conquered, as it were, simultaneously with his father, in the campaigns waged? Indeed, gentlemen of the jury, the defendant was in Asia, in the company of a very brave man, his own father, as a great ally in danger, a comfort in distress, and in victory a further reason for the father's being congratulated. And if "Asia" carries with it some inevitable suspicion of luxury and loot, Murena is to be applauded for never having looked upon "Asia," but to have lived frugally in the realm of Asia. So, the name and reputation of Asia ought not to have been cast in Murena's teeth, a place from which the fame of his family, the memory of his family stock, the honor and glory of his own name derives great lustre— he should have been accused of something else, either undertaken in Asia, or imported from Asia, something that might rank as offensive and disgraceful. To have honorably completed his military service in the war against Mithridates, the greatest and only war then being fought by the Roman people, was a proof of his

---

[13] The province of Asia Minor was a notorious temptation to Roman governors, as well as to later emperors, because it offered many opportunities for getting rich quick and for yielding to self-indulgence. Cleopatra remarked how different Antony seemed whenever "a Roman thought struck him."

manly courage; to have completed it voluntarily under his father's command was a proof of his piety; to have combined the end of his military service with the victory and ensuing triumph of his father was a proof of his good fortune. It is quite unlikely, therefore, that slurs have any place in these deeds, when praise of Murena has invested the entire subject.

6   Cato labeled Lucius Murena a "dancer"[14]—the sort of mountebank who climbs up on the table at parties or generally kicks up his heels. If true, this is the accusation of a bold prosecutor: if it is false, it is a piece of vindictive slander. And, it is unworthy of so respectable a person as you, Marcus Cato, to pick up any sort of foul gossip based on the suggestive repartee of disreputable men about town. Perhaps you ought not refer so ill-advisedly to the consul of the Roman people as a dancer and ought to look into the problem of what other vicious habits are usually said to characterize a man who goes by that name. No one, unless he were drunk, would be caught dancing or kicking up his heels—except, of course, if he were quite mad—either at a quiet friendly dinner party or in private. Of ordinary sensibly congenial parties, of pleasant surroundings, of delightful atmosphere, dancing is the last companion. You seize on the one shortcoming that, of necessity, is the least and most remote of faults, and you say nothing of other indulgences, in the absence of which, this matter of tripping about lightly doesn't seem to be an aberration at all. No debauch; no love affairs; no nocturnal revels, with music; no lechery; no ruinous spending—none of these are adduced as evidence. And, when things that have the name of pleasure, although they are, in fact, harmful, cannot be discovered, do you think you can find self-indulging extravagance in a man in whom not a single shadowy symptom[15] of it can be identified? Therefore, gentlemen

14 *Saltator:* one who jumps about and kicks out his legs. Perhaps Cicero's tone is ironic here—disgraceful as such behavior was considered to be—as today one might refer to a discothèque as "a den of iniquity."

15 *Umbra,* shadow, can mean a constant attendant, for example, the parasite who follows his patron like a shadow and shows up beside him at a banquet to which only the patron has been invited.

of the jury, nothing can be urged against the life and
personal conduct of Lucius Murena, I assure you: absolutely nothing. I seem to have a consul-designate to
defend, against whom no item of fraud, avarice,
treachery, cruelty, or licentious expression can be offered in disparagement of his character. I must say
I'm in luck.[16] Our defense rests firmly on such foundations. At present, we do not make use of certain praiseworthy facts which will be introduced later, but, practically by the admission of his adversaries, we defend
this good and upright man. This having been established, it is easier now for me to move on to the matter
of the respective merits of the candidates for the consulship, which forms the second section of the charges
against him.

I observe in you, Servius Sulpicius, the finest   7
degree of family background, of probity, of diligence,
and of all the other accomplishments it is fair and just
to rely on when seeking the office of consul. To an
equal degree, I recognize the same qualities in Lucius
Murena, so equivalent that neither does your worth
surpass his nor is his outclassed by yours. You have
run down the family background of Lucius Murena,
and played up your own. But, as to this point, if you
assume that no man is born of a good family unless
his father is a patrician, you will create the circumstances again wherein the plebs once voted to withdraw
to the Aventine.[17] If, however, there are fine and honorable plebeian families, both Murena's great-grandfather
and his grandfather held the office of praetor; and his
father magnificently and nobly earning a triumph at the
end of his praetorship, left the step of gaining the
consulship simpler for the son who was seeking what
was owed to his father. But your noble ancestry, Servius
Sulpicius, although of the highest degree, is more
familiar to historians and antiquarian researchers, less

16 *Bene habet:* a colloquialism not used elsewhere by Cicero
(although *belle habet* is found in the letters), but used widely
by the comic poets, and by Livy (in the speeches).

17 As Livy writes (II.32), there were conflicting accounts, one
being that the secession (in 494 B.C.) was to the Mons Sacer,
another that it was to the Aventine. Later, he seems to accept
the Aventine tradition (III.54).

familiar to people at large and to supporters with the
power to vote. Your father was of equestrian rank,
your grandfather famous for nothing especially memorable. Therefore the remembrance of your noble ancestors will have to be resurrected from musty ar-
chives,[18] rather than deduced from the conversation of
our contemporaries. I usually associate you with our
group of "new men,"[19] because, by dint of energy and
valor, you have succeeded in public life to the point
of being considered eligible for the highest office, although you were but the son of a Roman knight.
There never seemed to me to be any less virtue in
Quintus Pompeius,[20] a new man and a steadfast one,
than there was in the high-ranking aristocrat Marcus
Aemilius Scaurus.[21] It is of the same valuable character and high intention to hand on, as Pompeius did,
to his descendants the elevation of the family name and
to do as Scaurus did: resuscitate a nearly lifeless memory of his family's nobility by virtue of his own admirable deeds. As a matter of fact, gentlemen of the
jury, I was thinking that, not having their lowly origins
cast in the teeth of many excellent men, was due to
my efforts, for I have been eager to praise, not only
such great heroes of old as Curius,[22] Cato,[23] and Pom-

8

18 The oldest of the Roman annalists were Quintus Fabius
Pictor and Lucius Concius Alimentus. The annalists formed Livy's
chief authority.

19 Sulpicius, like Cicero, would be the first of his family to
gain the consulship; this is the special meaning of the term *novus
homo*, "new man."

20 Quintus Pompeius Rufus (the first of his family to hold the
consulship), consul in 141 B.C. and the first plebeian censor, in
131 B.C. Said to have been the son of a flute-player, he fought
against the guerilla chieftain Viriathus in Spain and before
Numantia (taken by Scipio Africanus Minor after a long siege,
133 B.C.).

21 Marcus Aemilius Scaurus (163–89 B.C.). Twice consul (115
and 107 B.C.), the first of his family in four generations to hold
the consulship, censor in 109. He constructed the Via Aemilia
that is a continuation of the Via Aurelia from Volterra to Dertona
and Vada Sabatia. The other, better-known, Via Aemilia was an
extension northwest from Rimini to Piacenza, and, later, as far as
Milan, of the great northern highway, the Via Flaminia, extending
209 miles from Rome to Rimini. The builder of the northwest
Via Aurelia was Marcus Aemilius Lepidus, consul in 187 B.C.

22 Manius Curius Dentatus, conqueror of Pyrrhus at Bene-
ventum in 275 B.C.

23 Marcus Porcius Cato, the censor. Consul in 195 B.C.

pey, all new men, but also such recent examples as
Marius,[24] Didius,[25] and Caelius.[26] When I had broken
through the barrier, behind which nobility of birth had
been entrenched these past thirty years, so that the
approach to the consulship would hereafter be, as it
was in the era of our ancestors, not more accessible to
nobility of birth than to excellence of ability, I did not
think that when a consul-designate, from an old and
famous family was being defended by a consul, the son
of a Roman knight, his accusers would speak out
against the newness of his family origins. It happened
that I myself competed for the office against two patricians,[27] one an arrogant and shameless type, the other
a modest and exemplary person: nevertheless, I surpassed Catiline in personal merit and Galba in popularity. But, if that victory constitutes ground for criticism against a new man, surely envious and hostile
forces would be plentifully arrayed against me. Let us
cease, then, speaking of family background, which is
sufficiently impressive for both men, and look to the
rest of the charge.

"He ran for the office of quaestor with me and I
was the first to be named as elected."[28] All objections
do not have to be answered. Since many equal in rank
were elected, you all realize that only one man can,
after all, be named first as having the most votes, and
the order of importance is not that in which the elected
officials are announced. The reporting of the votes must
be done in succession, but the ultimate distinction and
rank of all the quaestors chosen is ordinarily the same.
And, the quaestorial assignments for both of you were
appointments of practically the same weight. Murena
obtained, by the *lex Titia*, a quiet and tranquil prov-

24 Gaius Marius (157–86 B.C.), conqueror of Jugurtha (107–
105), of the Teutones at Aquae Sextiae (Aix-en-Provence), in
102, and of the Cimbri at Vercellae, in 101. He held the consulship
seven times, in 107, 104–100, and 86 B.C.
25 Titus Didius, consul in 98.
26 Gaius Caelius Caldus, consul in 94.
27 Lucius Sergius Catiline and Publius Sulpicius Galba. The
other four candidates for 63 were plebeians.
28 The quaestors were elected at the assembly of the thirty-five
tribes (*comitia tributa*), and the candidate who first got the votes
of eighteen of the thirty-five tribes taken in order was declared
elected before the others.

ince,[29] you, the one which the quaestors usually
grumble at when it falls to their lot, the department of
Ostia, which does not so much confer influence and
fame on its supervisor as cause him inordinate trouble
and worry. During your term, both your names took a
quiet rest during your quaestorships. The lot drawn
gave neither of you any field[30] in which your particular
talents might be displayed to the point of receiving
some unusual recognition. The discussion next pertains
to the time between the quaestorship and praetorship.
It was spent in quite different ways.

9   Servius spent it here with me in the city waging
the wars of the law courts, giving advice to his clients,
drawing up documents, advising those involved in lawsuits how to avoid injuring their case, worrisome and
exasperating maneuvers. He applied himself to the study
of civil law, lost sleep, worked hard, helped many, put
up with a good deal of stupidity, withstanding the arrogance and swallowing the insults he was offered, living
according to the wishes of others, not of himself. It is
praiseworthy and deserving of recognition by all for
one man to apply himself diligently to that learned profession which is beneficial to many. Meanwhile, what
of Murena? He was the staff officer of a most courageous and intelligent man, the eminent general Lucius
Lucullus. In this role, he led an army; advanced the
battle standards; came to grips with the enemy; scattered large units of the enemy's forces; took cities;
some by assault, some by siege; and marched through
that wealthy and effeminate land of Asia you mock
him with without a trace of greed or self-indulgence.
He so extended himself in that third Mithridatic War
as to have waged numerous and great campaigns successfully in the absence of his commander-in-chief, and
the commander waged none without him. And, although I say this in the presence of Lucius Lucullus,
himself here at this trial, still, so that we do not appear
to be indulging in exaggeration, which would permit us
to invent details under pressure, all that I say is amply
confirmed by the evidence given in the official dis-

---

29 *Provincia* is here used in its early sense of "sphere of action,"
or department, not in its later sense of a district, like Sicily, conquered and subsequently administered by Roman magistrates.

30 *Nullum campum:* the noun *campus* is here used to signify
"scope," "room for action," like our metaphorical "field."

patches, wherein Lucius Lucullus communicated such praise of Murena as no ambitious or envious commander would be under obligation to attribute to another person who shared his glory. So, in both Servius and in Murena, there is the highest reputation and the highest character. If Servius allowed, I would go on to single him out in terms of equal praise, but he does not permit it. He keeps discussing the military career of Murena, attacks this whole subject of his military mission, and considers the consulship primarily consists of his being constantly present and doing the day's work. "See here," he says, "are you, off with the army so many years and never setting foot in the forum, away all this time and now returning after so long an interval, daring to put yourself on the same basis as those who have lived in the forum?" But first, as for that plodding routine of yours, you fail to realize how much loathing and boredom it causes your fellow men time and again. For me, of course, it has proved extremely practical to be popularly on view. When they grew tired of me, I overcame that by hard effort, and, perhaps, you did also. Still, wanting to see us because we were absent might not have been a bad thing for either of us. But, letting that pass and getting back to the respective merits of your pursuits and careers, who can doubt that the distinction of a military career is a more advantageous qualification for the consulship than the glory of civil law? You are up late at night to advise those who consult you, he that he may reach the destination he is headed for with his army; you are awakened by roosters crowing, he by bugles blowing; you draw up a case, he a line of battle. You are on guard that your clients may not be taken in, he that cities or camps may not be taken. He understands and knows how the enemy's troops may be kept at bay, you know how to sue for damages if the roof gutters of a neighbor's house are directed so as to drain water[31] onto your client's property. He is trained in ways of enlarging our territories, you in defining the boundaries of your clients' property. No wonder, then—I must say

[31] *Ut aquae pluviae arcentur:* if anyone diverted the rain water from his own property to his neighbor's and caused any damage, it was open to the injured party to bring an *actio pluviae arcendae.* This applied only to land; a man who possessed the right of turning the dripping from the eaves onto his neighbor's land was said to have a *ius stillicidii.*

what I feel to be so—that the excellence of the military
profession overshadows all others. This is the art which
has given a name to the Roman people and brought
everlasting glory on their city, which has forced the
whole inhabited earth to obey our rule. All the many
activities of our city life, these celebrated skills, we
claim, our famous "forensic" style and our energetic
craft in applying it, huddle in the protective shade of
our military prowess. Let but the suspicion of a conflict be noised about, and straightway our civilian arts
fall silent.

Inasmuch as you seem to me to embrace that legal
profession of yours as if it were your own daughter, I
will not let you persist in so great an error as to go
on thinking that it is something unusually famous because you have learned it. I deemed you worthy of the
consulship, and of other high office on many other
counts: your continence, gravity, sense of justice, reliability. The knowledge of civil law you gained through
study I will not call a waste of time, but simply remind
you that the path to the consulship is not particularly
well reinforced by that sort of discipline. All our civilian arts which, as intellectual pursuits, win for us the
support of the Roman people, ought to manifest both
an admirably dignified character and a kind of pleasurable usefulness. The very greatest respect is due those
who excel in renown for military prowess: everything
in our empire and in the conditions of our state we
consider protected and strengthened by our men of
war; also, our being able to enjoy our republic and the
conduct of our affairs results from their far-ranging
plans and exposure to danger. Another significant and
respectable capacity which has often been decisive in
the choice of a consul is the ability to influence, by
means of wise advice and eloquence, the minds of the
Senators, the people, and those who act as jurors. The
consul is in demand who can, by his power of speech,
thwart the impassioned utterances of the tribunes, turn
aside the excited masses, stand firm against bribery.
Small wonder, then, that, in view of this capacity, men
not of noble birth have attained the consulship, especially, when this very same power earns them widespread favor with the public, strong and firm friendships, and devoted attachments. None of these possibilities, Sulpicius, are contained in that minor technical

accomplishment of yours. First of all, there is no room for dignity in that slender talent: the subjects are trivial and largely a matter of quibbles about words, and letters, and punctuation[32] between words. Then too, although our ancestors first found something to admire in the legal art, when your secrets were unveiled, the thing was held in contempt and disregarded. Formerly, few had knowledge of whether or not an action could be legally conducted; the calendar of "legal days"[33] was not publicly known. Those who gave decisions were in a position of great power, and were asked to show the day on which a suit could be preferred, as if they were Chaldean astronomers. A certain clerk, Gnaius Flavius,[34] "who could hoodwink a crow," as the saying goes, was found, who published the calendar so that the people could learn what the legal days were; Flavius robbed the legal authorities of their inside knowledge. They became angry because they were afraid that lawsuits could be conducted without their help, once the calendar phasing of days became widely known and available; so, they invented certain legal verbal formulae that they themselves might have a hand in everything. When it could be phrased with complete clarity as follows: "The Sabine property is mine"; "No, it is mine": yet, at the trial, they were unwilling to agree to so simple a phrasing. "The property," your lawyer intones, "which is in the territory[35] hereinafter

12

32 *Interpunctionibus verborum*, "by means of divisions between words by points"; this is the only time the word *interpunctio* appears in Latin, and refers, not to punctuation in the modern sense, but to the separation of words where continuous letters would confuse the meaning, for example: INCULTOLOCO, which could be *in culto loco*, or *inculto loco*.

33 On certain days, the *Fasti*, legal business could be transacted, on others, *Nefasti*, it could not. In the public calendar (*Fasti calendares*), these days were marked N and F.

34 He was the clerk of the lawyer Appius Claudius Caecus, who had worked out the schedule of the *dies Fasti* and *Nefasti*. Flavius either stole or copied the book containing this "inside knowledge" (literally, "robbed the lawyers' desks of their wisdom"), and made it public. Livy's account of the episode is given in Book IX, Ch. 45.

35 In earlier times, the praetor went with the litigants to the place in question and gave his judgment. When this was no longer feasible, the parties went from the court to the place in dispute and brought, for instance, a piece of turf (*gleba*), to represent the whole estate, which was handed over to the person in whose favor the praetor decided the case. When this custom was discontinued, a new form of procedure, verbose and elaborate, was introduced by the lawyers, which Cicero satirizes here.

referred to as the Sabine territory as it was hereinbe-
fore known." That's wordy enough, isn't it? Shall I
omit the later development of these formulae? "I say
that it is mine by indigenary title." What next? "From
this place, I summon you to that place thence to contend in law with me." The defendant was at a loss to
find words to answer words like those. But then, the
legal consultant went across to the other side like a
Latin flute-player[36] accompanying the actors as follows: "From the place where you," he intones, "have
summoned me to contend in law, from thence I, in
turn, summon you to that place thence." For the praetor, meanwhile, so that he may not be thought to be
happily off and ready to say something naturally or
even impromptu, a chant has been composed with
many silly things in it, especially the following: "I say
to both parties in the presence of their witnesses; that
is the path[37] I show you; now set out on the path." He
certainly had great presence of mind to be showing
them the path that lay right before them. "Now, return
ye by the path." And, with the same fine person leading
them, they retraced the path. I am sure these things
must have looked ridiculous to our bearded ancestors,[38]
when men, having assumed their correct place in court,
were ordered to withdraw, only to be made to return
immediately to the same place from which they had
withdrawn. All those formulae are discolored by the
same awkward phraseology: "Inasmuch as I formally
recognize you present in the court"; and this one: "Will
you say on what grounds your claim to the property
rests?" As long as these matters lay hidden, it was
necessary to seek them out from those who had knowledge of them, but after they became widely known and
frequently handled, when tested and thoroughly shaken
down, they were found to be empty of wisdom, but
full of guile and stupidity. For, although many things
have been aptly defined by law, more than a few of
these have been ruined and degraded by the brilliance
of their legal practitioners.[39] Our ancestors wanted all

---

[36] The *tibicines*, who accompanied the actors on the flute,
crossed from one actor to the other on the stage.

[37] I.e., to the farm or estate, to bring the *gleba*.

[38] Barbers were not introduced into Rome until 300 B.C., when
they were brought in from Sicily. The emperor Hadrian (reg.
117–138 A.D.) revived the custom of letting the beard grow.

[39] The general term for lawyer or jurist is *iuris consultus*.

women, because they were weaker, to be under the
power of guardians.[40] Lawyers, in turn, discovered types
of guardians who are in the power of women. Our
ancestors decreed that sacrifices for the dead[41] be continued in perpetuity, but the genius of lawyers discovered how to use old men for partners in a civil
marriage that would allow the sacrifices to lapse.
Finally, in every part of the civil law, they abandoned
the spirit of equality, while keeping to the letter. Because they had found that name in the books of some
legal advisers as a model, they thought that all women
who made these marriage bargains were called "Gaia"[42]
in formal conveyance of themselves. For a long time,
it has seemed to me remarkable that so many men,
after so many years, could not decide whether "day the
third" or "day after tomorrow"; "judge" or "referee";   13
"case" or "dispute", ought to be the word used. So,
as I have said, the legal branch of learning has never
exerted any real claim to the consulship, a learning that
rests on contrivance and pseudo-problems: it has, in
fact, alienated the respect of the public. What lies open
to all, and is equally accessible to me and to my opponent, is unlikely to secure influence. You have lost,
not only your former hope of conferring favors, but
even the opportunity you once had of individuals coming to ask if they "might consult" you. None can be
considered wise in the possession of a knowledge which
is of no value whatever outside Rome, or at Rome
when business is legally suspended. Therefore, no one
is considered skilled because, in something all are well-
versed in, one cannot be distinguished from another.
And a subject is not thought to be difficult, because it
is contained in a few far-from-obscure documents. If

40 All women, even those of legal age, were obliged to be under
the control of a guardian, supposedly incapable of managing their
affairs because of being weak minded. A way was found of letting
them choose their own guardian, on whom they could impose
their conditions beforehand.

41 Inherited property was often burdened with the obligation
of performing certain private religious rites, and as these entailed
considerable expense, the woman entered into a kind of mock-
marriage (*coemptio*) with a poor and childless old man, who
acquired her property and assumed the responsibility for keeping
up the rites. She then received her property back piecemeal by
way of a gift (*dono*). The indemnification of the rites remained
with the old man until his death, when they became extinct,
because he had no property to leave, and no children.

42 In the formula of *coemptio* the woman was called *Gaia*.

you provoke me, busy as I am, I predict I will be a full-fledged lawyer in three days. For everything concerning a written subject has been recorded somewhere, and nothing is so narrowly defined by the precedents that I cannot simply add "as in the case we are dealing with . . ." to the brief I am preparing. Where it is a question of individuals consulting you for verbal advice, you can answer as you should with the minimum risk. If you answer as you should, you will appear to have answered in your own person of Servius; if you return an unexpected answer, it will appear that you are equally familiar with the other side of the question and its various dubious points. Therefore, not only should the glory of a military career be ranked above your formulae and lawsuits; but also ability in public speaking takes precedence when it is a matter of advancement. Many persons seem to have, at first, preferred the profession of public speaking, but being unable to succeed in it, fell back on the pursuit of law. As among Greek musical performers, they say that those who sang to the accompaniment of the flute were those who were not good enough to sing to the harp, so here we see that those who could not make progress as orators dropped into the study of law. Great is the effort an accomplished speaker must exert, great are the subjects with which he is concerned, great is his status in life, but greatest of all are the public rewards he may win. From you, a specific cure is solicited, from those who speak in public, life itself. Also, your verdicts and decisions can be upset by someone's speaking against them and cannot be strong and firm without someone's speaking on their behalf. Were I proficient in the art I would speak more sparingly of it; as it is, I am referring not to myself, but the present and past masters of the art of public speaking.

14   The two arts, then, which can carry a man on toward the highest stages of recognition are that of the military commander and that of the authoritative public speaker. By virtue of the one, the flourishing pursuits of peacetime are preserved, by the other the dangers of war are repulsed. Several other excellent human qualities are intrinsically valuable: justice, honor, decency, temperance—all men realize that you, Servius, are distinguished by these. But at present, I am contesting your claim to high office on the basis of your

professional equipment, not those good qualities which anyone may develop. All those fine studies of yours are knocked loose from your grip the moment some new disturbance sounds the signal for war. As our marvelous poet Ennius,[43] a trustworthy authority, puts it: "When battles begin, all else is driven from our midst"; not only the wordy imitation of knowledge you lay claim to, but "wisdom" herself, the true mistress of things; "matters are settled by force, the orator is disregarded": and not only the untrustworthy speaker, the master of harangue, but also "the good man, skilled in speech: the rough soldier only finds favor." Then your whole art lies prostrate. "They settle things by the clash of steel, not by trial in the courts." If this is the case, I imagine, Sulpicius, that the forum must yield to the camp, leisure to military service, the pen to the sword, the retired life to the active: so in the end let that be primary in the life of the state, by virtue of which the state itself has won its preeminent position.

But Cato here endeavors to prove that we are making too large a thing of that in our argument and forgetting that the whole war with Mithridates was fought against a womanish enemy. I consider the matter far otherwise, gentlemen of the jury, and will expand on a few points, if I may: only a few, for the case does not turn on this issue. For, if all the wars we waged with the Greeks are to be scorned, let the triumph of Curius over King Pyrrhus be ridiculed, Flaminius' over Philippus, Fulvius'[44] over the Aetolians, Paulus'[45] over King Perses, Metellus'[46] over Pseudophilippus, Mummius'[47] over the Corinthians. But, if these wars have been very significant and the victories gained in

---

43 Quintus Ennius of Rudiae in Calabria (239–169 B.C.). The lines Cicero introduces here are from his *Annales,* a hexameter poem about the history of Rome from earliest times to his own day (Book VIII, ll. 276 ff.).

44 Marcus Fulvius Nobilior, who celebrated a triumph over the Aetolians in 187 B.C. They had assisted Antiochus, king of Syria.

45 Lucius Aemilius Paulus Macedonicus, who defeated Perses (Perseus), king of Macedonia, at the battle of Pydna in 168 B.C.

46 Quintus Caecilius Metellus celebrated his triumph over Andriscus, a youth who pretended to be the son of Philip, in Macedonia in 146 B.C.

47 Lucius Mummius celebrated a triumph in 146 B.C. for his victory over the Achaeans and his capture of Corinth, when Greece was reduced to a Roman province under the name of Achaia.

these wars widely celebrated, why are the Asiatic nations and our enemy Mithridates scorned by you? Yet, I observe from the records of ancient history that the Roman people fought one of their major wars against Antiochus the Great:—the victory in this war was shared equally by Lucius Scipio and his brother Publius Scipio:—the type of glory which Publius attached to this sort of triumph is evident in the cognomen he took after his victory over Hannibal, as a result of which he was called Publius Cornelius Scipio Africanus Maior; and his brother assumed this same kind of glorious title by virtue of his triumph over Antiochus, after which he was called Lucius Cornelius Scipio Asiaticus. Also, in the war against Antiochus,[48] Cato, the remarkable prowess of your ancestor, Cato the Censor,[49] shone dazzlingly: and, since he was, as I myself would conclude, the same impressive sort of man I take you to be, he never would have set out on that campaign, if he had considered the war one that was to be fought against a womanish enemy. Nor, indeed, would the Senate have called upon Publius Scipio "Africanus" to go out as a lieutenant-general to aid his brother Lucius, when he had just shortly before driven Hannibal out of Italy and then out of Africa and, bringing Carthage to terms, had liberated the republic from its extreme danger, unless they held that war against Antiochus to be an extremely serious and violent challenge.

15   If you reflect carefully over what sort of man Mithridates was, and what he was capable of, you will rank him above all the kings the Roman people had made war on. He was a man Sulla negotiated a peace with, after finishing up the war he had carried to every part of Asia, Sulla at the head of a very powerful and very courageous army, himself an aggressive, tough, skilled field commander, to say nothing else about him. Mithridates was a man whom Lucius Murena, the

[48] The king of Syria, who crossed the Hellespont into Europe. Hannibal joined him and tried to rouse Carthage to invade Italy, while Antiochus attacked Greece. Antiochus delayed, and, after having been defeated at Thermopylae in 191 B.C., withdrew to Asia. In 190, Lucius Scipio Asiaticus completely defeated him at Magnesia.

[49] At Thermopylae, in 191 B.C., he commanded the right wing of the Roman army under Manius Acilius Glabrio against Antiochus.

defendant's father, forcibly and vigilantly harried and kept in check, for the most part, but whom he left undefeated; and a man who, as king, having spent some years building up his forces and his pretexts for declaring war, was so effective in his ambitious efforts as to think he might join the Atlantic Ocean with the Black Sea and the troops of Sertorius in Spain with his troops in the East by launching a double attack simultaneously from both sides. When two consuls, Lucius Licinius Lucullus and Marcus Aurelius Cotta, were sent out against him with orders that one, Lucullus, attack Mithridates, and the other, Cotta, safeguard Bithynia, the province of which he was then governor, the calamitous defeat of Cotta on both land and sea contributed vastly and suddenly to the resources and reputation of the king. Lucullus' maneuvers, however, were so extensive that we can call no war more important, or more strategically and energetically fought. For, after the fury of the whole war had concentrated itself under the walls of the inhabitants of Cyzicus, and Mithridates thought that this city would prove to be the doorway for him to all the provinces of Asia, and when it was broken and torn from its hinges, the whole realm would lie open to him, every detail of the campaign was so conducted by Lucullus that the city of these, our faithful allies, was successfully protected, and all the resources of the king were used up in the protracted siege. And what, too, of the sea fight off Tenedos, when the enemy's fleet, racing at top speed for Italy under the command of its ardent admirals with hope and spirits high, was trapped and annihilated by Lucullus? Do you estimate that a run-of-the-mill battle was joined there, a minor engagement? I say nothing of additional battles, and omit mention of the various siege operations by which towns were reduced. Mithridates was, at long last, routed, but still commanded so much influence by virtue of his canniness and prestige that he allied himself with the king of the Armenians and replenished his troops and materiel.

If it were now in order for me to describe the campaigns waged by our army and its commander, I could review the many major battles such as Tigranocerta and Artaxata; but we are not arguing this. I will content myself with saying merely that, if this war, if this enemy, if that once-formidable king had been

16

objects to dismiss with scorn, the Senate and the Roman
people would not have thought they should be dealt
with, with so much energy and thought, and Lucullus
would not have fought so long with such glorious
results; nor would the Roman people have transferred[50]
the commission to put an end to this war to Gnaeus
Pompey. And of all Pompey's battles, numberless as
they are, that night engagement at Nicopolis in Armenia
against Mithridates seems to me to be the sharpest and
most bitterly contested he ever fought. When the king
had disentangled himself from this defeat and fled to
the Crimea where an army was unable to maneuver,
even then, in the direst circumstances and in full flight,
he proudly preserved his royal name. And so, Pompey,
after having occupied the kingdom of Pontus and
routed his enemy from all his coastline and well-known
hiding places, still put so high a value on the life of
the one person alone that, although he now held by
means of his victory everything the king had possessed
or had been encroaching upon, or had hoped to take,
he did not call the war finished until the king had been
deprived of his life. Is this the enemy you refer to so
slightingly, Cato? One with whom so many commanders
fought so many engagements in so many wars for so
many years, and a man whose life, when he himself
was driven back and routed, was of so great a price
that when his death was announced, then and then
only, was the war thought of as actually finished?
Therefore, we would maintain in defense of Murena
that he is known to have been a field commander in
this war, an officer of most courageous temper, highest
intelligence, and unsparing effort; we maintain that the
fulfillment of this work constitutes a qualification for
election to the consulship no less worthy than my
forensic activity.

17   But you object: "Servius was proclaimed first in
the elections for the praetorship." Do you persist, as
though you were holding the people to a promissory
note, in arguing that whoever has been given this
precedence ought to have the same priority in all other

50 Lucullus was recalled and Gaius Manilius proposed a bill
conferring the command on Pompey. This is the subject of
Cicero's speech, *Pro Lege Manilia* (or, *De Imperio Pompeii*).
The measure was opposed by the patricians, but generally favored
by the people, and was passed in 66 B.C.

offices? For what seething strait or narrow channel like the Euripus[51] do you think is subject to so many currents, such great and varied swellings and choppings of its waves, as great as the squalls and tides that characterize the deliberations of the assembly? One day later, or one night intervening, often upsets everything, and one slight breeze of rumor frequently alters the entire sentiment. Often, without any overt cause, something quite different from what you had thought is done, and the people are amazed that it happened this way, as if, indeed, they had not brought it about. Nothing is more unreliable than the public, nothing darker than the will of the people, nothing more misleading than the collective behavior of the assembly at elections. Who thought that Philippus,[52] a person of the greatest gifts, energy, and public esteem, and noble rank, would be defeated by Herennius? Who thought that Catulus,[53] a man superior in culture, wisdom, and character, would be defeated by Mallius? Or Scaurus, a serious, sober, dedicated citizen, outstandingly effective and strong as a Senator, by Quintus Maximus?[54] Not only was it not to be thought that anything of this sort would come to be, but even when it had, we could not understand how. Just as storms are often set in motion in conjunction with some constellation in the sky and often spring up with no apparent warning, so in this popular weather of the popular elections, you are often given some indication of what is brewing, but often the event is so obscure as to seem to have arisen quite by chance. Still, if some explanation is to be given of why Murena was not announced first for the election, there were two things seriously lacking in his campaign for the praetorship, both of which have been very advantageous to him in his pursuit of the consulship. One of these was that the people expected to be offered public shows: this expectation was increased by general impression and by the promises and publicity spread about by his

18

---

[51] Used of any narrow channel, but especially the channel between the coast of Attica and Euboea (Negropont) and the *fretum Siculum*, or Straits of Messina.

[52] Lucius Philippus, defeated by Herennius for the consulship in 93 B.C., gained the office two years later.

[53] Quintus Lutatius Catulus, defeated for the consulship in 105 B.C., was elected consul with Marius in 102 B.C.

[54] Scaurus was defeated by Quintus Fabius Maximus Eburnus in 116 B.C.

competitors for office as to their intentions to produce
lavish spectacles; the other was the fact that the friends
and supporters he had made in his praetorship and in
his military mission, the beneficiaries of his bounty and
witnesses to his sterling character, were in the city.
Lucullus' army, which had assembled for his triumph,
was itself a supporting force for Murena in the assembly, and the very generous public spectacle he
produced for the *ludi Apollinares*,[55] which had been
lacking when he was a candidate for the office, was
presented during his praetorship. Surely, such things
do not seem to you to be trifling as a means of assistance and support for the consulship? And what of the
good will of the soldiers? This carries much weight
with the masses by virtue of the influence the soldiers
have with their friends, and indeed, in the matter of
declaring for a consul, the support of the soldiers has
great influence on the whole body of the Roman people;
military commanders are chosen as consuls rather than
interpreters of words. Therefore, talk like the following
is significant: "When I was wounded, he gave me time
off to recover fully before going back into combat. . . .
I had my share in the plunder. . . . With him as our
leader, we stormed their camp and captured their
battle standards. . . . He never assigned a soldier more
work than he took on himself. . . . He was as lucky
as he was brave. . . ."[56] How much do you think this is
worth in gaining reputation and good will for men?
For, if there is such a scrupulous regard in those assemblies that the vote of the century that casts the
first ballots is considered a definite omen of how the
election will result, and the "prerogative" vote, therefore, virtually assures election, what wonder is it that
a man's reputation for luck is also powerfully influential?

19   If, however, you take lightly these things which do
carry weight, and rate the votes of the city populace
above the military, do not scorn the elaborate style of
the *ludi Apollinares* produced by Murena and the very
luxurious scale of his theatrical entertainment—for they

55 The public games in honor of Apollo, established in 212
B.C. and celebrated annually on July 13. They lasted for eight
or nine days and consisted for the most part of theatrical exhibitions.

56 The Romans felt that a soldier had to be not only brave
(*fortis*), but also lucky (*felix*).

were a distinct advantage to him. Need I say that the people and the untutored masses take great delight in entertainment? This is hardly amazing, although in consideration of the case at hand the point is worth noting, that the election assemblies are in the hands of the people and of the multitude. So, if a splendid display of public entertainment is a source of pleasure to the people, it is no marvel that it was an advantage for Murena in the eyes of the people. But, if even we men of business, kept by our affairs from normal amusement, can find many other pleasures in our business itself, and we are nevertheless enchanted by public shows and drawn to them, why do you express surprise at the unlearned multitude? My gallant friend and close associate Lucius Roscius Otho,[57] restored to the equestrian order its privilege and its pleasure: his law pertaining to the spectacles is in high public favor, because the reward of pleasure was restored along with the honor due that most reputable order of knights. And so, believe me, public entertainment pleases people mightily, both those who admit that it does and those who pretend not to be interested, as I was fully aware in my campaign for the consulship: I had to compete against a rival's theatrical bid for publicity. And if I, who had presented the three usual performances of public games during my aedileship, still felt under a strong pressure from the games that my rival Antonius was offering, do you think that there was no disadvantage to you, who had presented none, in that lavishly gilded spectacle of entertainment produced by your rival?

But let us suppose that all these elements come out evenly for both sides, that civil and military conduct are equal, the votes of the military and the votes of the civilian populace the same, that it is all the same whether one puts on magnificent public entertainment or offers none. Do you, nevertheless, think there was no difference between your career and Murena's during the term of your praetorship? He drew the assignment which all your associates were wishing you would get, 20

57 Otho, as tribune of the people, passed a law in 67 B.C. assigning the first fourteen rows of seats in the theatre to the knights. The places in the orchestra were reserved for the Senators. This recognition of the equestrian class was a sign of the rising status of the order, membership in which required a property qualification of 400,000 sesterces (roughly $20,000 dollars).

of presiding over courts; in this position, the importance
of the duty confers renown on the judge, and his free
application of equity in terms of the spirit, rather than
the letter of the law, only earns him grateful apprecia-
tion. When a position like this is assigned to him, a
sagacious praetor like Murena avoids offense by impartiality in his decisions and wins a store of good will
by the kind spirit in which he hears evidence. It is a
sphere of duty excellently suited to groom a man for
the consulship, as one in which praise for fairness,
integrity, and courtesy is rounded off and summed up
in the pleasure conferred by the games he provides for
the public. What was your assignment in the praetorship? The bitter and fiercely contested problems of
misappropriation of public money that form the agenda
of standing courts of inquiry such as that to which
you were appointed, cases featuring tears and poverty of
dress on the one hand, and prison and informers on
the other; unwilling jurymen who have to be persuaded
and kept on to serve against their inclinations; the instance of a notary being condemned and the whole guild
of notaries thereby alienated; the instance of the largesse
distributed by Sulla having to be confiscated, and many
good men and a considerable part of the state thereby
offended; the frequent imposition of crippling damages;
the realistic fact that the man whom the judgment favors
forgets you and the man it hurts remembers you. Then
too, you were unwilling to undertake the government
of a province. I cannot criticize you for that, something I approved of in my own case when I was praetor
and subsequently consul. But still, Murena's province
earned him the good wishes of many, along with their
highest respect. When he entered upon his assignment,
he levied troops in all Umbria; the state of affairs there
gave him the opportunity for generous action, and by
capitalizing on this, Murena won for himself the allegiance of the many tribes in the provincial towns of
Umbria. In Transalpine Gaul, also, he worked hard and
honestly to enable investors to collect debts they had
despaired of receiving. You, meanwhile, were undoubtedly of service to your friends at Rome. I admit
that; but still, think of this: the interest of friends
often sags when they learn that their friends have no
ambition to govern provinces.

21   Now that I have shown, gentlemen of the jury, that

the merits of these contestants for the consulship were
equal, but the lot they drew in their realm of responsibility as praetors quite unequal for Murena and
Sulpicius, let me now openly state how my close associate Servius was the less effective official, and repeat
to you who hear me now, when that period has gone
by, what I often said to him when there was still time
to do something about it. I told you, time and again,
Servius, that you did not know how to go about running
for the consulship. I used to say to you in the midst of
those very complaints you kept raising boldly and
spiritedly about corrupt practices in elections that you
were rather the great investigator than the shrewd
candidate.

First of all, the scare tactics and threatening accusations which you were applying daily do constitute the
brave man's ammunition, but they both divert people's
opinion from your hope of attaining office and weaken
your friends' support. In some way or other, it happens
(as will be noticed, not in just one or two cases, but in
the majority) that as soon as a candidate seems to be
thinking only of accusing others, he seems to have lost
hope of being elected. And what of it? Is it not fully
justified to prosecute wrongdoing? Indeed, it is right and
just. But there is a time for seeking office and a time for
righting wrongs. I expect a candidate for office, especially
one seeking the consulship, to be conducted into the
forum and the Campus Martius with high hopes, high
spirits, large groups of supporters; it is displeasing to me
if he seems to be only bent on piling up evidence and, as
a candidate, thereby gives advance notice of his failure
to attain the office. It is not his witnesses that impress me
as much as the number of voters he can round up, not
his threats as much as his alluring promises, not his lurid,
violent harangues as much as his going around from one
person to another to solicit their support, especially, since,
in the modern fashion, people generally flock to the
homes of almost all the candidates and draw their con-
clusions from the looks on the candidates' faces about
how much confidence and chance of success each one
seems to have. "You notice how worried and depressed
he looks? He's taking it lying down; he doesn't care; he's
thrown his spears aside." So a rumor glides through the
crowd. "Do you realize that he is planning to prosecute
and investigate his competitors and is rounding up wit-

nesses? I'll go for another candidate: this one has obviously given up hope." Close friends are hampered by this kind of rumor about their candidate and lose interest; they either give up the whole thing or their part in it and reserve their support for the trial and prosecution. Also,

22 in the same circumstances, the candidate is unlikely to concentrate his whole attention, interest, effort, and activity on his campaign for office, for he has the additional labor of planning out his charges, no minor concern, surely, but the biggest of all the things he has to do. For it is a serious task to prepare the materials that will enable you to thrust out a man from his state, especially, when he is not a resourceless or helpless figure, but one who may be defended by himself, or be helped by his friends and associates, even by strangers. For we all run to meet dangers that have to be fended off and, unless we are openly hostile, offer our services and time to friends, even strangers, who are in serious difficulties.

And so I, rather experienced in this troublesome business of running for office, in defending and prosecuting, have come to realize that, in seeking office, the critical thing is initiative; in defending a client, the sense of duty; in prosecuting someone, grinding work. I therefore conclude that it is in no way manageable for one and the same person to be busily enhancing his race for the consulship and drawing up charges for a prosecution. Few men are capable of sustaining the one effort alone: none can do both. When you had diverted your attention from your race for office and transferred it to investigating, if you thought you could discharge both activities handily, you were very much in error. What day was there, after you had embarked on that declared course of bringing charges, which you did not utterly use up in the furtherance of that scheme? You

23 called for a law against bribery, which was, in fact, not lacking to your purposes, for there was the crushingly severe law written by Calpurnius.[58] Out of deference to

58 Under the *lex Calpurnia,* passed during the consulship of Gaius Calpurnius Piso and Manius Acilius Glabrio in 67 B.C., anyone found guilty of bribery was removed from the consulship if he had been elected to it, and required to pay a heavy fine; he was forbidden to hold any office in future or to show himself in the Senate. The rival candidates who made the charges against him would be nominated to replace him. The law also seems to have prescribed a punishment for the *divisores,* or election agents who distributed the money, referred to here by Cicero as "the common people (plebeians) implicated in bribery."

your wishes and position, it was granted in the form of the *lex Tullia*. That whole law would have, perhaps, reinforced your accusation strongly, if you had a guilty defendant. Against Murena's innocence it ruined your candidacy. A harsher penalty against the common people implicated in bribery was demanded and secured by your importunate demands for it; the anger of the lower classes was aroused, there was exile for us, in the senatorial order; the Senate acceded to your demand, and unwillingly decided on the harder role it was to impose on the generality of men at your instigation. A penalty was decreed for someone excusing himself from appearing in court on account of sickness; and, here again, many were offended, for, by making an appearance when unwell, they would worsen their chance of recuperation, or by the difficulties of illness, they would risk losing the other benefits of life, by being condemned *in absentia* to exile. And what more? Who carried these measures through? I, the consul in office, I, who had nothing whatever to gain by the enactment of such laws. Do you consider as only mildly disadvantageous to you the provisions refused by the Senate over my enthusiastic backing? You demanded a general election,[59] instead of the usual voting by tribes or centuries, the passing of the Manilian Law to establish the popular veto, the equal extension of influence, voting power, and rank to all. Men of position and influence in their towns and districts bore it ill that someone should try to erase all distinctions of worth and status. You wanted the jurors chosen by the plaintiff bringing on the accusation (who might conceivably select his judges from among the personal enemies of the accused); the effect was that smoldering antagonisms, so far confined to silent disagreements, might flare up in the faces of decent citizens. All these moves fortified your means of accusing your fellow candidate, but jeopardized your chances of gaining office.

The most crushing blow delivered to your candidacy was the ominous presence of Catiline, as I often warned you. My talented and eloquent colleague Q. Hortensius has already discussed this matter in the most convincing terms in the brief presented here earlier. It is more difficult for me to speak of it in this place when both he and Marcus Crassus, whose excellence, application,

---

59 I.e., quantitative voting by individual citizens, rather than by tribes or centuries.

and skilled delivery are familiar to all, have spoken before me. I, as the last speaker, am not to argue special aspects of the case, but to present a general summary brief for the defendant in such terms as seem to me appropriate. And, although I must go over some of the same ground again, gentlemen of the jury, I will do my 24 best to avoid wearying you. Nevertheless, Servius, do you realize what a death blow you gave your candidacy when you led the Roman people into that fear that alarmed them with the thought that Catiline might be made consul, while you were busy compiling evidence for your prosecution of Murena, having laid aside and abandoned your own suit for office? For they saw you investigating him, they saw you depressed and your friends worried. They saw you keeping other candidates under surveillance, they marked your sworn statements, your taking aside of witnesses, your secret conferences with your juniors. This unnerving procedure made the candidates in their whitened robes look darker. Meanwhile, they saw Catiline, sprightly and cheerful, closely followed by a band of young men, walled in by informers and henchmen, buoyed up with his hope for soldiers, then by the promises, as he himself says, made him by my colleague, with an army of farmers from Arretium and Faesulae flowing round him, a mob with a few very different sorts of men in it, legitimate victims of the Sullan regime. His face was flooded by fury, his eyes glared criminally, his speech was insolent, as if he were certain of the consulship and had it already safe at home 25 under lock and key. He scorned Murena, and regarding Sulpicius as his prosecutor, not his rival, bullied him and threatened the republic. Do not let me remind you of how fear was instilled in the hearts of all good men by these actions, how hopeless the case of the republic would be if he were elected consul—you can recall it by yourselves. For you remember when the bully's threats became more talked about, said to have been voiced at a private meeting in his own home, that no faithful defender of the oppressed poor could be found, except one who was himself poor. He said that the victimized poor ought not to trust the promises of the wealthy and secure; and that those who wished to replenish their expended funds and to recover what had been taken from them should look at what he himself owed, what he owned, and what he would risk. That he ought to be the least fearful and in the most disastrous position, who was to be the future leader and standard bearer of victims of disaster. You will remember then, that, when these intentions were heard of and made known, a decree of the Senate I proposed was carried through that the elections be not held the next day, so that we might deal with the matter in the Senate. And, in the crowded chamber the next day, I called on Catiline to rise to speak of the things that had been reported to me. And he, frank as always, did not clear himself of the charges, but admitted them and walked right into the trap. He said at that time that there were two bodies of the republic, one weak and with a weak head, the other strong but lacking a head; but that a head would not be lacking to the latter as long as he was alive, if it deserved one. The crowded Senate groaned, and yet issued a decree insufficiently drastic in proportion to the shamelessness of his actions. Some Senators were not capable of a bold decision, partly because they feared too little what was actually threatening the state, partly because they feared it too greatly. Catiline bounced out of the Senate gloating, a man who should not have left there alive. It was the same person who, in that same senatorial gathering a few days earlier, had answered the gallant Cato, when Cato was formally announcing his intentions of bringing Catiline to trial, that if anyone set fire to his hopes he would put out the fire, not with water, but with total ruin.

Alarmed by these events, and because I knew men 26 already in the conspiracy were being paraded about the Campus armed with swords by Catiline, I went into the Campus with a stout bodyguard and wearing that splendid broad cuirass of mine, not to protect myself—I knew full well that Catiline habitually thrust his dagger at the head or neck, not at the side or stomach of a victim—but, so that all good citizens might notice it, and seeing their consul in fear and peril speed to his rescue and support, exactly as it turned out. Therefore, Servius, when they began to think that you were slacking off in your candidacy and to see Catiline inflamed with hope and greed, all who wished to drive that disease out of the republic immediately came over to Murena. Great is the sudden swerving of wills in the consular elections, especially, when the choice falls upon a good man, endowed with many other advantages and means of assistance for his candidacy. A man who—graced by a distinguished father, a most irreproachable career as a young man, a most famous military mission, a praetorship that met with approval for its equity, favor gained by presenting public spectacles, a distinguished provincial record—had actively sought election, and so sought it as neither to yield to one threatening him nor to threaten anyone; is it any wonder that the sudden hope Catiline entertained of winning the consulship was an additional advantage to a man like this?

Now remains the third section of my speech, that concerning the charges of bribery already discussed and disproved by the previous speakers. In accordance with Murena's wishes, I would review and sum up these matters. In this section, I will address a few words to my close associate, Gaius Postumus, my gifted fellow citizen, about the evidence given by the alleged distributors of the money and about the money that was seized; to Servius Sulpicius, that talented and fine young man, about the centuriate assembly of the knights; to Marcus Cato, a man possessed of every outstanding quality, about his own accusation, about the decree of the Senate, and about matters of state. But first, let 27 me air a grievance concerning the fate of Lucius Murena which has just come to my mind and I feel urged to mention briefly. For, although often before, gentlemen of the jury, both on the basis of the troubles of others and on the basis of my own worries and daily labors, I have judged those well off who led lives of peace and quiet, far removed from the desire for public office, indeed, in the midst of these sudden dangers looming so large for Murena, I have been so moved in my heart as to be unable to sympathize enough, either with the common fate of all men or with the outcome and fate of this one man. First, a man who here tries to ascend one rung higher in the ladder of public service than the grades to which his family and ancestors have risen, now runs the danger of losing both what was left to him and what he has gained by his own efforts; and then, because of his energetic pursuit of additional glory, is led into the crisis of losing even his former gains. And if these are serious concerns, gentlemen of the jury, that is surely the bitterest pill, to have as his accusers, not men who have come to accuse him because they mistrust him, but who have come to mistrust him

because they are accusing him. To leave out Servius
Sulpicius, who, I know, does not attack out of desire
to hurt Murena, but is impelled to it by contesting the
office with him, he is accused by Gaius Postumus, an
old (as he says himself) neighbor and close associate,
who has many reasons to be his friend and can recall
no point of personal grudge here. Servius Sulpicius
accuses Murena, Sulpicius whose father was a member
of the same sodality[60] as Murena, and whose father's
close friends deserve staunch support. Marcus Cato
accuses him, who, not only has never been estranged
from him, but, indeed, who has been born into such
circumstances in this state of ours that his wealth and
character should protect many, even those totally unknown to him, and hardly a cause of destruction even
to any enemy. I will answer Postumus first, who appears
to me when, as a candidate for the praetorship himself,
he contests the claim of a consul, to be like a circus
rider[61] trained to leap from the back of one horse to
another who drops down to take the reins behind a
four-horse chariot and drives right into another team.
If Postumus' competitors have committed no illegality,
he conceded their prior claim to the office when he
left off canvassing for it. But, if some one of them has
been rather liberal with money at election time, Postumus
is a friend to be clung to, who investigates the harm done
someone else like Sulpicius rather than that done
him.[62]

I come now to Marcus Cato, the main strength
and support of this entire accusation. Despite his un-
doubted powers as a prosecuting counsel, I fear his
personal influence and authority more than the charges

28

---

[60] Murena and the father of the younger Sulpicius belonged to
the same political society (*sodalitas*), the members of which were
not permitted to appear against one another in court. This relationship was considered to be passed on from father to son, so it
is unworthy of the younger Sulpicius to be accusing Murena.

[61] A *desultorius*, who rode two horses joined together, leaping
from the back of one to the other. Postumus' awkward stance in
withdrawing from the candidacy for the praetorship and interfering in matters concerning only a candidate for the consulship is
like a *desultorius* turning himself into a charioteer.

[62] A heading in the manuscript, *De Postumi Criminibus de Servii
Adulescentis* (*Concerning the Charges of Postumus and the
Younger Servius*), survives as a title only, indicating that Cicero
developed further material in the course of his speech which he
omitted from the published version.

he has made. In view of the fact that Cato is Murena's
accuser, I beg your consideration, gentlemen of the
jury, so that Cato's authority, his position as tribune-
elect, the great prestige and sobriety of his life as a
whole, do not put Murena at a disadvantage, and finally,
that those good qualities themselves, which Cato has
developed so markedly, do not militate against this
one man alone, qualities acquired to benefit mankind.
Publius Scipio Africanus Minor had twice been consul
and had neutralized the twin threats to our empire,
Carthage and the Spanish Numantia, when he prosecuted Lucius Cotta.[63] In him, there were the greatest
eloquence and uprightness, irreproachable consistency,
and an influential authority as great as that of the empire
itself of the Roman people, which, in fact, was being
maintained by his devoted work. I often heard our
elders point out, though, that the very outstanding
quality of Scipio's personal prestige was beneficial to
Cotta in this case. Perfectly wise as were the men who
then sat in judgment on that case, they were unwilling
for anyone to lose his case, if it seemed that he were
overwhelmed by the superior strength of his opponent.
And, what of this other famous instance of Servius
Galba,[64] that has been handed down to our memory
in that speech of your ancestor, Marcus Cato the Censor,
transcribed in his book of *Origines?* Cato was the adversary of Galba and doing his utmost to convict him,
but the Roman people rescued Galba from destruction,
despite your great ancestor's powerful and impressive
prestige. In our state, both people as a whole and wise
judges looking far into posterity have been proof against
the unfairly advantageous wealth and resources of a
prosecuting counsel. I am unwilling to have a prosecutor
bring his own power into play in a matter before the
court, or any greater influence than usual or personal

---

[63] Between 132 and 129, the younger Scipio brought charges
of extortion against Cotta, who was defended by Quintus Marcellus Macedonicus. After the trial had been adjourned seven
times, Cotta was acquitted, the jury having been bribed.

[64] Servius Sulpicius Galba, when praetor in 151 B.C., had massa-
cred 30,000 Lusitanians and provoked the war with Viriathus. On
returning to Rome in 149 B.C., he was accused by the tribune,
Libo, but was acquitted. Libo was assisted by Marcus Porcius
Cato the Censor, who died soon afterward. Cato had written
his speech out and inserted it in his history, the *Origines.* The
Galba mentioned here was an ancestor of the emperor Galba.

prestige or exceptional popularity. Let all these things qualify in saving the innocent, helping the weak, aiding the needy, but be rejected as a means of endangering or ruining citizens. And, if someone were to make the point that Cato would not have deigned to enter into this prosecution, unless he had already judged the case in his own mind, he would be establishing an unfair principle, gentlemen of the jury, and a most unfortunate situation for men against whom serious charges have been preferred, to think that the judgment of an accuser ought to prevail as a form of prejudice.

In view of my singular regard for your character, 29 Cato, I cannot find fault with your declared intention in this case; perhaps, I can set a few things in better order and improve them slightly. His old teacher Phoenix says to the heroic Achilles (in the play *The Myrmidons* by Accius), "You are not greatly in error, but you are in error. I can correct you." But, I cannot correct you, Cato. I think I can truly say that you do not make mistakes, that you deserve not to be corrected, but restrained. Nature itself has formed you for uprightness, sobriety, temperance, largeness of mind, justice, in short, has made you a great man loftily endowed with all excellent qualities. To your natural qualities your Stoic teaching has contributed neither moderately nor mildly but, as it seems to me, rather more harshly and unbendingly than either the realities of practical life or human nature sanction. Inasmuch as this speech is not being delivered to the ignorant masses nor at a meeting of country folk, I will discuss a bit more frankly the general subject of those intellectual pursuits which you and I have been pleased to experience. Gentlemen of the jury, you realize full well that those excellent, godlike qualities we discern in Marcus Cato are entirely his own possession. What we find missing are defects due, not to his natural instincts, but to his teacher. There was a certain man, Zeno of Citium, the greatest sort of genius, the followers of whose dogmas are called Stoics. His proverbial sayings and teachings are of the following sort: a wise man must never be emotionally influenced by good will; he must excuse fault in no one; no one feels pity except the foolish or fickle man; a true man is never open to entreaty or flattery; only philosophers are, however weird, handsome, however impoverished, rich, however enslaved to servility, monarchs; us, however, who are not Stoics they nominate runaways, exiles, enemies, even mad; all faults are equal; every misdemeanor is a dastardly crime, and he who strangles a poultry cock, when there is no need of it, transgresses as much as he who suffocates his own father; the philosopher never "thinks," he knows; he never experiences regret; never makes a mistake; never changes his mind.

30   Misled by the authority of most learned men, our brilliant Marcus Cato has seized on these paradoxical aphorisms not, as most of us do, to dispute them, but as his way of life. If the tax collectors petition the Senate for something, he reminds us: "Be on guard against making any allowances based on favoritism." Some unfortunate victims come forward in humble need: "It would be criminally wrong of you to act when influenced in any way by sympathy." Someone confesses that he has done wrong and asks pardon for his misdeed: "It is criminal to forgive a wrong." But the misdemeanor was slight: "All faults are equal." You say something: "It is completely settled and decided." You were influenced by your opinion, not by the facts of the case: "The wise man never gives an opinion, he knows." You made some mistake in estimating the facts: he thinks he is being insulted. Here is a sample of this sort of philosophy. "I said in the Senate that I would impeach some candidate for the consulship." But you spoke in anger. "The philosopher," he says "is never angry." Well then, you said it on the spur of the moment. "It is the behavior of a wicked man," Cato says, "to deceive by a lie: to change one's opinion is disgraceful; to be won over by talk a sin, to be sympathetic a crime." But those teachers we had (for I will admit, Cato, that I, also, when young and unwilling to trust my own mind, sought the help and assistance of education), our teachers, I say, men trained in Plato and Aristotle, cautious and conservative, say that it is the part of a philosopher to have occasional recourse to the feeling of gratitude, of a good man to show pity, that the types of misconduct are different and punishments for them correspondingly inequal; that there is always in a stable man room for pardoning wrong; that the philosopher himself may often think about something he does not know; that he may occasionally become angry; that he can be the subject of entreaty and appeals to his friendly instincts; that what he has once declared he may eventually alter his

opinion of, if that is the more correct course; that he can occasionally change his mind; that all virtues are tempered by a certain spirit of moderation.

If chance had brought you, with your native **31** qualities, into contact with those teachers, you would certainly be, not a braver, more temperate, more just man—that is hardly possible—but one slightly more inclined to kindness. Incited by no animosity, untouched by any personal hurt, you would not be prosecuting a most reliable man, one graced with the highest dignity and integrity; you would think that since fortune had placed both you as tribune-elect and Murena in positions of responsibility for the same year, you had been linked with him by your common duty to the republic; the words you uttered so ferociously in the Senate you would either not have said, or if you had, would have given a milder construction to. Indeed, insofar as I may hazard an opinion, you yourself are, at present, impelled by a certain intensity of spirit, and elevated by the strength of your native intelligence, and fired by a fresh study of your teachers' doctrines. Soon, experience will make you more pliable, the course of time soften and age mellow you. Indeed, those teachers of yours seem to me to have themselves extended the boundaries of moral duties beyond the limits nature intended—for when we have striven in thought to reach the utmost limit, we should nevertheless stop where we ought to. "Forgive nothing," you are instructed. But what that means is, pardon some things, but not all. "Concede nothing to your friendly disposition." What that means is, when duty and honor so demand, resist your inclination to return a favor, but, otherwise, do not deny this impulse. "Let yourself not be influenced by pity." I quite agree, when it would involve an undue relaxation of severity; but make some concession to it in other cases, for there is something praiseworthy in human kindness. "Abide by your convictions." By all means; unless a still better conviction conquers that conviction. Scipio Africanus Minor[65] was not a man to take anything but delight in doing what you do, when he invited the celebrated Stoic

---

[65] Scipio Africanus Minor (185–129 B.C.) formed a circle of eminent philosophers and men of letters, including Panaetius of Rhodes, Gaius Laelius Sapiens (consul in 140 B.C.), Lucius Furius Philus (consul in 136 B.C.), and Gaius Sulpicius Galus (consul in 166 B.C.).

philosopher, the learned Panaetius, to live at home with him. Panaetius' persuasive speech and instructions, although they were the same as those that please you, did not, nevertheless, make Scipio a man of harsher temper, but, as I have heard from our elders, a milder person. And, by concerning himself with the same philosophical pursuits, who became more sophisticated a man than Gaius Laelius, more affable, or more sage and serious? I can say the same for Lucius Philus and for Gaius Galus, but I will direct your glance homeward. Can you think of anyone more kind, more sociable, more congenial, than your great-grandfather, Cato the Censor? When you spoke of his outstanding character, you said that you had an example from your own home to imitate. To be sure, that example was offered to you at home, but, although the likeness to that nature could register on you more indelibly than on any one of us —as you are descended from it—to imitate that example is as much open to me as it is to you. If you season Cato's sophisticated urbanity with your sobriety and dignified severity, those qualities will not be improved, which are as they stand undeniably excellent, but they will certainly be more palatable.

32   Therefore, to return to the point I began with, take from my sight the name of Cato as connected with this case; remove your authoritative presence, which ought either to carry no weight with the judges or contribute to his acquittal, and retrace with me these criminal charges themselves. What is it you charge him with, Cato? What do you bring up for judgment? What do you accuse him of? You charge Murena with bribery. I do not defend him against that. You reproach me for defending the very thing I myself have applied the penalty of the law to. I have punished bribery, but I have not punished innocence. Bribery itself I will prosecute together with you, if you wish. You said that a decree of the Senate had been issued, with me as its proposer: if they were bribed to meet the candidates, if they were paid to follow in his train, if a place for gladiators had been generally given to all in the tribe, and likewise free dinners, it would seem to have been done in violation of the Calpurnian Law. Therefore, if the Senate judges that these things are illegal if they have been done, its decision is a mere formality however convenient to the candidates. But, whether it was

actually done or not is the matter being fiercely debated. If it was, no one doubts that this was a violation of the law. It is absurd for the Senate to specify a thing as doubtful and leave it uncertain, when no one can be doubtful about it. And that resolution was passed at the demand of all the candidates, so that from the decree of the Senate it cannot be known which of them it benefits or harms. Therefore, show that those things were done by Murena; then I will concede to you that they were done in violation of the law.

"Many people went to meet him as he returned to **33**
Rome from the province he had been administering." But that is the usual courtesy extended to a candidate for the consulship, and is it not usual to greet a man who is returning home? "But why was there so great a group of people?" First, even if I cannot offer you a satisfactory explanation of that, let me merely observe that there is nothing the least remarkable in the fact of many persons thronging to greet a man of such status, a consular candidate, returning to Rome. It would be remarkable, rather, if no one had done so. And, I suppose, I might add, that many were invited to go (not an uncommon event)—is that a cause for suspicion or alarm? In our city it is usual for many to rise in the dead of night and form an escort for the young sons of citizens of low rank, even from the outlying regions, who are about to don the *toga virilis*. Is it strange that men should be prevailed upon to proceed to the Campus Martius at the third hour of the day to greet a person of such rank and reputation? If you consider the members of the multitude who escorted Murena, you will find members of the various groups of trade associations;[66] many of those here seated among the judges in this case; members of our honorable equestrian order; and, of course, that officious, fussy crew who refuse to let a candidate enter the city unacclaimed, the tribe of office-seekers; last, but not least, would be our prosecuting attorney here, Postumus, with a large group of his own retainers. Is this so astonishing? I omit as too obvious to call for mention, Murena's clients, immediate neighbors, fellow tribesmen, the whole army of Lucullus which was then here to enjoy its delayed triumph. I only want to point

---

66 *Publicani*, knights who formed companies to provide funds for purchasing the rights to farm taxes.

out this: that a crowd of friends and interested well-wishers has never failed to assemble on occasions like this to pay respect to and gratify the desires of a friend, and this out of disinterested motives.

34   "But many partisans followed him about constantly wherever he went in public." Can you show that they were paid to do so? If you can, I will concede that the law has been violated. But, if you cannot show that, why should you reproach him for it? "What need is there," the prosecutor inquires, "for a tribe of partisans to follow him about in public?" Do you ask that of me about something that is conventional and customary with all of us? The underprivileged members of our society have but this one opportunity for returning the favor and showing the gratitude they feel toward the members of our order, precisely this assiduous daily attendance upon us in our campaigns for office. It is not demanded—and could not be held to—by us of the senatorial order or by those of the equestrian order, that their dependents accompany them day and night. If our home is frequently visited by them, if we are occasionally accompanied by them to the forum, if we are honored by their taking a single turn with us in the basilica,[67] we are being scrupulously looked after and cared for. This attendance on others by those of slender resources, who are not otherwise occupied, constitutes their friendly attention; and no good and generous man is without a supply of his less fortunate followers. Therefore, Cato, do not try to deprive this underprivileged group of the one way they have of offering something in return for the favors they have received. Let those who have placed all their hopes in us also have something of their own to contribute to our needs. If this is nothing but their votes, it is hardly worth much, for few of them ever have influence. As they themselves say, they cannot speak on our behalf or plead our case in the courts; they cannot pledge surety for us; they cannot invite us to their homes. They expect these services from us, and believe that they can repay us for the benefits we confer by giving

    [67] The building whose architecture most influenced the later structure of the Christian church; a large roofed building with a long central axis, the roof supported by columns, and one side furnishing a portico. In the forum, justice could be administered and business conducted in either of the two basilicas, the one built by Cato in 184 B.C. and the Fulvian (179 B.C.).

us their loyal attendance. So, they have disregarded
the Lex Fabia concerning the limiting of the numbers
of attendants, and the decree of the Senate passed in
the consulship of Lucius Caesar. For there is no punishment which can keep the poor proletarian orders from
observing an old-fashioned, time-honored custom.

"But seats for the public entertainments were
handed out to all members of the tribe, and invitations
to the banquets distributed to the people en masse."
Although this was not, gentlemen of the jury, in fact,
the work of Murena himself, but done by his friend
according to the usual custom and in due moderation,
I nevertheless recall being warned by this very incident
how many of the Senate's votes these complaints were
considered to have lost for us, Cato, at the time when
I supported you for your candidacy for the praetorship.
Has there ever been a time within our memory or that
of our fathers when this habitual form of generosity
—or is it bribery?—has not prevailed, whereby places
at the circus or in the forum for attending the gladiatorial contests are provided free for friends and some
members of the candidates' tribe? His impoverished
supporters obtained these rewards and special privileges
in the old-fashioned, time-honored, usual manner from
the fellow members of their tribe.

But if Murena's accusers charge him with having 35
assigned the places reserved for the chief public en-
gineer to the members of his own tribe, what will
they claim against those men of first rank who set up
whole booths in the circus for the use of their own
tribesmen? People attributed all these grave misde-
meanors pertaining to attendants, feasts, entertainments,
Servius, to your overeager spirit of inquiry. Murena is
protected against them by the authority of the Senate
—for, mark you, does the Senate hold it wrong that a
returning candidate was met by an escort? No; you
argue, rather, that people were paid to do so. But
prove that, if you can! Does the Senate hold it illegal
that many persons attended him in public? No; you
argue rather that they were hired to do so. Well, show
us your evidence for that! Or, does the Senate hold it
delinquent that seats were provided for the shows or
invitations to feasts extended? Not at all, you argue,
unless this was done indiscriminately. How do you
mean that "indiscriminately"? Inclusively, that is, for

everybody, say you. But take the instance of Lucius
Natta,[68] whom we see to be a young man of highest
rank, endowed with a fine character, and headed for
a promising future. He wanted to be of service in the
assembly of the knights, both by supporting the candidacy of his friend and by storing up good will for his
own political future. And this gesture cannot be charged
against his stepfather Murena as prejudice or as a misdemeanor. When one of Murena's relations, a Vestal
Virgin, gave him, for the use of his friends, her own
privileged place at the gladiatorial games, her own
integrity was not thereby compromised. Nor is Murena
to be blamed for accepting the favor. This procedure
is inevitable as a matter of friendship, of doing a favor
for one's less fortunate retainers, a matter of a political
candidate's obligations.

Cato takes me severely and Stoically to task, saying that it is not right for good will to be won by feast-
ing one's friends, that men's judgment must not be
tampered with by offering the magistrates pleasurable
entertainments. And so, if someone, in the interests of
his campaign, invites friends to a banquet, is he to be
condemned? "You don't believe, do you," Cato replies,
"that you can solicit the noblest offices of government,
the highest and grandest position of authority in the
land, by catering to men's pleasures, relaxing their
minds, and fondling their senses? Is it," he continues,
"a sleazy master of revels you are selecting, from the
crowd of pampered youth, or the commander of the
world, to be chosen from among the Roman people?"
A devastating speech, that. But the ordinary traditions
of our society, our way of life, our general conduct,
our state itself, would cast it back in his teeth. Not
even the Spartans, themselves the originators of an
austere style of life and speech, men who recline at
meals on the hard surface of uncushioned oak—nor
even the citizens of age-old Crete, who did not even
recline but sat up at meals—maintained their government in better order than the Romans, who allot time
for work and for the normal pleasures of existence.
The nation of Crete was totally subdued by one assault of our army, and Sparta has preserved its char-

[68] The stepson of Murena and brother-in-law of Publius
Clodius. Later, when pontifex, Natta helped Clodius wreck Cicero's
house.

acteristic discipline and constitutional rights only under our protection.

Therefore, Cato, refrain from reproaching in such [36] caustic eloquence the customs of our ancestors which our national life evidently and naturally endorses. The learned and respected aristocrat, Quintus Tubero, was inclined to a similar excess of zeal in our fathers' day. When Quintus Maximus was offering a funeral banquet to the Roman people in honor of Publius Africanus, his uncle Tubero (the son of Africanus' own sister) was asked to prepare the couches. And he, skilled philosopher that he was, used goatskin covers for the wretched wooden stools he provided; he set the tables with cheap Samian pottery, as if it were Diogenes the Cynic they were honoring at the hour of his death, not the great man Africanus. On the day of the funeral, when Maximus was pronouncing the eulogy, he thanked the immortal gods that this great man had been born in this state rather than elsewhere, for where he was, the seat of government over the whole world would inevitably be. In the celebration of the rites held at Africanus' death, the Roman people were offended by Tubero's display of sour Stoic wisdom, and so, this honored man and respected citizen, although he was the grandson of Lucius Paulus and the son of Africanus' sister, as I have said, was defeated for the praetorship because of those goatskins. The Roman people despise private luxury, but favor public magnificence. They loathe overindulgent banqueteering, but they are even more contemptuous of conspicuous austerity and self-neglect. With due regard for circumstances and duties, they can identify the need for an alternation of work and pleasure. When you argue that nothing but inherent worth should influence men in the choice of their magistrates, furthermore, you contradict your own political behavior. For why then do you solicit the interest and support of persons like myself in your candidacy? Ought not *you* to be requested by *me* to undertake the trials of public office in my own better interests? Is it proper for you to ask me to support you? Why do you employ a nomenclator? Thereby you deceive and mislead us. If the honorable course is for you to call your fellow citizens by name, it is surely a disgrace that they should be better known to your slave (who remembers their

names and says them to you), than they are to you
yourself. And if, even though you are acquainted with
them, their names must be called by your nomenclator,
why ask who they are before he has called their names
out? And why, when you have been prompted, do you
hail them as if you yourself actually knew them? How
is it, that after you have been elected, you greet your
constituents so much more negligently? If you conceive of these matters according to the rule of what
political behavior calls for, they are quite straightfor-
ward. But if you wish to make them depend on the
philosophical standards of your Stoic discipline, they
will be found to be hypocritical in the extreme. So,
neither should the populace be denied the enjoyment
of their entertainments, gladiatorial contests, public
feasts—all of which our ancestors instituted—nor
should the candidate for office be denied that liberality
which signifies generosity rather than graft.

37   You will, perhaps, argue that you entered this
case out of zeal for the public interest. I can well
believe, Cato, that you came into it from that spirit
and estimate of the situation; but you will fall because
of your impetuosity. What I do, gentlemen of the jury,
I do not only for the sake of my friendship for Murena
and the dignity of his reputation, but for the sake of
peace and quiet, of order, freedom, safety, and, indeed,
the very life and welfare of all our citizens; this I insist
on, and call you to witness. Hear a consul, fellow
citizens, the consul who makes no arrogant demands
upon you, but simply states that he has watched day
and night over the well-being of our state! Lucius
Catiline did not so underestimate and despise our
republic as to think he could overthrow the government with that supply of troops he took away with him.
The contagion of his conspiracy is more widespread
than anyone quite realizes, and infects many. The
Trojan Horse, I tell you, is now here, right inside our
city walls: you will never be overcome by it in your
sleep, so long as I am your consul. Is it Catiline himself I fear? you may ask. Of course not: I have taken
measures to see that no one need fear him; but his
forces I see here in our midst; these are the ones we
must fear, I tell you. The army of Catiline is not to
be feared so much as those who are rumored to have
deserted from that army. They have not deserted, but

have, in fact, been planted here and lie in waiting in caves and points of ambush, lurking behind our backs, ready to spring at our throats. These it is who want to see a fine consul and good commander, linked to the safety of the state by both his strong character and his independent position, cast down from the guardianship of the city and dislodged from the care of the state by your decision against him. If you betray one of the two consuls to the men whose swords I blunted in the Campus Martius and whose boldness I daunted, whom I sapped of strength in the forum and fought off time and again in my own home, these men, gentlemen of the jury, will have won more by your decision than they gained by flourishing their swords. Of the greatest importance, gentlemen, was the effort and toil I expended to ensure that there should be in this republic of ours two consuls on the Kalends of January —and I fought for this against strong resistance. Do not think that they are acting in the usual way or by half-hearted measures. It is not a question of an unfair law, or harmful bribery that we are hearing, of some projected future injury to the state. Plans are underfoot in this state, gentlemen of the jury, calling for the destruction of our city, the butchering of its citizens, the extinguishing of the Roman name. Such plans are being made, as they have been made, by our citizens— if so they may be rightfully called—against their native country. Day after day, I thwart these men's machinations, I blunt the edge of their boldness, I stand firm against their criminal subversion. But, gentlemen, let me remind you, that my term of office as consul is now coming to its close: do not, then, take from me the compatriot who will take my place as a zealous advocate of the public good; do not reject him to whom I would hand over the republic intact to be protected from such enormous dangers.

And, gentlemen, do you not see what else will be 38 added to these present troubles? I call on you, Cato: do you not yourself see the storm approaching your year as tribune-elect? In yesterday's meeting of the assembly, the voice of your colleague in office as tribune-designate[69] thundered ominously. Your judgment, and that

---

[69] Quintus Metellus Nepos. He tried to secure the return of Pompey to help put down the conspiracy. Later, when consul, he was instrumental in obtaining the recall of Cicero from exile.

of all right-minded citizens who called on you to seek
the office of tribune, has strongly opposed him. All the
nefarious schemes under way these past three years,
ever since the day you are well acquainted with, when
the design of Catiline and Piso was formed of murdering the Senate, are ripening during these days, these
months, at this very moment. Is there a place or a
time, gentlemen, day or night, when I am not being
rescued from their ambushes, or managing to scrape
past the edge of their swords, thanks to my own sense,
and thanks even more, to divine providence? It is not
so much on my own account, of course, that they want
to murder me, as it is that they wish to get a consul
out of the way who is constantly on the alert for the
country's well-being. They would do as much for you,
Cato, by whatever means, if they could! Take my word:
this is a matter they are hard at work on, at this very
moment. They recognize how generous a degree of
spirit, talent, authority you possess, and how dedicated
a defender of your country you are. They count on
crushing you the more easily, when you are exposed
and weakened by having your tribunician power
stripped of authoritative support from the office of the
consul. They do not worry about another consul's being
elected, for they see that this is in the power of your
colleagues. They hope that Silanus, fine man that he is,
can be gotten at, without the support of his colleagues,
you without a consul, the state without its protection.
At such a dangerous crisis in affairs, it is your duty,
Cato, as a man who seems to have been born, not for
your own sake, but for the country's, to see clearly
what is going on and to retain as your ally and fellow
defender and colleague in the government a consul who
is not self-seeking, a consul of the kind the moment
urgently calls for, well constituted to promote peace,
by his knowledge equipped for waging war, by his
temperament and experience ready for whatever may
be required.

39   However, the power in this case rests entirely with
you, gentlemen of the jury; in your hands you hold the
republic; you are the governors of the state. If Catiline,
with the conspiring assent of the criminal associates
he has led from the city with him could cast sentence
in this case, he would find Murena guilty; if he could,
he would kill him. Catiline's interests are that the re-

public may be deprived of protection, that the supply
of generals to oppose his fury may be diminished,
that a wider opportunity may be given to the tribunes
for stirring up unrest and sedition, by removing the
man who could resist them. Will the wisest and finest
men, selected from the highest ranks, the classes of
knights and Senators, arrive at the same decision as
that savage gladiator and enemy of the state? Believe
me, gentlemen, in this event, you will be passing sentence, not only on Murena, but on your own life. We
have come to the ultimate point: there are no longer
any resources from which we may rebuild our strength
or, once having slipped, regain our footing. What
forces we now have must be somehow added to, if at
all possible, not allowed to diminish one whit more.
The enemy are not standing like Hannibal at the Anio,
three miles from Rome—that was seen to be a critical
enough juncture in Roman history. They are within
the city itself, in the very forum (and, O Gods, I cannot utter that statement without a groan!). Some few
lurk in that very innermost shrine of our government,
the Senate chamber, some few are right there. May
the gods see to it that my colleague,[70] Antonius, courageous man as he is, defeat this criminal band of
thugs with his army. I, clad in the citizen's toga, with
the help of all you good citizens here, will, by my
timely warnings, squeeze the life out of this dreadful
thing the republic has conceived and brought to birth.
What will happen in the end, if the elements that escape
our hands flood back upon the state in the ensuing
year? There will be only one consul, and he will be
fully engaged, not in conducting the war against the
conspiracy, but in finding a replacement for his colleague. That monstrous plague, the savagery of Catiline, will break out, which has been menacing good
citizens with destruction for some time now; it will
spread through the outskirts; passion will dominate the
rostra; fear will run riot in the Senate chamber; conspiracy will be rife in the forum, an army will be
conjured up in the Campus Martius; destruction will
rain on our crops. We shall stand in constant fear of
flame and sword, from every building and every quar-

[70] Gaius Antonius Hybrida (the uncle of Mark Antony). Cicero
had won his cooperation by assigning to him the lucrative province
of Macedonia.

ter wherein they have been planning long since to make their attack. But each of these crises can be met by the concerted thought of the magistrates and the careful planning of private citizens, if the government is duly outfitted with its protecting officials.

40   This being the situation, I, first of all, advise you, on behalf of the republic—whose cause should outrank any other cause—and warn you, by my own efforts, the utmost exertion of which is known to you; by my authority as consul, I beseech you; by the presence of so great a danger, I call on you yourselves to witness the need for seeing to the public peace and order, to your safety, to your very lives and those of your fellow citizens. Secondly, brought to this by the duty of defending a friend, I beg and beseech you, gentlemen of the jury—do not overwhelm with cause for new grief the new cause Murena has had for rejoicing, suffering as he is from physical and mental anguish. Just now he seemed to be happy, graced and honored with the highest rewards the Roman people can bestow, being the first man to have brought the consulship to his old family and to his ancient municipal town. Now, the very same person lies a suppliant at your feet, gentlemen of the jury, in rags and tatters, in tears and sorrow; he calls on your honor, begs your mercy, looks anxiously to your power and support. By the immortal gods, do not, I pray you, gentlemen, deprive this man of the success whereby he thought that he would be even more honored, and of the other honors he has previously won, and of his whole station and means. Murena asks and implores you, gentlemen, if he has hurt none unjustly, taken advantage of no one's wishes and receptivity, if, to put it mildly, he has no enemies at home or abroad—let there be in your hearts a place for the modest, a refuge for those in distress, a help for the decent. The prospect of being deprived of the consulship should evoke great pity, for everything else is lost with it. Indeed, in times like these, the consulship itself offers little to envy; opposition mounts, in the minds of traitorous schemers, in the ambushes planned by conspirators, in the weapons of Catiline; the consul alone is exposed to every sort of insult and injury. It is hard for me to see, gentlemen, why Murena or any of us should be envied for holding this renowned position, the consulship. But, what is rather to be pitied is

all too evident to me, and perfectly visible and perceptible to you.

If you condemn him (Jupiter forbid!), where will the poor man turn? Home? Only to see there the funeral bust of that eminent man, his father, only a few days earlier wreathed with laurel in congratulations, now stripped and humiliated by his disgrace? Or to his mother who, having but a moment ago bestowed a kiss on her son, the consul, is now troubled and torn by the thought that she may soon see the same young man shorn of every dignity of office? But why mention his mother or his home, when ten years of exile, by the new penalty[71] of the law, deprives him of home, of parent, of the company and sight of all his friends? Will the unfortunate victim then go into exile, and, if so, where? To the East, where he was an officer for so many years, commanded armies, and performed great deeds? It is particularly painful to return to the same place in humiliation, which you have recently left with great honor. Or will he take refuge in the opposite corner of the earth, and let Transalpine Gaul look upon the grieving, sorrowing countenance of one in exile, whom it but recently gazed happily on vested with the supreme power? In what spirit will he there exchange looks with his brother Gaius? What will be the grief of the one, the bitter laments of the other, the tearful sorrows of both together? How different their situation and their talk in the very place where, only a few days earlier, messenger and documents from Rome brought the news that Murena had been elected consul, and friends and associates had rushed to Rome to congratulate him! Will Murena reappear there to bring news of his downfall? If things of this sort are pitiable to you, bitter, grievous, if they are completely foreign to your natural and habitual sympathies, confirm the honor conferred by the Roman people; give back this consul to the republic that elected him; grant this much to the man's own decency, to his dead father, to his tribe and family, to the noble municipality of Lanuvium, his town of origin which you have seen represented during this case by its anxious crowds. Do not keep her most important consul and fellow-townsman from performing the sacrificial rites due Juno the Pre-

41

71 The *lex Tullia* imposed a penalty of ten years' exile.

server[72] in the traditional ceremony at Lanuvium. I, a consul, commend to you, gentlemen of the jury, this man as consul—if my recommendation carries any weight or influence—I solemnly promise that he will be a person most eager to secure peace and order, most attentive to the needs of all good citizens, most keenly alert to counter any act of treason, unflinching in war, and intransigently hostile to this conspiracy which would now subvert the state.

[72] *Juno Sospita*, whose worship was inaugurated in Rome in 338 B.C.

In Defense of the Poet Archias

INTRODUCTION

By the provisions of the Lex Plautia-Papiria, passed in
89 B.C., Archias was qualified to claim Roman citizenship.
His claim, as Cicero explains in this oration, was allowed.
Archias thereupon took the full name of Aulus Licinius
Archias, adopting the Licinius name of the Lucullus gens,
who were his chief patrons. From 89 to 62 B.C., Archias
enjoyed the rights and privileges of Roman citizenship, and
was closely associated with Lucius Lucullus, on whose East-
ern conquests he wrote a poem. In 62 B.C., Archias had also
begun a poem on Cicero's suppression of the Catilinarian
conspiracy; but he was still working on the panegyric for
Lucullus and had promised to write another poem celebrating
the achievements of the Metellus gens. A year after this
oration was delivered in 62 B.C., Cicero himself wrote a
Latin poem on his consulship, then translated it into Greek*
and sent it to Archias for criticism and comment. Archias
expressed admiration for so superior a specimen of verse
and said that he no longer felt that he could compete with it.

---

* Cicero was fluent in Greek. Shakespeare's eye lit on the fact:

Cassius   Did Cicero say anything?

Casca   Ay, he spoke Greek.

Cassius   To what effect?

Casca   Nay, an I tell you that, I'll ne'er look you i' the face again.
But those that understood him smiled at one another and
shook their heads; but for mine own part, it was Greek to
me.

(*Julius Caesar*, I,ii,ll.281 ff.)

He never wrote the poem that Cicero hopefully refers to in
the course of this oration.

The prosecution of Archias was primarily a means of
harassing his patron Lucullus, instigated by the rival party
of Pompey the Great. After Lucullus had finally been permitted to celebrate his long-delayed and well-deserved triumph, the friends of Pompey took this minor means of
discrediting Lucullus, invoking an old and seldom used
statute, the *lex Papiria de peregrinis exterminandis*. This
rare law, an alien act expelling all foreigners from Rome,
was hardly enforceable, and as Cicero shows here, hardly
relevant to the situation of the defendant. The prosecutor,
Gratius, is otherwise unknown to us. Cicero, as sole counsel
for the defense, thereby associates himself clearly with the
party of Lucullus in the Senate and indicates his dissent from
the partisans of Pompey. Not only did the old aristocratic
party, represented by Lucullus, at this juncture stand for
constitutional government and Cicero's prized "concord of
the orders"; Cicero himself had been attacked since the end
of his year as consul by Pompey's irresponsible adherents—
with the tacit consent of Pompey—on the grounds that he
had taken illegal measures in executing the conspirators.

We notice how skillfully and sensibly Cicero deals with
all the relevant matters before the court and with the prickly
issues of political association, as well as with literature in the
brief course of this speech. Lord Brougham said:

> Cicero's speech for Archias, which is exquisitely composed,
> but of which not more than one-sixth is to the purpose,
> could not have been delivered in a British court of Justice.

Actually, Cicero deals very directly with the legal issue at
the beginning and goes on to convey the significance of
Lucullus' position—referring in passing very diplomatically
to Pompey—before expanding on the occupation of the
writer who happens to be the defendant. In a three-phase
exposition, Cicero defends the poet Archias, shows his association with Lucullus to be a cause for congratulation, and
descants upon the relevance of literature to life. The most
Gratius could contend was (1) that Archias had no documentary evidence of his original admission to citizenship
and that (2) he had not been enrolled on a census register.
Cicero refutes the first charge by witnesses to the fact, and
shows that the reason for the second was the fact of Archias'
absence in the East with Lucullus when the census rolls were
revised, both in 86 and in 70 B.C. The case against Archias

was dubious to begin with and insufficient to end with. He was acquitted, and he continued to reside in Rome as a citizen. At the age of seventy-five, he was still flourishing, and Cicero affectionately refers to him as "noster Archias."

Like the harassment of Murena, this suit gave Cicero a chance to unbend his mind. In the former instance, he had delivered himself of a long, lively, intricate speech on the vagaries of law and the vicissitudes of political innocence and guilt by association. Here, Cicero trims his words neatly to the occasion with a short, powerful defense, not only of the poet, but of poetry. It is an opportunity for the statesman and orator to ventilate his humanism, and he does so airily, but with a sure-handed grasp of his subject. Perhaps Archias, most recently described as "a very minor Greek versifier," did not deserve so generous an accolade on his talents and career. But to Cicero's audience he was renowned as a prodigious artist, an accomplished improviser as well as a prolific composer of verses. And the incident of an artist's being haled into court to defend his qualifications as a citizen is precisely the sort of trial that is likely to arouse interest because of its wider implications.

Cicero saw that to some extent poetry was on trial that day in Rome in 62 B.C., and his speech is as much a consideration of art as it is of the predicament of a continental Greek writer. The general Lucullus and the poet Archias could well symbolize thought and action in close and fortunate conjunction. For all that action can bring to pass, "this intellectual being, those thoughts that wander through eternity," play their part in the larger view posterity deserves to have of what is worth doing.

An intelligent portrait painter of the soul like the poet Archias is a candidate for citizenship in the human state, not just in the Roman state. His gifts are at the service of the community of the human spirit. By rendering his fellow citizen the service of his legal talents, Cicero has also added a page to the humanist's notebook. He has handed down a portrait of the artist as a fifty-seven-year-old Greek poet, for future generations to see. Archias' poems have perished, but the purpose and spirit of the artist's life have been made memorable in a short speech written by a man of action.

In Defense of the Poet Archias

1   Gentlemen of the jury, perhaps I have attained
some skill in public speaking; if so, both the talent
and its application (in which I can claim some experience), as well as the knowledge of the principles and
technique derived from my continuing study of rhetoric and the other liberal arts, ought to be entirely at
the disposal of Archias Licinius. For as long as I can
remember, looking back over that whole tract of time
past since childhood, I see clearly how Archias was the
leader who guided me to the cultivation of this profession. Thanks to his steady counsel and careful teaching, my own voice has been shaped as an instrument
for the defense of others. And, if he has endowed me
with the ability to serve and to save others in their
time of trouble, surely, I ought to offer him such help
and hope of safety as it may be in my power to command in his time of need. Should you be wondering
that I say this of Archias, a poet rather than a rhetorician and professional speaker, let me remind you that
I am not a man exclusively trained as a lawyer and
advocate. All the liberal arts, humanistic in their purpose, are closely related and have a common bond.

2   Do you find it strange that I should approach the
case in so different a manner from the lawyer's usual
brief, at variance with the general style of legal argument? And that I do this at a regular session of the
court, at a public trial being heard before a distinguished praetor[1] and a dedicated jury, in the presence
of so vast an assemblage? Then I bespeak your indulgence, for the defendant, and for myself speaking on
behalf of this talented and learned poet, on an occasion
where so many cultivated men are gathered—you yourselves, gentlemen of the jury, and our distinguished
judge not the least among them—for I know you will
bear with me while I speak particularly of literature
and the liberal arts. On behalf of an eminent person,
Archias, so seldom involved in the intricacies of legal
action, thanks to his artistic pursuits, I adopt a virtually
new and untried method of presenting the case. If,

[1] Quintus Tullius Cicero, the orator's brother.

then, I may so proceed, I will establish the fact that Archias Licinius, not only should not be deprived of his citizenship, but, even if he were not a citizen, should rather be considered by you as worthy of immediate acceptance into the ranks of Roman citizens.

After his early years of primary education, leaving *3* those first studies by which the young are normally prepared for a civilized life, Archias turned to the study of literature and composition. At his native Antioch, then famous for its many humanists and scholars, he swiftly surpassed all in reputation for literary genius. His arrival in other regions of Asia Minor and Greece aroused so much interest that eager curiosity about the man himself outweighed even his reputation for genius. His personal appearance on the scene and the admiration he excited, furthermore, surpassed all expectations. Southern Italy was, at this time, also exposed to the influence of Greek literature and philosophy: the subjects were, as a matter of fact, more intensively pursued in Latium than they are at present in the same towns, and they were far from being neglected here at Rome during that peaceful phase in the life of the Republic. The townspeople of Tarentum, of Locri, of Regium, and of Naples, conferred citizenship and other honors on Archias. All men in a position to judge his talents deemed him worthy of their hospitality and acquaintance.

Because of his widespread fame, then, known even to those far removed, he came to Rome during the consulship of Marius and Catulus. He found these men to be of such a sort, that one furnished ample material for heroic verse, the other fully represented good taste and literary sympathies. Archias, then a mere youth, was immediately received into their own home by the family of the Luculli. It was a result, not only of his literary gifts, but also of his natural disposition and character that such a home which looked on him with favor in his youth would also prove to be his home in later years. But, already at that early date, he came into favor with Quintus Metellus Numidicus and his son Pius; he was listened to with respect by Marcus Aemilius; he lived on familiar terms with the Quinti Catuli, both father and son; his company was cultivated by Lucius Crassus. And, although the Luculli, Drusus, the Octavii, Cato, the entire household of the

Hortensii, fell regularly under his spell, it was perhaps an even more unusual distinction that, not only those eager to learn from him and hear him lionized Archias, but also those who had no such specific qualifications were drawn to him by the influence he exerted on these famous personages.

4   Next, when Archias had, some time later, gone on a tour of duty in the retinue of Marcus Lucullus to Sicily, and was returning from it, he arrived in Heraclea. When he wished to be enrolled as a citizen of Heraclea, which enjoyed favorable privileges and treaty rights as an ally of Rome, his request was promptly granted by the citizens of Heraclea, both because Archias was thought well worthy of the right and by virtue of the influence of Lucullus. This citizenship was granted in accordance with the Lex Plautia-Papiria, in the following terms: "To those (1) admitted into citizenship in allied cities who (2) resided in Italy at the time the law was passed and (3) had declared their intentions for a period of sixty days in advance to the praetor." Archias had maintained a residence here at Rome for some years by then, and had declared his intentions officially before the praetor Quintus Metellus, an intimate friend of his.

Were I to speak of nothing but the legal status of Archias' citizenship, which clearly satisfies the three necessary conditions, I should have nothing more to say, and the case would be closed. What can the prosecutor Gratius offer to weaken it in any way? Can he deny that Archias was enrolled as a citizen of Heraclea? Lucullus is present, to state on unimpeachable authority and personal responsibility, not an opinion, but his knowledge of the fact; not that he heard of the event, but saw it and was a party to it, not simply an observer. Representatives from Heraclea are also with us who have come bearing official documents in support of the facts. Do you ask to inspect the bronze state records of Heraclea, which we all know were destroyed by fire during the Italic War? How absurd, to say nothing about the evidence we do present and to inquire after documents of which all trace has been destroyed! Failing to acknowledge the conscientious testimony of a significant public figure like Lucullus or the reliable attestations under oath of the representatives of an honorable municipality, neither of which can in any way be controverted, you ask for official records, which you yourself admit can be tampered with. Did Archias not establish residence in Rome, having, for some years prior to the granting of his Heraclean citizenship, settled here with all his possessions and property? Did he not make the required declaration of intention? He did so, and, indeed, on those very records which alone retain the authority of public documents, all the others being untrustworthy except those executed during the praetorship of Metellus.

The records kept by the praetor Appius Claudius were, people well knew, carelessly handled. Those of Gabinius, so negligently kept, were insignificant prior to his trial for extortion: after his conviction they became utterly worthless. By contrast, an example of how faithfully and scrupulously Metellus looked after his records is shown by his bringing to the attention of the praetor, Lentulus, and the other judges his concern for the fact that one name was deleted from the list. On these records, you observe that the name of Archias Licinius has not been deleted.

Since these things are as I have stated, then, how can you entertain any doubts concerning the citizenship of Archias, especially, when he has long since been enrolled as a citizen in other municipalities of our nation? Can it be thought that, when men of little consequence, endowed with a minor talent or none at all, have freely gained citizenship in Greece, the good people of Regium, Locri, Naples, or Tarentum would not want to accord to a man of genius and reputation the privilege they were in the habit of bestowing even on actors? And what do you make of the fact that others, under duress as to the legality of their citizenship, not only after it had been conferred, but even after the Lex Plautia-Papiria, somehow managed to have their names entered surreptitiously on the town registers? Shall the defendant, who never makes use of those other affiliations, but always prefers his status as a citizen of Heraclea, be stricken from our list?

You ask about our census rolls—but it is hardly a secret that Archias was in the retinue of the renowned general Lucullus at the time of the most recent census. At the previous census, he was also with Lucullus, then quaestor in Asia during Sulla's campaign against Mithridates. At the time of the first census, held after the passage of the Lex Plautia-Papiria, during the censorship of Lucius Julius Caesar[2] and Publius Licinius Crassus, none of the population was in fact rated, the next rating being held only three years later. But, inasmuch as a census roll does not legally confirm the right of citizenship, and only identifies the person listed as one who has been performing the duties of a citizen, at that very period, the man you allege was conducting himself not as a Roman citizen (even in his own judgment) made his will in accordance with the law, and named Roman citizens as his inheritors, and was among those recommended for reward by the proconsul Lucullus. Suggest what arguments you wish: he will never be overborne by them, either in his own judgment or in that of his friends.

Now, Gratius, you may inquire as to why I am so enchanted by this man in particular. He offers the mind an opportunity to regain its strength after a noisy session in the courts, and gives something to ease the ears limp with vituperation. Do you imagine I could supply the resources I lavish daily in such variety on public discourse, without stocking my mind with ideas? That my mind could bend to such sustained tension, without its being regularly relaxed by turning to the study of the very same ideas? I readily admit to being addicted to the study of philosophy. Others may, perhaps, feel a little guilty to bury themselves in literary studies and not bring forward any fruitful results of their labor to share with their fellow men, and have nothing to bring to the light to be seen; but why should I feel in the least embarrassed? I, who have lived all the days of my life in such a way that my own leisure has never yet kept me from responding to the danger or to the strategic aid of anyone who needed my services, I, whom pleasure has not kept aloof, nor sleep made sluggish?

Will anyone find fault with me or, in all fairness, begrudge me my diligent labor in pursuit of philosophical and literary studies, when I have only put as much time into that as others devote to their respective interests, to the observance of holidays for entertainment, to rest and recuperation, or as some spend on long dinner parties beginning in the middle of the day, or on gambling, or on playing ball? Perhaps, it will be all the more conceded to me, be-

[2] The father of the dictator.

cause, thriving on these disciplined pursuits, my powers
of oratory, such as they are, have never been in abey-
ance when any of my friends was in danger. My own
skill may seem to some to be of no great weight; I,
nevertheless, know for certain how fundamentally important are those philosophical principles and rules of
practical conduct from which, as from a pure spring,
I refresh my life. Unless I had been convinced from
the time of young manhood by the counsels and writings of many philosophers that nothing in life should
be aimed at but glory and honor, I would never have
subjected myself to every sort of physical strain to
achieve them, or thought the danger of death or exile
to be of little consequence in comparison. I would never
have exposed myself to so much extended combat on
behalf of your welfare, my fellow citizens, or to those
attacks day after day from Catiline and his desperate
crew. Books are filled with descriptions of the merits
of the course I chose to follow; the sayings of wise
men abound with them; antiquity is full of examples
demonstrating them. And yet, the virtue would lie in
darkness still, had not literature brought it to the light.
How many portraits of noble men traced for us, not
only to look at, but to emulate, have Greek and Latin
authors bequeathed us! It was always these that I held
up to my mind's eye as I conducted affairs of state:
I shaped my own mind in accordance with the very
thought of excellent men.

    Someone may say, "What is this? Were those men   *7*
of outstanding character, whose merits have been traditionally conveyed to us by literature, learned in the
same doctrine and discipline you praise so highly?"
That would, of course, be difficult to establish for all
of them, but I am still perfectly certain of how I should
answer the question. I admit that there have been
many, of excellent mind and character, not made so
by schooling, but by their natural disposition, with an
inborn and virtually divine capacity for sage and serious conduct. I say, further, that nature can confer
glory and greatness without the aid of scholarship more
frequently than learning can without the natural en-
dowment. I would also maintain that, when an excellent
and unusual natural gift has been combined with the
exercise of reason and disciplined training, a unique
and brilliant effect usually results. In that number would

be the godlike person our ancestors saw, Scipio Africanus, as would be Laelius and Furius, exceptionally well-balanced and self-controlled beings, not to mention the noblest and most learned man of his day, Cato the Elder. If humanistic studies had not been of service to these men in comprehending and cultivating virtue, they would not have turned so eagerly to them.

Even though no such compellingly prosperous a result were forthcoming, if only delightful absorption were to be aimed for in these studies, I dare say you would still adjudge such mental recreation to be a most civilizing and broadening pastime. Other things are not for all times and all ages and all places. But the study of literature stocks and invigorates youth, brings joy in old age, adorns prosperity, and offers refuge and comfort in adversity. The things of the mind we can enjoy at home, and we find them to be not at all burdensome when we are out. They while away the hours of the night, they travel well, they make themselves at home in the country.

8   If we cannot become accomplished ourselves in the practice of the arts or participate directly in them, we should all the more admire seeing others do so. Who of us was so uncouth and stony-hearted as to be untouched by the recent death of Roscius?[3] Although he died at a ripe old age, it still seemed as though, because of his supreme talent and grace, he ought not to have died, really. Here was a man who had won all hearts by the motion of his body. Can we then remain inattentive to the fascinating activity of cultivated minds and the swift intuition of genius? I have often seen our Archias, gentlemen—I impose on your good will, for you are hearing me out most courteously in my novel presentation of the case—without a single letter being written down, improvise a series of first-rate verses on some topic currently under discussion. I have often seen him, when asked to do it again, express the same subject, changing the words and varying the ideas. Had he deliberately written out the material carefully and fully, I saw that it would be an achievement considered worthy of praise by the ancient masters of style. Therefore, shall I not cherish this man and artist, wonder at

3 Quintus Roscius, who died in 62 B.C., had been the most celebrated actor of the time. He had earned a large fortune.

him, and think of him as one to be defended with every argument at my command?

We have been informed by the greatest scholars that the learning of other things rests on methodical study, attention to principles, and development of skill, whereas nature herself endows the poet with his ability, and generates strength of mind in him, breathes in him, as it were, with a kind of divine inspiration So, our great Ennius rightly called poets sacred, because they appear to be committed to us by some gift and dispensation, as it were, of the gods. Let the name of poet therefore, be revered also by you, men of the highest culture, for it is a name no savage race ever desecrates. Hills and rocks and the solitary places resound to the effect of the human voice; huge animals stand still and are governed by the cadence of a voice; shall we, in our highly civilized atmosphere, be impervious to the voice of poets? The people of Colophon say Homer was their citizen, the people of Chios claim him as theirs, those of Smyrna insist that he is theirs and have dedicated a temple to him in their city. Many others quarrel and compete for the possession of Homer. Thus it is, that they strive to have a poet after his death, even though he was an outsider.

Shall we cast out a poet who is still alive and is 9 very much our own by his choice and the benefit of our law, especially an Archias, who has applied all his study and his art to the end of rehearsing the glory and honor of the Roman people? As a young man, he essayed an account of the war against the Cimbri; Marius himself, hard as he was on poetry, took pleasure in it. No man is, in fact, so disinclined to the Muses as not to be perfectly willing to have the timeless proclamation of his own strenuous accomplishments fashioned in lasting verse. They report that the great Athenian hero Themistocles, when asked what music or whose voice he most delighted in, said "his, by whom my merits are recited." This is why our Marius also had a soft spot in his heart for Lucius Plotius, by whose poetic genius he thought his own achievements could be entered in the annals of fame.

Archias composed an epic on the war against Mithridates, a war which was, as you know, vast and perplexing, with many vicissitudes and a long series of engagements fought on land and sea. The books of

Archias' poem embellish, not only the name of the heroic and illustrious Lucullus, but also the name of the Roman people. It was the Roman people who, under Lucullus' generalship, opened up the regions of the Black Sea, formerly closed and protected by princely fortifications and by the very nature of the terrain. The army of the Roman people, under the same leader, scattered vast hordes of Armenians with a modest expeditionary force. It is to the glory of the Roman people that our closely allied city, Cyzicus, was rescued by the strategy of Lucullus from every assault by the barbarian king, and snatched from the mouth and jaws of the war. That amazing naval engagement off Tenedos[4] will ever be remembered and made glorious as the occasion when Lucullus, in swift pursuit, crushed the enemy fleet and destroyed its captains. But ours are the trophies, ours the monuments, ours the triumphs. The fame of the Roman people is carried far and wide by the genius of the men who bring these matters into the light. Our poet Ennius was so loved by Africanus that he is thought to have had his portrait sculpted in marble on the tomb of the Scipios. And, in praising Scipio, Ennius adorned, not only that person, but the name of the Roman people. Cato, the great grandfather of the Cato here present today, was praised to the skies by Ennius, and thereby great glory accrued to the Roman people. To cite the accomplishments of the various great men of the day—Fabius Maximus, Claudius Marcellus, Fulvius Nobilior—was to enhance the glory all Romans shared in common. The man

10　who did that was a native of Rudiae in Calabria, and our ancestors admitted him into citizenship. Shall we cast out this citizen of Heraclea, who has been invited into many other cities, but has taken up his residence here at Rome?

If someone thinks that the account of our fame is less effectively grasped when written in Greek rather than in Latin verse, he is woefully wrong; the fact is that Greek is read almost everywhere, and Latin is confined to our borders, which are, as everyone knows, small. If the mighty accomplishments we claim end only at the farthest limits of the civilized world, we might want our glory and fame to extend as far as the

4 An island off the coast of Asia Minor, near which Lucullus gained a great victory in a naval engagement in 73 B.C.

weapons brandished in our hands have reached. To celebrate these actions in literature is not only honorable for the people concerned in them, but, surely, for those who fight for their lives and for glory, this is the greatest incentive in the face of peril and hardship. How many writers Alexander the Great is said to have had in his train! But still standing at the tomb of Achilles in Sigeum, he observed, "How lucky you were, young man, to have found a Homer to herald your valor!" A point well taken. If the *Iliad* had not been composed, that very same tomb which enclosed his body would have buried his name as well. Did not our own Magnus Pompey, when his good fortune still kept pace with his merits, confer citizenship on the writer of his deeds, Theophanes of Mytilene, at an army assembly? And, did not those fine men of his, rough-hewn and soldierly as they were, moved by a certain sweet sensation of glory, cheer the act in loud approval, as if they shared also in the leader's praises? If Archias were not a legal Roman citizen, no doubt he would be unable to have citizenship bestowed on him by a military commander! Sulla, who granted the right to men of Spain and Gaul, would, no doubt, have refused it for Archias! When a poor poet from the common people showed Sulla a manuscript in which he had written an epigram in his praise in an elegiac couplet, the general immediately ordered a reward paid out to the poet, from the funds he was amassing from the sale of confiscated property; but ordered it paid on the condition that this poet never again write a line. A man who considered the efforts of an eager, if incompetent, poet still worth rewarding would have yearned, would he not, for the talents, facility, and literary power of an Archias? And indeed, could not Archias have received citizenship from Quintus Metellus Pius, his close friend, who did grant it to many, by means merely of his own efforts or those of the Luculli? Metellus was so concerned to have his campaigns consigned to a literary record, that he listened avidly to poets from Cordova, speaking in their colorful and thick foreign accent.

Let us have no pretense, either, about a matter 11 which cannot be hidden, but, rather, ought to be openly avowed. We are all of us led forward by an eager desire for praise: every exemplary man is particularly excited by the prospect of fame.[5] Even philosophers in the books they write, pouring contempt on glory, sign their names to their work. By simply displaying their scorn for praise and renown, they expect to earn commendation and to be honored by name. Decimus Brutus,[6] a heroic general, embellished the entrances of his own temple and monuments with the verses of Accius, a very close friend of his. When Fulvius waged war against the Aetolians and was accompanied on the campaign by Ennius, he showed no hesitation in offering up the spoils of Mars to the Muses. Therefore, in a city where generals, still in their battle-dress, honor the name of poets and pay their respects at the shrines of the Muses, shall these judges, clad in the civilian toga, decline from regarding the glory of the Muses and the well-being of their servants, the poets?

To offer you some excuse for declining, gentlemen, let me betray my own feelings to you and confess to a definite yearning for fame. Perhaps, this is too readily, but even so, all the more honestly, admitted to. The great deeds performed in our consulship with your support, and on behalf of this city and its government, on behalf of the citizens and of the republic as a whole —these achievements are the subject of a poem Archias is at present composing. When I had listened to some of the lines, which seemed to me powerful and extremely pleasurable, I urged him to proceed to bring the poem to completion. True merit asks for no other reward for the effort and danger it undergoes than this token of honorable fame. Take that away, gentlemen, and what motive have we for so great an expenditure of time? Of course, if the soul took no thought for

---

5 *Trahimur omnes studio laudis, et optimus*
quisque maxime gloria ducitur.

Milton, in *Lycidas,* considers the complexities of fame:

> Fame is the spur that the clear spirit doth raise
> (That last infirmity of noble mind)
> To scorn delights and live laborious days . . .
> Fame is no plant that grows on mortal soil,
> Nor in the glistering foil
> Set off to the world, nor in broad rumour lies,
> But lives and spreads aloft by those pure eyes,
> And perfect witness of all-judging Jove.

6 Consul in 138 B.C., and a distinguished general, conqueror of the Lusitanians.

posterity, and all its ideas ended at the boundaries to which our lifespan is confined, it would not exert itself so strenuously; it would not be troubled so often by anxiety and sleepless nights; it would not fight, time and again, for its very life. But, as things are, a certain noble instinct abides deep in the heart of every worthy man, which animates the soul, day and night, with an incentive toward glory and reminds us that the story of our fame must not be given up when the term of life ends: it must be made coexistent with all future time.

Are we to let ourselves appear so craven-hearted, **12** we, who work for our country and labor amid the perils of this life, that, when we have brought to the final bourne a soul always active and vigorous, we conclude that all things die with us? Many great men have been concerned to leave statues and portraits behind them, likenesses not of the soul, but of the body. Ought we not much rather wish to leave behind us an image of our thoughts and of our good qualities, molded and finished with artistic skill? I believed, even when I was doing them, that the things I accomplished were seeds I cast and planted in the soil of the world's everlasting memory. Whether this memory will lie beyond the reach of my consciousness after my death or whether, as philosophers have maintained, it will be present in some part of my soul, I take delight in the very hope and anticipation of it.

Therefore, gentlemen of the jury, preserve in safety this entirely modest, entirely worthy man, whose friends you see vouch for him by the very dignity, as well as the long-continued intimacy, of their association with him. He is a man, moreover, whose great talent, whatever estimate you may have formed of it, you see clearly to be sought after by men of the highest ability. Let his request meet with your approval, as it has already conformed to the demands of the Lex Plautia-Papiria, found favor with the officials of Heraclea and been corroborated by the records of Metellus. We, therefore, beseech you, judges—if, not only human, but also divine, sanction for men of great genius ought to be of any weight—to accord this man your protection, so that he appear exalted by your generous understanding, not swept aside by a harsh ruling. Surely, this is the due of a man who has always celebrated the deeds of your field commanders and the achievements of the Roman people, who is now preparing to enhance, with the undying testimony of artistic glory, the events surrounding the recent domestic crisis in political affairs, which you and I saw through to a successful conclusion, and a man who, by his profession as artist, is held in esteem and awe in the minds of all men.

So, gentlemen of the jury, as is my custom, I have held forth briefly in demonstration of the three points which I trust have been proven to the satisfaction of all. I have also discoursed in general terms about things lying outside the immediate boundaries of the legal matters at issue, the man's genius and the poet's profession. I can only hope, gentlemen, that these remarks will be taken in good faith on your part, as I know for certain they will be by the praetor invested with the duty of presiding over this trial.

In Defense of Caelius

The trial of Marcus Caelius Rufus took place on April 3 and 4 of 56 B.C. Caelius, then in his late twenties, spoke in his own defense, and was also represented by Crassus and Cicero. The summing up for the defense was done by Cicero, whose speech *Pro Caelio*, has been part of the repertoire of classical oratory since the day it was delivered.

After his apprenticeship with Cicero in 66–63 B.C., Caelius became temporarily involved in the Catilinarian movement in the year 63 B.C. He soon dropped his associations with that group, and, in late 62 or 61 B.C., went to Africa as an aide-de-camp in the military retinue of the proconsul, Quintus Pompeius Rufus. Returning to Rome, Caelius won his first public recognition by a successful prosecution of Gaius Antonius Hybrida (Cicero's fellow consul in 63) for mismanagement of the province of Macedonia. After this achievement in March, 59 B.C., Caelius moved out of his father's house and leased a house of his own in the fashionable Palatine quarter of Rome. His home happened to be near that of Clodia, the recently widowed wife of Quintus Metellus Celer. She was the sister of Publius Clodius Pulcher, who, as tribune in 58 B.C., had passed the law that drove Cicero into exile. Clodia's siren powers provided the inspiration and substance of many of the lyric poems of Gaius Valerius Catullus (c. 84–c. 54 B.C.), who was deeply in love with her, but, to his sorrow and anger, was eventually spurned as Clodia's exclusive admirer. It was probably

Caelius who supplanted Catullus in the affections of Clodia,
Caelius, whom Catullus ruefully addresses in poem 77,

Rufe mihi frustra ac nequiquam credite amico:

Rufus, whom I, your friend, trusted in vain, and to no purpose
—in vain? Nay, rather at a great and ruinous price—have
you stolen into my heart and, burning into my vitals, torn
away, alas, all my blessings? Torn away, alas, alas! you the
cruel poison of my life, alas, alas! You the deadly bane of
my friendship.*

For some two years, Caelius and Clodia conducted a
love affair that ended when Caelius cast her off. Until then,
it had always been Clodia who jettisoned her cargoes of men,
and Caelius' refusal to continue subject to her undoubtedly
prompted the defamatory prosecution Caelius found himself
facing in April, 56 B.C. Scholars have even suggested that
the prosecutor, the young man, Atratinus, then only seventeen years old, was, himself, strongly under the influence of
Clodia. The fact is, that at the beginning of that year, Caelius
had prosecuted Atratinus' father (Lucius Calpurnius Bestia)
for *ambitus,* and when Bestia was acquitted, had begun new
proceedings against him for another trial.

Cicero seems to have been justified in making Clodia's
animosity to Caelius the central issue of his final speech
for the defense. Caelius was acquitted, and abandoned his
plans for a second prosecution of Bestia. He was elected
tribune in 52 B.C., and allied himself informally with Milo,
Cicero's chief protector against the harassments of Clodius.
When Clodius was murdered near Bovillae, January 18,
52 B.C., Milo "was prosecuted before a court so heavily
guarded that Cicero did not dare defend him (but subsequently published his speech *Pro Milone*)."† Milo retired
into exile at Marseilles. Although Cicero's attempt to defend
Milo had not been successful, he and Caelius appeared together before the court at the trial of Saufeius, the leader of
the gang which had murdered Clodius, and secured his acquittal. Cicero then took up his duties as proconsular governor of the province of Cilicia in Asia Minor, and from this
point on, we can follow the fortunes of Caelius as they are
reflected at first hand in the correspondence between him and

* Translated by F. W. Cornish, *Catullus.* Cambridge, Mass.: Harvard
University Press, Loeb Classical Library Edition, revised 1964.
† G. E. F. Chilver, in the *Oxford Classical Dictionary.*

Cicero that begins in this year and lasts until late January, 48 B.C. Volume VIII of Cicero's *Letters to his Friends*, consists entirely of seventeen letters from Caelius to Cicero, written between the years 51 and 48 B.C. Cicero's letters to Caelius are distributed elsewhere in the published correspondence. The image of Caelius that emerges from the letters has been aptly registered by R. G. Austin.*

Caelius' sense of the political realities led him to side with Caesar in the civil war against Pompey. On January 1, 49 B.C., Caelius, having voted against the motion in the Senate that Caesar be declared a public enemy, left Rome to join Caesar, who was then proceeding from Ravenna to Rimini, crossing a small river, the Rubicon, en route. Soon after, under Caesar's orders, Caelius was assigned a rather insignificant mission, to put down a revolt at Intimilium in Liguria. In April, he accompanied Caesar to Spain. When, a year later, Caelius was appointed *praetor peregrinus* by Caesar, the more substantial post of *praetor urbanus* having been awarded to the more reliable Trebonius, he expressed his dissatisfaction by making so much trouble for Trebonius that the consul and the Senate finally relieved him of his office. Pretending that he would appeal to Caesar, Caelius left Rome—actually he had a rendezvous with Milo in Southern Italy, and intended to lead an armed revolt against Caesar. But Caelius and Milo could only rally a small group of slaves and gladiators to their rebellious standard, and, in April of 48 B.C., Caelius was captured and put to death after an engagement with some of Caesar's troops near the southern town of Thurii.

So, in its thirties ended the life of the young man whose career, Cicero had assured the judges in the speech for his defense, would be "dedicated, devoted, and deeply committed" to the Roman state. It was certainly a committed career, an engaged life, one in which Caelius' personality, ambition, literary talents, and political and social convictions, conspired to compel him to take part in, not withdraw from, the revolutionary crisis that was enveloping Rome. In his speech in defense of Caelius, Cicero limns the rising action of a heroic revolutionary who can shoulder aside such seething social and political antagonisms as his self-realization

---

* M. Tullius Cicero, *Pro Caelio*. Translated by R. G. Austin. Oxford: Clarendon Press, 3rd ed., 1960, pp. x–xi. Austin's edition of this oration is a masterpiece of scholarly analysis. Caelius' character and "style" are also amply discussed in *Correspondence of Cicero* by R. Y. Tyrrell and L. C. Purser. London: vol. iii, 1890.

have provoked. The older statesman did not portray the reversal of fortunes and final defeat of the dynamic spirit on which he had delightedly focused his attention in April, 56 B.C.

When Cicero was on his way to Cilicia to assume the governorship of the province, in June, 51 B.C., Caelius wrote a letter to him from Rome that begins:

> Is it so? Have I won? And do I send you frequent letters, which, as you were leaving, you said I should never take the trouble to do for you? . . . not only do I feel myself to be all alone, but now you are gone a desert seems to have been created at Rome; and I who in my carelessness omitted paying you a visit on many days, when you were here, am now daily tortured to think that I have not got you to run to.

There follow some political and domestic items, but the letter concludes with a request:

> What I now have to ask of you is that, if (as I hope) you get any leisure, you would compose some treatise dedicated to me, to show me that you care for me. "How did that come into your head," say you, "a modest man like you?" I desire that out of your numerous writings there should be something extant handing down to posterity also the record of our friendship. "What sort of thing do you want?" I suppose you will ask. You, who are acquainted with every school of thought, will hit upon the suitable thing sooner than I. Only let it be of a kind that has some appropriateness to me, and let it contain practical instruction, that it may be widely used.*

Cicero had already done just that, when he wrote the speech justifying the young man's right for a continued career in Roman politics.

---

* *Ad Familiares*, vol. VIII, no. 3, translation by E. S. Shuckburgh.

In Defense of Caelius

Gentlemen of the jury, if some stranger unfamiliar **1**
with our laws, our courts, and our way of life, were
to chance upon us here today, he would, I know, wonder what heinous crime is on trial. Seeing this case
being conducted on a national holiday[1] when all other
legal business is suspended, he would not hesitate to
conclude that the defendant stands accused of so enormous an offense that, were it neglected, the state would
collapse. If the visitor learned that our law governing
crimes of violence against the state by subversive citizens who have laid siege to the Senate under arms,
offered violence to the magistrates, or attacked the
republic, requires immediate investigation, he would
see the point of the law, but he might inquire what the
particular charge is now before the court. Were he then
to learn that no heinous crime, no reckless action or
act of violence is in question—but, that rather, a
talented, reputable, and energetic young man is being
prosecuted by the son of a man he himself is prosecuting and has prosecuted in the past, that, moreover, the
main source of the opposition is a notoriously loose
woman—hearing that, our visitor will not find fault
with the prosecutor, young Atratinus, for performing
his filial duty, but will think the woman and her lust
should be restrained and he will find you much put
upon who cannot enjoy your leisure even today when
the rest of the community are enjoying theirs.

If, gentlemen, you give your close attention and
total objective judgment to this case, you will conclude
that no one, with any real choice in the matter, would
have stooped to such an accusation nor, when he had
embarked upon it, would have harbored any hopes of
success, unless he relied upon the uncontrollable passions and extraordinarily bitter hatred of someone else.
I quite forgive my good friend Atratinus, a generous
and fine young man, who can plead duty to his father,

[1] The *Ludi Megalenses,* a festival instituted in 204 B.C. in honor
of the Magna Mater. It now lasted from April 4 to 10, and was
the holiday during which plays were shown and public entertainments given.

necessity, and youthfulness. If he himself wanted to take the case, I attribute it to his sense of filial duty; if it was forced on him, to necessity; if he hoped to gain some advantage thereby, to his immaturity. To the others involved in the impeachment, however, I give no quarter, but promise a fight to the bitter end.

2 As the best approach to the defense of my young client, Marcus Caelius, gentlemen, I will first reply to what his accusers have said in their efforts to distort, degrade, and defame his character. His father's name has been introduced in several ways: he was a person who allegedly brought no credit upon the equestrian order; or he was called a person whom his own son treated with disrespect. To those of you who know him and to the older persons here present, Marcus Caelius the elder can answer sufficiently for his own dignity without uttering a word, and with no need of my speaking on his behalf. To those who do not know him so well—for, with advancing years, he has appeared less frequently among us in the forum—let me say that whatever dignity can pertain to a Roman knight (and that is a large measure), Marcus Caelius is considered to possess, not only by his close associates, but by all who have had any contact with him whatsoever. The fact of a man's being the son of a Roman knight ought not have been brought up as a species of charge by the prosecution; nor is it likely to impress the jurors or myself, the counsel for the defense. As for what the opposition has said about Caelius' filial piety or lack of it, we may form some estimate of it, but the decision must rest with the father. What our opinion of it is you will hear from the witnesses. The touching grief and tears of the mother you see here, the sorrowful father garbed in mourning, make clear what the parents feel.

As for the allegation that the young man is in disfavor with his fellow townsmen, let me merely remind you, gentlemen of the jury, that the citizens of Interamnia have paid no greater compliment to any resident than they did to Caelius when he had moved away; although he was no longer living there, they elected him to their highest governing body and conferred honors on him, without his requesting them, which many others have solicited and been denied. And the same citizens have sent a picked delegation of Senators and Roman knights to this trial to attest to Caelius' character in a prepared statement couched in the most eloquent and convincing language.

I do believe that I have now laid the foundations of my defense very solidly by resting them on the testimony of those closest to the defendant. For the young man could not be recommended to you so unqualifiedly, if he were unfavorably regarded, not only by his eminent father, but also by so renowned and respected a township.

Indeed, I, if I may say so, myself have proceeded *3* from similar origins to win a good name among men; my work in the law here and the manner in which I have conducted my public career have found favor in men's eyes and attained wide recognition by the good opinion and approval of my friends.

As for the attacks on his moral behavior, harped on long and loud, rather than specified as charges, Caelius will not take them so to heart as to regret not having been born without his good looks. For this is the sort of envious criticism generally launched against all whose youth has been generously endowed with beauty and attractiveness. An accusation would require a criminal act to define the status of the event, identify the man, prove the case by argument, corroborate it by witnesses; vindictive criticism has no intention beyond that of simple slander. If it is done spitefully, it is called abuse. If amusingly, sophisticated wit. I indeed wondered at that section of the accusation, and took it amiss that it had been entrusted to Atratinus above all men. It was unbecoming to him and his own youth, as you could well perceive, to have his natural modesty suffer the outrage of being the agency of vituperation like that. I would have preferred one of the older and more robust members of the prosecution to draw the assignment of impugning the defendant's character. Then I might have proceeded to dispose of the unwarranted and false exaggerations contained in this slanderous indictment and completely crushed it in my usual way. I will, of course, handle you, Atratinus, more leniently, both because I would temper my tone to your innocence and because I would preserve the good will I bear you and your father. I do warn you simply, first, to let people think of you as you, in fact, really are, and detach yourself from the degrading aspects of the case as you do from the use of licentious language. Next, do not say anything against another that would make you blush to hear falsely imputed of you. For this path lies open to anyone, does it not? Who cannot find fault in some niggling way with a man of your age and rank like Caelius, and carp at him with some apparent basis for argument, although without any real grounds for suspicion? The actual blame for the unseemly nature of the prosecution lies with the men who wanted you to play this role. Only praise is due your natural modesty, when we see that you uttered these slanderous statements quite unwillingly, just as praise is due to your exceptional talent for having phrased them in so decorous and courteous a manner.

4   To the whole speech you delivered, my reply can be brief. Insofar as Caelius' youth could create the suspicions you raised, he was well protected against them both, by his genuine good character and by the care and discipline afforded him by his father. When the toga of manhood was conferred on Caelius (to say nothing here of my own role, which you can judge quite adequately for yourselves; I merely remark that he was immediately brought to me as a pupil by his father)—from that time on, no one saw Marcus Caelius, in the flower of his youth, unless he was with his father or with me or in the upright house of Marcus Crassus,[2] and when he was being instructed in the most exemplary branches of learning.

People were wont to say that the many virtues of Crassus were darkened by the one vice of avarice . . . at first he was not worth above three hundred talents ($300,000), yet, though in the course of his political life he dedicated the tenth of all he had to Hercules, and feasted the people, and gave to every citizen corn enough to serve him three months, upon casting up his accounts, before he went upon his Parthian expedition, he found his possessions to amount to seven thousand one hundred talents ($7,100,100); most of which, if we may scandal him with a truth, he got by fire and rapine, making his advantages of public calamities, observing how extremely subject the city was to fire and falling down of houses, by reason of their height and their standing so near together, he bought slaves that

_____

[2] Of Marcus Crassus, the famous millionaire politician of Cicero's day, Plutarch writes:

were builders and architects, and when he had collected these to the number of more than five hundred, he made it his practice to buy houses that were on fire, and those in the neighborhood, which, in the immediate danger and uncertainty the proprietors were willing to part with for little or nothing, so that the greatest part of Rome, at one time or another, came into his hands. . . .

Crassus was very eager to be hospitable to strangers; he kept open house, and to his friends he would lend money without interest, but called it in precisely at the time; so that his kindness was often thought worse than paying the interest would have been. His entertainments were, for the most part, plain and citizenlike, the company general and popular; good taste made them pleasanter than sumptuosity would have done. As for learning, he chiefly cared for rhetoric, and what would be serviceable with large numbers; he became one of the best speakers at Rome, and by his pains and industry outdid the best natural orators. For there was no trial how mean and contemptible soever that he came to unprepared.

Life of Crassus, translated by John Dryden, *ad init.*

As for the objection that Caelius was an associate of Catiline, he ought to be far from any such suspicion. You all know well that, when Caelius was still a very young man, Catiline stood for the consulship the same year I did. If Caelius had gone over to Catiline's support or ever had left my party—and to be sure, many well-brought-up young men did become partisans of that worthless and wicked man—then, indeed, Caelius would be thought of as having been too closely associated with Catiline. But afterward, we knew and we saw that he was also among the friends of Catiline. And who denies that? I am defending his conduct at an age when a young man's nature is not yet strong in itself, but an easy prey to the passions of others. He was constantly in my entourage when I was praetor; he had not known Catiline. Then Catiline was assigned the province of Africa as praetor. The next year came, and Catiline stood trial on charges of extortion. Caelius was of my party; he did not go to Catiline, even when summoned as an advocate of his cause. The next year was the one when I was a candidate for the consulship; and Catiline also. Never once did Caelius leave me to support him.

5   So many years, therefore, having been engaged in public business without suspicion or slander attaching to him, he supported Catiline when the latter sought office for a second time. How long do you think his youth should have been kept in tutelage? In my young days, a single year was customary, during which our arms were confined as, clad in tunics, we took our athletic practice on the Campus. If we then entered upon our military service, the same routine prevailed in camp and on campaigns. At that stage of life, unless a young man protected himself by great sobriety and self-control, and not only by the native sense of decency instilled at home, but also by a decided natural instinct for good behavior, no matter how well he was looked after by his friends, he could hardly escape some slights upon his character. A person who passed that first period of his manhood pure and unblemished would be the object of no one's slurs on his reputation and chastity when he had at last grown up to be a man among men.

Caelius favored the party of Catiline, when he had been launched for some years on the tide of public affairs. But many others, of every rank and age, followed the same course. The creature Catiline had, as you all remember, many potential hints of greatness, contained as it were in outline and never fully fleshed out. While he was the intimate of many unscrupulous men, he also made a pretense of giving his allegiance to many men of the better sort. There was about him always the lure of debauchery, but at the same time he generated a certain excitement of energy and stimulus to effort. Depravities of passion raged in him; yet he showed a marked ability for soldiering. I think there was never before on earth such a hybrid as this person combining such opposite, conflicting, incompatible natural instincts and desires.

6   Who was at one time more congenial to the finest men and at another more closely linked to the worst? What citizen was at times more sound and reliable than he and at times a more loathsome enemy of the state? Who was ever more dissolute in pleasure, or again more inured to hard work? Who more rapacious in grabbing other people's money and possessions or more free-handed in sharing out his own? And besides, gentlemen, there were these paradoxical qualities: his ability

to embrace many men in his friendship and retain their devotion by being attentive to them; to share his possessions with them all; to meet his friends' needs with his money, and assist them with his influence, with his own physical efforts, with his crime and daring, if necessary. He could control and guide his own nature as occasion dictated, turning it this way, bending it that way. With the sad he was serious, with the cheerful gay, sober with the old, amusing with the young, bold and reckless with the criminal, extravagant with the spendthrift. Having employed that many-sided, complex character to bring together unscrupulous types from everywhere in the world, he also commanded the respect of many good and brave men by the impression of gallantry he created. Never could the criminal intent to destroy the state have originated with him, if the enormity of so many vices had not been based on a foundation of great patience combined with wily adaptability.

So let the charge of Caelius' intimacy with Catiline count little in your judgment, gentlemen. It applies to him in common with many others and some of them the best people. I myself—yes, even I—was once nearly deceived by Catiline, who seemed to be a good citizen, eager to win his fellow citizens' admiration, and a loyal, strong, and faithful friend. In fact, I saw his evildoing before I quite realized what it meant; I sensed the need for direct action before my suspicions were fully aroused. If Caelius, therefore, was among his friends, it is more a reason for his being disgruntled at having fallen into such an error—as I also regret having been so mistaken about the same person—than a reason he should fear the accusation of having been his friend.

And then, your speech sank lower, from its insulting slurs on Caelius' chastity to its attempt to fasten guilt on him by association with the conspiracy of Catiline.[3] Your premise, although tentatively advanced and shakily insisted on, was, that because of his friendship with Catiline, Caelius must have been involved in the conspiracy. On that point, not only did the charge fail to hold good, my eloquent young friend, the prose-

[3] Although Caelius had supported Catiline's candidacy for the consulship in 63, he undoubtedly withdrew his support of Catiline's party when Crassus and Caesar did.

cutor's argument failed to hold together. For what revolutionary frenzy, what great flaw in character, or instincts, what inadequacy in his fortunes or prospects disabled Caelius to such a degree? And furthermore, was his name ever heard in connection with any such suspicion?

I am not sure whether I need to reply in the same way, now that I seem to have arrived at this point, on the subject of the corrupt electoral practices and on the charges of belonging to political bribery-clubs. Caelius never would have been so foolish as to prosecute another man on charges of bribery, if he had contaminated himself by the same immoderate practice, or try to cast suspicion on someone else for doing what he himself wanted to feel free to engage in, nor if he thought he might face trial even once for bribery, would he himself indict another man on this charge a second time over. His prosecution of Bestia on this charge seems to me to have been ill-advised; nevertheless, it represents the sort of eagerness that shows him to be thinking of attacking another man's innocence, not entertaining any fears about his own.

Turning to the matter of the debts he is reproached for having incurred, the extravagance he is rebuked for, and the account books demanded in evidence, I will reply, please note, very briefly. A son who is still legally a minor is not required to keep account books. Caelius did not contract a single loan. The lavish expenses attributed to him all come down to one matter: the house rent he paid, cited as 30,000 sesterces. Oh! Now I see why Clodius is offering that block of apartments for sale; Caelius lives in one of them at a rent I would imagine to be about 10,000 sesterces. And you, the prosecutors, in an effort to please Clodius, have agreed to falsify the figure more accommodatingly.

Then, you rebuke Caelius for having moved away from his father's residence. But, for a man of his age, this is not the least cause for reproach. Entering on his public career, he prosecuted Antonius: I admit this was an annoyance to me, but it was a great triumph for Caelius, and after that, he could appropriately begin to pursue public office. His father, not only permitted, but encouraged Caelius' making himself independent; and the father's house being rather distant from the forum, Caelius leased quarters on the Palatine at a modest rent.

On this point, I may rehearse the quotation offered earlier in the case by my distinguished colleague, Marcus Crassus, in a disparaging reference to the arrival of King Ptolemy. He cited the opening lines of Ennius' tragedy, which run: *8*

Would that the firs in the forest of Pelion
Had never been cut to fashion the Argo's planks, etc.[4]

Actually, I would remind you more fully of the context which goes on:

Then my wandering mistress would have never . . .

as the poet says, given us so much cause for trouble, my mistress:

Medea, heartsick, savagely wounded by love.

You will find, gentlemen, when I come to deal with the topic, that it was precisely Caelius' move to this region, and this Medea of the Palatine,[5] which have been the cause of all the evils afflicting the young man, or rather, of all the things that have been said to afflict him.

Therefore, gentlemen, relying on your common sense, I feel undaunted by assertions contrived and invented by the prosecution to bolster up their case. They said a Senator would come forward to testify that he had been forcibly driven away from the pontifical elections by Caelius. If the man does appear, I will ask him, first, why he took no action immediately, and then, why, if he preferred ruing to suing, he is dragged in by you instead of coming forward himself, and why he waited so long after the event instead of voicing his complaint immediately. If he answers shrewdly and to the point, I may then inquire as to the source the Senator has sprung from. If he proves to be himself, the main source and supply, I will be impressed, as I

4 The lines are from the beginning of Ennius' *Medea in Exile*.
5 Atratinus had called Caelius a "pretty little Jason," *pulchellum Iasonem*, implying that Caelius had won his golden fleece (the gold he took from Clodia) and then deserted his Medea. In the speech for his defense, Caelius had called Atratinus "the curly-haired Pelias," *Pelia cincinnatus*, equating his accuser with Pelias, who tried to ruin Jason.

usually am. If, on the other hand, he is a mere rivulet, drained and drawn off from the fountainhead of the prosecution, I will be happy to note that, although your indictment has such powerful and wealthy backing, only one Senator has been found willing to gratify you.

Nor do I worry in the least about that other class of night witnesses. The prosecution states that there will be men to testify that their wives have been criminally assaulted by Caelius when returning from dinner parties. They will be important people to state this on oath, when they are forced to admit that they have never begun proceedings for redress of such wrongs, not even by some amicable settlement out of court.

9   By now, gentlemen, you can grasp quite clearly the entire spirit of the attack being made on my client, and when it is offered, you will find it your duty to reject it promptly. Marcus Caelius is not being prosecuted by the same persons by whom he is being attacked. The shafts are hurled openly, but the ammunition is being supplied secretly. I do not say this to arouse hostility against the members of the Claudian family, who are entitled to assert their pride. They are behaving dutifully, they protect themselves and do as the bravest will: injured, they grieve; angry, they are drawn into retaliating; challenged, they fight back. But it lies within your wisdom, gentlemen of the jury, to see that, although the reasons for courageous opposition to Caelius may be justified, you have no reasonable ground for consulting someone else's spite, rather than your own honor as a jury. You see what a great throng is assembled here in the forum, comprising people of different classes and different interests. From this vast gathering, how many do you think are there who are willing to volunteer their services to influential, popular, and eloquent men when they think these leading figures want something, and who offer to work and to bear witness for them? Should some of this sort, by chance, have pushed into this trial, shut out their greedy self-interest from your considered judgment, gentlemen of the jury, so that you appear to have taken thought for both the safety of the defendant and for your own sense of responsibility, in guarding the general welfare of all our citizens against the dangerous influence of powerful men. Indeed, I will lead you away from these witnesses and not allow the unalterable truth of this

trial to depend on the willful testimony of witnesses, which can be easily shaped and manipulated and twisted in any direction. We shall conduct our case by arguments and refute the charges brought against us with proofs clearer than daylight. Facts will be met by facts, motives by motives, reasons by reasons.

Of course, I am very pleased to let stand that part **10** of the case[6] discussed fully with dignity and eloquence by Marcus Crassus, the portion of the attack concerning the seditions at Naples, the demonstrations against the Alexandrians at Puteoli, and the seizure of Palla's property. I only wish Crassus had also dealt with Caelius' alleged involvement in the murder of Dio. What statement can you expect to hear, except one which the man responsible, not only is unafraid of, but readily admits to? For he is a king, Ptolemy. The man named as his agent, Publius Asicius, has been tried and acquitted. What sort of crime is it that the man responsible for does not deny, and the man tried for has been absolved of, but another person unconnected with the event and never suspected of having been a party to it should fear being accused of? If Asicius profited more by the publicity he gained in being acquitted than the damage done him by being accused, will your abuse descend on a person untouched by the faintest suspicion of being implicated, even the suggestion that he was? Asicius' acquittal was secured by means of collusion? It is simple enough to meet that point, especially for me, who defended the case. But Caelius himself thinks Asicius' case was perfectly sound; whatever its quality, he considers it to have no bearing on his own. Not only Caelius, but Titus and Gaius Coponius, also, find the case of Dio to have no connection with the present trial. They are young men of the most cultivated sensibility and scholarship, with the advantage of the finest literary training and the most virtuous principles. More than anyone, they lamented the death of Dio, for they were close to him, not only by the relationship of hospitality, but by his devotion to scholarship and to the principles of human conduct. Dio lived for some time at the home of Titus,

---

6 For guidance to the concatenation of charges involved in the prosecution of Caelius under the *lex de vi,* I refer the reader to Austin's incomparable discussion.

whom he had come to know in Alexandria. You will
hear what Titus, or his equally gifted brother, think of
Caelius from them themselves, if they take the witness
stand. Let us, therefore, dismiss these irrelevant con-
siderations so that, finally, we may come to the actual
facts behind the case.

11   I noticed, gentlemen, how closely you listened to
the presentation made by my friend of the opposition,
Herennius. Although you were wrapped up mainly in
his talented manner and style of speaking, I was worried
that his speech, tellingly planned for an incriminating
effect, would, imperceptibly and slyly, insinuate itself
into your minds. He discoursed at length on overindulgence, sensual cravings, vice, and, generally, the misconduct of the young. Normally, Herennius is the soul
of kindness, and displays the disarmingly affable and
civilized manner so highly appreciated today, but in
discussing this case he became a sternly moralizing
uncle, a censor, a teacher. He scolded Caelius as no
father ever lectured his son, and expatiated grandly
upon loose and intemperate conduct. In short, I more
than sympathized with the attention you paid his
words, when I found myself wincing at his glum and
grim manner of speaking. I was not very impressed by
the drift of his opening remarks about Caelius' being
on friendly terms with my associate Bestia, that Caelius
dined there often and frequently visited at his house,
and supported his candidacy for the praetorship. I am
not impressed by statements that are patently false. He
said that others, too, dined in their company, who are
either nowhere to be found, or who must say just what
Herennius tells them to. Nor was I particularly impressed by his assertion that Caelius was a member of
the Lupercalian fraternity. This Wolf-Priest group is a
wild and woolly brotherhood, a guild of savages made
up of those genuine wolf-men whose famous woodland
pack antedates law and civilization. The members of
the fraternity, not only inform against one another,
but boast of their membership in the fraternity when
they do so. I suppose, they are afraid someone might
be left in ignorance of the fact. I disregard such things,
preferring to answer the matters that do cause me some
concern.

12   His lengthy tirade against dissipation, being uttered
in steely quiet, had more subtlety than ferocity in it,

and was, therefore, heard all the more carefully. My good friend Clodius, after all, ranted and raved, displaying such force and effort, glowing white-hot throughout his speech, using caustic terms and shouting at the top of his voice, that I gave him a good grade for eloquence, but saw no reason to fear anything in his argument. In previous cases, I had noticed how ineffective his technique of prosecution was. But with your permission, Balbus Herennius, I will try to answer you, if it is judicial for me to defend someone who has not refused an invitation to dinner, who has been known to stroll in a private park, and who had made visits to Baiae. I have, of course, known many men in this republic of ours, who devoted their entire youth to pleasures, and did not merely dip into them and sample them, but who eventually turned over a new leaf, and, in maturity, became serious, leading citizens. Everyone is willing to grant a young man a few love affairs; nature herself develops desires in us during this period of youth. If the desires find expression in such a way as not to ruin anyone's life or wreck anyone's house, they are considered to be manageable and endurable. You seemed to me to be using the common elements of youth's bad reputation to weld together a definite prejudice against Caelius. The utter silence in which your oration was heard out derived from the fact that we were thinking about the vices of many with reference to the one defendant in the dock. It is easy enough to inveigh against profligacy. Daylight would fail me before I could list the necessary points in an argument on that subject. A mighty oration remains to be delivered on corruption, adultery, lascivious conduct, extravagance. Even when no specific person is being accused, but only the vices in general, the subject offers room for ample and serious attack. But, it is the better part of your wisdom, gentlemen, not to have your attention sidetracked from the defendant. As sober, responsible persons, you have the sting of your verdict to apply, which the prosecutor has now diverted to generalizations about the decadence and immorality of the age. You should not turn it on the individual on trial, when it is not through his own fault, but through the irresponsibility of many that he is confronted with an accusation he does not deserve. As for your harsh indictment, Herennius, I dare not meet it

as it should be met. I might have pleaded for the concessions a young man is entitled to, and have asked
forgiveness for him. But I dare not, I say, do that. I
do not take refuge in the plea of his youthfulness: I
disregard everyone's right to such allowances. I merely
request that, whatever general prejudice our generation
attaches to debts, profligacy, and the debauched ways
of young men—and I know that it is a large measure—
the sins of others or the depravity of the times or of
the age-group be not used to Caelius' detriment. And
I, the same person who make this demand, have no
objection to answering to the fullest of my ability the
accusations legitimately leveled at the defendant in
person.

13   There are two charges before us, one having to do
with gold ornaments and the other with poison. One
and the same person stands accused of both. The allegation is that the gold was obtained from Clodia, and
the poison procured to be administered to Clodia. All
the other accusations are not criminal charges, but
slander, the matter of merely personal invective, irrelevant to a public hearing. To call a man an adulterer,
an unscrupulous agent of bribery, is an insult, but not
a legal accusation. There is nothing behind such charges,
there is no basis for them. They are quarrelsome noises
rashly uttered by an angry prosecutor, with no specific
person authorizing them. But, as for the two criminal
charges, I see their author; I see their source; I see the
name of the person behind them. He needed the gold,
so he acquired it from Clodia, procured it in the presence of no witnesses, and kept it as long as he wished.
Here, I detect the clearest indication of a phenomenally
familiar relationship. He wished to kill the same woman;
he procured the poison, suborned the slaves, prepared
the potion, established the rendezvous, secretly brought
the stuff there. After all, I see utter hatred formed on
the breaking-up of their relationship. The whole matter
before us, gentlemen of the jury, has to do with Clodia,
with a woman, who is not only one of the nobility, but
notorious. I shall say nothing about her reputation,
except what may be necessary to introduce for the
purpose of refuting the charges. But you know quite
well, by dint of your exemplary foresight, Domitius,
that our business concerns her exclusively. If she claims
not to have loaned Caelius the gold, if she maintains

that the poison was not bought by this means, we are grossly at fault in using the term of "Roman lady" in a way far different from what the respectable status of matron requires. But, if the woman is left out of the case, and then there remains neither any criminal charge nor the funds needed to continue the proceedings against Caelius, what else are we as his counsel to do, but refute those who are attacking him? Indeed, I would do this very thoroughly, if I were not so mindful of the hostility that exists between me and her lover—I beg your pardon, I meant to say "her brother"; I am always making that mistake. As it is, I will act with restraint and take no longer than my obligation in the case demands. I hardly think I ought to engage in any hostilities with a woman, especially, a woman usually thought of as the friend of all men rather than the enemy of any one.

But still, I will ask her, first, whether she prefers **14** me to conduct the case solemnly, weightily, in the old-fashioned way, or freely, amusingly, in the smart contemporary style. If she prefers the old-fashioned approach, I will have to summon up some figure from among those bearded patriarchs of bygone days, not the little goatee-type she is infatuated with, but the bristling sort we see in statues or on ancestral busts, who can bring down his wrath upon the woman's head and speak in place of me, so that she will not by chance become angry at me. Let someone materialize, some member of their own family, chief of all, perhaps, Appius Claudius Caecus.[7] At least, his being blind will diminish the pain he might feel when he saw her. Suppose him now, to have come back to life. Surely, he would take the stage and speak in the following way.

"Woman, what have you to do with Caelius, with a young man like him, unrelated to you? How can you have been so intimate with him as to put gold ornaments at his disposal, or then so hostile as to fear poison from him? Had not you seen that your father was a consul or heard that your uncle, your grandfather, great-grandfather and great-great-grandfather, were consuls? Did you not realize that you were joined in

7 Appius Claudius "the Blind," Censor in 312 B.C., consul in 307 and 296 B.C., the builder of the Via Appia and the Aqua Appia. Clodia and her brother were members of the Claudian gens.

marriage to Quintus Metellus,[8] an eminent and noble patriot who, the moment he set foot outdoors, surpassed nearly all citizens in merit, honor, and reputation? When you had married from a most noble family into an aristocratic one, why was Caelius so closely connected with you? Was he a relative, a neighbor, an associate of your husband? He was none of these. What was involved, then, if not plain reckless lust? Are you not moved, if not by the masks of our male descendants, by my descendant, the Claudia[9] who advised you to rival her in the honor of the family? Or by the Vestal Virgin Claudia,[10] who refused to allow her father to be dragged from his triumphant chariot by a hostile tribune of the people, clutching him in her protective arms? Why do your brother's dissipated ways influence you, rather than the virtues of your ancestors and the merits found so often since my day, not only in the men, but especially in the women? Did I abrogate the treaty with Pyrrhus so that you might daily strike the most debased bargains with your lovers? Did I bring water to Rome in the great aqueduct so that you might use it for lust and sin? Did I build the Via Appia for you to ride along attended by other women's husbands?"

15   But why, gentlemen of the jury, have I brought on to the stage so impressive a speaker, and one who may well now make me fear that the same Appius might wheel on my client and confront him in the same somber censorious tones? I will explain later on, in such a way as to vindicate Caelius' character against its most caustic critics. But now, woman, I speak to you directly, without bringing any other imagined person on stage: if you mean to substantiate your actions,

8 Quintus Metellus Celer, Clodia's cousin and husband, praetor in 63 B.C. and consul in 60 B.C. His sudden death in 59 B.C. prompted the suspicion that Clodia had poisoned him.

9 *"Quinta illa Claudia,"* as Cicero puts it, Quinta Claudia, who performed a miracle. When in 204 B.C., the image of Cybele (the Magna Mater) was being conveyed to Rome and the vessel stuck in the shallows at the mouth of the Tiber, soothsayers announced that only a chaste woman could move it. Claudia, who had been accused of incontinency, seized the rope, and the vessel followed her.

10 *"Virgo illa Vestalis Claudia,"* as Cicero puts it. The daughter, or perhaps sister, of Appius Claudius Pulcher, consul in 143 B.C., who protected him from attack when the people tried to prevent him from celebrating a triumph.

statements, charges, maneuvers, you must give a clear account of the close association and intimacy that existed between you and this young man. His accusers cite instances of orgies, love affairs, adultery, trips to Baiae,[11] beach parties, dinner parties, musical entertainments, boating parties—and indicate that they make these charges with your full consent. Since you, because of some mad obsession, wanted these actions introduced into a public trial in the forum, you must either show them to be false and withdraw them, or admit that neither are your charges nor is your testimony allowable. If you prefer me to adopt a more gentlemanly approach, I can proceed to dismiss from the scene the dour and uncouth ancestor, and summon another sort, from the ranks of our more sophisticated contemporaries, your youngest brother, whose taste is unerring in these matters. He is so inordinately fond of you that, even as a little fellow, being somewhat anxious and fearful of the dark, he always liked to sleep with his big sister. So, now, imagine Clodius saying to you: "Why are you making all this fuss, sister? What's got into you?

"Why raise such huge noises with your words? That a small matter becomes vastly important?"[12]

You laid eyes on this young man next door. His fair, tall body, his face and eyes, made a strong impression; you wanted to see him more often; you were in your park every now and then when he was. As a woman of a good family, you would like to gain the upper hand by lavishing your resources on this son of a frugal father of modest means. But you are not successful. He kicks, stalls, refuses, and decides that your gifts are not worth all that much. So, try somewhere else. Your own landscaped lawns on the banks of the Tiber where all the young men may come to swim. You can have an appointment there with a different man every day. Why trouble yourself over this one who's turning you down?"

Now I come to you, Caelius, in your turn, myself assuming the righteous indignation of some fatherly

16

---

[11] A fashionable seaside resort near Naples.
[12] The author of these lines is not known.

figure, just which one I am not quite sure to select, but perhaps some fire-breathing worthy from the comedies of Caecilius[13] will do, when he says:

"Now is my soul ablaze, my heart o'erwhelmed with

wrath." Or, perhaps the one who declaims:

"Oh graceless, ruthless, rogue!"

Those are hard-hearted fathers, who speak such lines as these:

"What can I say, or wish? Your dirty deeds
Frustrate my every prayer."

Their anger can hardly be borne. A father of this sort would surely say: "Why did you frequent the neighborhood of so notorious a loose woman? Why didn't you keep clear of her well-known charms?"

"Why make friends with a woman who means nothing
to you?
Scatter and squander your money: that's all right with me;
When you are in trouble it will be your pain not mine.
For me it's enough to enjoy what days I have left."

To so morose and blunt an old father, Caelius would reply that he had not strayed from the right path because of passion. What evidence could he offer? He did not incur lavish expenses, throw money away, or borrow it. There were stories that he had, but how often can a man escape the slur of slander, especially, in so spiteful a city as ours? You are surely not surprised to hear that this woman's neighborhood had a bad reputation, when her own blood brother could not escape people's unfriendly talk. It was a gentle and forebearing father who said:

"He broke the doors? Well then, let us have them repaired. He tore her dress, did he? Let it be sewn back together again."[14]

And to him Caelius' case can easily be explained. In fact, is there any particular in which Caelius cannot

13 Cicero here cites some passages from the comedies of Caecilius (d. c. 166 B.C.), who apparently specialized in portraying grouchy old men.
14 Lines 120–1 from Terence's *Adelphoe* (*The Brothers*), spoken by an indulgent father.

candidly and simply defend himself? I am not discussing the woman in the case. I am merely saying that if there were a woman, utterly different from her, let us suppose, who made free with anyone and everyone, openly carrying on liaisons with the favorites of the moment, a woman whose private grounds, home, and place at Baiae were easily accessible to all manner of debauchery and made so by her own decree, a woman who met the financial needs of hard-pressed young men by generous outlays from her own inheritance; suppose that, although a widow, she lived merrily, and as a provocative type, conducted herself enticingly, just as her being rich meant being extravagant and carefree, and her being sensual in her tastes meant her adopting the courtesan's ways. Is a man who greets such a woman in a familiar and friendly fashion to be considered an adulterer?

I may be asked if this is the discipline and training *17* I prescribe for young men. Did his parent entrust me with the care of Caelius to devote his youth to love and pleasures and have me subsequently defend such conduct and such preferences? Let me say, gentlemen, that were there someone with a force of mind and native penchant for goodness and temperance compelling him to eschew all manner of pleasure and dedicate his whole career to physical work and mental effort, a person who took no delight whatsoever in rest, relaxation, the interests of his fellow men, entertainment or society, and who considered nothing worth striving for, except the kind of achievement linked to honor and glory—I should think of such a person as one formed by, and endowed with, certain divine powers. Of this stripe, I imagine were the Camilli, Fabricii, and Curii of our history, and all those who have risen to great heights from lowly origins. Extraordinary goodness of this caliber is rarely found in books, much less in life. The pages of ancient history denoting that pioneer austerity have themselves grown old; not only for us who have followed this principle and philosophy of life, in practice rather than in words, but also for the intelligent Greeks who, when they could no longer conduct themselves in this way, were still free to write and speak nobly, with true moral splendor. As the Greek atmosphere changed, other precepts came into being and held sway. Some of their philosophers asserted that

pleasure was the first principle of action, and learned
disputants did not shrink from uttering so loathsome a
statement. Others maintained that virtue should be allied
with pleasure, so that two things fundamentally opposed
might be reconciled by means of an opportunistic argument. The proponents of the straight and narrow path
to glory, paved with hard work, are now virtually alone
in their schoolrooms. Indeed, nature has produced many
enticements that can lull virtue to sleep at times and
make her close her eyes; nature points out to youth
many slippery paths, on which it can hardly set foot or
walk without risking a fall. She offers a variety of
extremely pleasant things to ensnare not only youth,
but the firmer time of life. If, by chance, you come
across someone who scorns the fair aspect of things and
is not impressed by fragrance, touch, or taste, who
shuts his ears to every sweet sound, I and a few others
like me will think the gods have smiled on such a man:
most people will think the gods are angry at him.

18   The pathway of austere virtue, therefore, over-
grown as it is with brush and shrubs, must be abandoned. And, as a matter of fact, some recreation is
rather desirable in early life. Not everything is ruined
by contact with pleasure. The true and straight principle
does not necessarily prevail at all times and in all places.
Occasionally, desire may dominate reason, provided
only, that the following rule and limitation is observed:
a young man ought to keep his good reputation and not
spoil another's; not pour out his inheritance like water
or become crippled by debts; not invade another's
house and home. He should not bring vileness on the
pure, a stain on the virtuous, disgrace on the respectable,
nor should he threaten anyone with violence. Finally,
when he has yielded to pleasures and spent some time
in love affairs and the idle joys of youth, let him then
remember his responsibilities to the family, to the forum,
and to the state, so that he seems to have learned from
experience to scorn, and from indulgence to disregard,
the very things he comprehended imperfectly by the
light of reason alone.

Many distinguished leaders, gentlemen, within our
memory and our fathers', have been of the sort to
display exemplary characters in mature life, when the
passions of youth had simmered down. I need not
mention names, for you will all readily enough recall

them, and I have no wish to connect even the slightest
foible with the great honor due a fine and eminent man.
If I wanted to do that, many of the outstanding talented
men of the day could be referred to publicly, in connection with some of whom, could be mentioned
excessive wildness in youth, in connection with others,
base indulgence, great debts, lavish expenditure, sensu-
ality of various sorts, which later on, having become
covered over by many virtues, anyone who wished
could use as a means of defense for making allowances
for youth.

But as for Marcus Caelius and his real interests—I
want to speak out very directly, since I entrust such
things as his weaknesses to your good judgment to
evaluate—no overindulgence will be found in him, no
extravagance, no debts, no passion for guzzling and
debauchery. Of course, the vice of gluttony is not
sloughed off with the years, but even grows on a man.
Flirtations and the things called love affairs, which are
not generally too much of an annoyance to a man of
mature mind—they bloom and wither quickly enough
—never hampered Caelius or held him in their grip.
When he spoke here initially in his own defense, you
heard what an orator he was, and you had heard him on
earlier occasions when he was the prosecuting attorney.
I say this to defend him, not to glory in my own
teaching. Being perceptive men, you clearly appreciated
his style, his fluency, the range of his ideas and expressions. There you saw the light, not only of talent (which
often, even when not being exercised, grows of its own
power), but, unless my good will toward him bemuses
me, you also saw the combination of theoretical knowledge instilled by liberal studies, and ability perfected
by practice and hard work. You may rest assured,
gentlemen, that those distracting desires cast in Caelius'
teeth and the intellectual pursuits I am now discussing
do not sit comfortably in one and the same man. It is
not possible for a mind bound by lust, love, desire, and
passion, at times overwhelmed by sensual satisfactions,
at times frustrated by their lack of fulfillment, to sustain
the tasks we orators assume, either in their physical
accomplishment or in their mental organizing. Can you
think of any other reason why, in view of the great
rewards of eloquence, the inspired pleasure of public
speaking, the honor, influence, and acclaim attendant

upon the skill, there are, and always will be, so few
men who become highly adept in this work? All pleasure
must be suppressed, the pursuit of amusement abandoned, love affairs, frivolity, society, conversation with
friends, forsaken. It is work on this scale that jars men
and scares them away from the profession, not any
lack of native talent or early training. Would the
defendant, if he had surrendered to the life of a
voluptuary have, when he was still quite young, challenged a man of consular rank to public trial? Would
he, if he wanted to avoid work and were enmeshed in
the toils of pleasure, daily do battle here in public?
Would he provoke antagonisms, instigate trials, and
expose himself to proceedings in a criminal trial, and,
with the Roman people looking on, fight for so many
months on end, either for the public welfare or for
his own honor and fame?

20   Does not a whiff of something come from that
neighborhood, a rumor about the kind of people it
harbors, does not Baiae speak? Baiae does not merely
speak, it shouts and resounds with the report that one
single woman's lust has sunk to such depths that, far
from seeking isolation and darkness, the usual con-
cealments for depravity, she revels in the most disgraceful conduct and flaunts her actions in public in
the full light of day.

Should someone think that affairs with prostitutes
ought to be forbidden to young men, he is taking a
good strong line, I cannot deny, but he is turning his
back on the normal allowances made, not merely in
our own day, but also by common consent and the
custom of our ancestors. Was there ever a time when
this was not regularly done, when it was under reproach,
when it was not allowed; in short, when the accepted
thing was unacceptable? I will only define the thing
itself and not mention any specific woman: thereby, I
can leave the application open. But, if some woman who
is not married has thrown open her house to the
desires of all men, established herself in the life of a
prostitute, and arranged parties for men who are utter
strangers; if, moreover, she does this here in Rome, or
in her private gardens, or in the notorious society of
Baiae; if, not only in her bearing, but in her dress and
choice of companions, and not only by bright glances

and lively talk, but with embraces and kisses, at beach parties, boating parties, and dinner parties, she acts so as to seem not merely a prostitute but a saucy and provocative one, would a young man, who happened to be in the company of such a woman, seem to you, Herennius, an adulterer or rather a lover, to be storming the fortress of virtue, or rather gratifying lust? I relegate to oblivion the wrongs you have done me, Clodia; I discard the memory of my grief: I discount the cruel way you and yours took advantage of me and mine, when I was in exile. Nor should you imagine that what I have just said was directed at you. But I do appeal to you because the counsel for the prosecution state that the charges originate with you and say that they have you as a witness for the crime with which Caelius is charged. If there were some woman of the sort whose picture I have just painted in vivid colors, one quite unlike you, a pure prostitute, would the fact that a young man should have had some dealings with her seem to you the height of depravity and disgraceful conduct? If you are not such a person, as I certainly hope you are not, why do the prosecutors berate Caelius? But if, by such a person, they mean you, why should we fear an accusation you treat with contempt? Either your sense of decency will support the statement that Caelius has not acted immorally at all, or your shameless attitude will offer him and the other men you make friends of an excellent means of excusing themselves.

My speech now seems to have steered safely away from the reefs and passed easily across the shoals, so the remainder of the voyage looks clear. Accusations of two heinous crimes have been made by one woman, concerning the gold allegedly acquired from Clodia and the poison they charge Caelius with having prepared, for the purpose of murdering the same Clodia. He obtained the gold, you assert, to give to slaves of Lucceius,[15] by whom Dio of Alexandria, then residing at Lucceius' house, could be killed. A major crime, either to set a trap for an envoy or to subvert slaves for

21

---

15 Lucius Lucceius, a Senator, and old friend of Cicero, most often remembered today for the letter (*Ad Familiares*, vol. xii) Cicero wrote, asking him to compose a laudatory account of the events of the year 63 B.C.

the purpose of murder in their master's household, a plan replete with base criminal intent and daring! Therefore, I ask, first, respecting the accusation, whether Caelius told Clodia why he was taking the gold or did not tell her. If he did not, why did she give it to him? If he did, she becomes an accessory before the fact. Did you, Clodia, dare despoil the image of your tutelary deity, Venus, of the gold ornaments she acquired as loot from other conquests, and take the ornaments from your safe, knowing full well for what purpose the gold was required—the murder of an official state envoy— and as an indelible stain on the character of Lucius Lucceius, an upright and respectable man? Your generous heart should never have shared in so shameless a deed, that open house of yours never have had a part in it, nor that hospitable Venus of yours have offered her help. Herennius Balbus apparently took this point into consideration when he claimed that Clodia was kept in ignorance, that Caelius gave, as his excuse, the need to furnish gold to finance a public entertainment contracted for by a friend. But, if Clodia was not on such intimate terms with Caelius, she would hardly have handed over her gold ornaments at his request. If Caelius told you the truth, you shameless woman, you gave him the gold for a criminal purpose. If he did not dare tell you, then you did not give it.

22   Why do I refrain from meeting this accusation with the countless facts available to refute it? I can cite the character of Caelius, utterly dissociated from the monstrosity of such criminal acts as these. We cannot believe that an intelligent and perceptive man would not realize, moreover, that a terrible deed of violence should hardly be entrusted to the slaves in an unfamiliar household. Also, I can address my customary inquiries to the prosecution, as the defense usually does: where, for example, Caelius met with Lucceius' slaves; what approach he worked out; whether he took the initiative, which would have certainly been a bold step; or, if he worked through an intermediary, who that was. By questioning, I can flush out of hiding every possible lurking suspicion, and not a trace of the terrible crime will be found anywhere: no motive, no place, no opportunity, no accomplice, no master plan, no hope of keeping the evil concealed. But, for the sake of brevity, I omit the deductive proofs a speaker commonly em-

ploys and which, had I prepared them on my own responsibility and adduced them as evidence, might have had results, not because of any talent of mine, but simply on account of the orator's normal training and practiced skill.

Instead, I can present a man whom you may freely accept as a colleague in your judiciary responsibilities under solemn oath, a completely conscientious and firmly reliable witness, Lucius Lucceius. He is not one to have been unaware of so dastardly a blow struck at his credit and fortunes, or to have failed to take action to prevent it, or to have tolerated it. Is it likely that such a man, graced with his sensibility and the advantages of his training in the liberal arts, with his accomplishments and learning, could have ignored the peril of the very friend he was attached to because of those same interests, and not have taken measures to deal with a crime done to a guest, the sort of crime that he would surely be revolted to hear of being committed against a total stranger? It would have pained him deeply to discover such a thing being done against people he did not know. Would he have paid no attention to it when it was tried by his own household servants? Would he lightly pass off a plot originating in his own house and home, which he would roundly condemn if it occurred in the countryside or in a public place? Something he would take seriously as endangering the merest uncouth rustic, would so educated a man think ought to be concealed, when it was a trap set for a most cultivated person? But why detain you further, gentlemen? Lucceius has himself given evidence on oath. Please note the serious tone of his sworn testimony, and attend carefully to every word of his deposition.

What more than this can you want? For the truth of the case to speak aloud in its own voice? Well, here is a defense of the innocent, a plea made by the case itself, the single utterance of truth. It reveals not a scrap of suspicion as to the crime, not a scrap of evidence as to the facts, not a trace of the transactions said to have taken place, of any talks being held anywhere at any time. Not a single witness is named, nor a single accomplice. Rather, the whole accusation has been dreamed up by a hostile, disreputable, ferocious, crime-ridden, lust-addled family. But the family assailed by this allegedly monstrous, criminal intent is secure in its integrity, dutifulness, and respectability. And, from the latter household is offered to you evidence sworn to on solemn oath that leaves no doubt of whether to think that a reckless, irresponsible, infuriated woman has preferred false charges or a serious, sensible, level-headed man has given conscientious evidence.

23 We are, therefore, let with the charge concerning the poison, whose beginning I cannot trace nor purpose disentangle. What was Caelius' motive for wanting to poison the woman? To avoid paying back the gold? But then she must have dunned him for it? To prevent being charged with having made an attempt on the life of Dio? But who accused him of that? Would anyone have mentioned Caelius if he had not prosecuted somebody? You heard Herennius state that he would not have troubled Caelius with a single word, if Caelius had not prosecuted his close friend on the same charge a second time over after he had already been acquitted. Is it plausible that so great a crime (as the poisoning of Clodia) had no motive at all? Do you not see that the charge involving one horrible crime (the alleged attack upon Dio) has been trumped up to lend weight to the suspicion of another? In whose hands was the scheme placed? Who was the helper, ally, accomplice he could entrust with so frightful a business, compromising himself and his safety? The woman's slaves? So we have been invited to believe.

Was he so out of his mind, this man whose intelligence you grant, although in the course of your hostile speech you denied him any other virtues, as to place his entire destiny in the hands of another person's slaves? And what sort of slaves were they? It makes a difference. Those who, he realized, did not know the usual condition of bondage, but lived on terms of frank and friendly familiarity with their mistress. We all know, gentlemen, that in a household like hers, where the mistress lives in the manner of a courtesan, in which nothing that goes on really ought to be spoken of outside, where odd sensual tastes and forms of over-indulgence prevail, where all imaginable and unimaginable forms of vice are rife—in such a home, the slaves are not servants, who have charge of everything; they play their part with her in her profligacy, share in all

her secrets, and get a considerable income siphoned off
from the daily extravagant outlays. Did not Caelius
notice this? If he was so intimate with the woman as
you make him out to be, he also would know the slaves
in the mistress' household. But if he did not have the
run of the place, as you imply, how could he have been
on such familiar terms with her slaves?

And as to the poison, what theory has been formed   24
about that? Where was it obtained, how prepared, how,
to whom, and where was it conveyed? They say he
tested its potency on one of the slaves in his house
selected for that very purpose. When the slave died
almost immediately, he was convinced of the poison's
effectiveness.

Immortal gods! How can you, at times, either close
your eyes to the greatest crimes men are capable of
or postpone the speedy punishment of deceit until
some future day? I saw—and drank the bitterest draft
of grief to see it—Quintus Metellus Celer torn from the
embrace and bosom of his fatherland. This fine man,
who thought himself destined from birth to leadership
in the state, who only two days earlier had been at the
height of his powers in the Senate, in the courts, and
on the political scene, in the prime of his life and at
the peak of his health and strength, was unworthily
wrenched away from all good citizens and from the
whole state. As he lay dying, his mind assaulted in many
different ways, he rallied his final consciousness to
remember the republic. He saw me there weeping and
indicated to me in broken and halting sentences how
great a storm was brewing for me, a tempest gathering
over the state. Striking the wall between his house and
Catulus', he repeatedly called on Catulus and on me,
and most often on the republic. He lamented not so
much his own death as the deprivation to me and to
the state of their staunch protector. Had not the force
of a sudden foul crime carried him off, with what
energy as a man of consular rank would he not have
stood up to his revolutionary cousin, one, who, as a
consul, was already making trouble and beginning to
rage and sputter, who had declared within the hearing
of the Senate his intentions of doing away with Metellus
by his own hand? Will the woman from that same house
dare speak of the *celerity* of poison? Does she not fear

the house itself and what it might say? Has she no fear
of the walls that were witness to her wickedness? Does
she not shudder to relive that macabre and dolorous
night? But let me return to the charge before us. The
mention of this fine and noble person and his achievements has racked my voice with sobs and harrowed
my mind with sorrow.

25   Still, where the poison was obtained or how it
was prepared has not been stated. Allegedly, it was
given to Publius Licinius, here present, a good
friend of Caelius, and an admirably modest young man.
Allegedly it had been arranged that they would meet
some slaves at the baths of Senius, that Licinius would
go there and give them the box containing the poison.
Now, the first question I pose is, why it had to be
transported to that place—why did not the slaves
simply go to Caelius' house? If the habitual intimacy and
easy familiarity between him and Clodia still prevailed,
what suspicions would have been raised by the appearance of one of the woman's slaves at Caelius' house?
If, however, jealousy was already undermining the
relationship, their closeness was over, and a falling out
had occurred, then that explains the shedding of all
those tears, and constitutes, in fact, the entire cause of
this array of charges and so-called crimes. "Oh, no,"
we are told, "when the slaves had informed their mistress of the whole evil business Caelius was plotting,
the resourceful woman instructed them to promise
Caelius anything he wanted but, so that the poison
might be seized openhandedly from Licinius when he
had conveyed it, she told them to arrange a meeting
at the baths of Senius where she dispatched friends to
lurk in hiding and, when Licinius arrived and handed
over the poison, to spring out suddenly and take hold
of him."

26   But these points, gentlemen, lend themselves to
easy refutation. Why, above all, select a public bathing
establishment? I see hardly any hiding place there for
people with their clothes on. If they were in the
vestibule, they were not out of view, and if they meant
to penetrate further inside the establishment they
couldn't very well have managed that fully clothed and
shod, and probably would not have been admitted—
although, of course, the persuasive, accommodating
Clodia may have earned the price of admission from the

chief steward and then given him back his quarter,[16] so that he would admit her men friends free. I was impatiently waiting for these good witnesses to be called, but so far, not a single one of them has been named. I am convinced that they are the most reputable characters, first of all, being on such intimate terms with so fine a lady, and then, volunteering for this mission to be stowed away in the public baths. She would never have gotten them to agree to such a proposition, strong as her powers are, unless they had been the most highly honored and respected characters. But why do I expatiate upon the high merits of witnesses such as these? Observe their valor, their self-denying energies: "They hid in the bathhouse." That's the sort of witness we like to have in court. "Then they suddenly leapt from concealment." There's self-control for you. So you can just imagine how, when Licinius arrived with the box of poison in hand, about to hand it over, but not yet having done so, at that very moment, these famous—if nameless—witnesses pounced; but Licinius hastily withdrew the hand he held stretched out with the box of poison in it, and in the face of the sudden attack, beat a quick retreat. Well, great is the power of truth to defend itself so nonchalantly against the canny intelligence, the skill, the carefully contrived snares of all!

16 *Nisi forte mulier potens quadrantaria illa permutatione familiaris facta erat balneatori.*

"Unless, naturally, that influential lady, doing the usual farthing deal, had turned into a crony of the bathman." (Austin)

Quadrans, a "quarter" = about half a cent, the price of admission to the men's bath. *Mulier quadrantaria,* i.e., "two-bit woman": Clodia had the price of admission, but had obtained it by *permutatione,* for services rendered to the bathman.

In the speech for his defense, Caelius had referred to Clodia as a *quadrantaria* Clytemnestra, alluding to the rumors that she had killed her husband and that she received her lovers for a *quadrans.*

Ovid's verses for the first of April, the month dedicated to Venus, are perhaps relevant:

"Duly do ye worship the goddess, ye Latin mothers and brides, and ye too, who wear not the fillets and long robe. Take off the golden necklaces from the marble neck of the goddess; take off her gauds; the goddess must be washed from top to toe." *Fasti,* Bk. IV, ll. 133–136.

Frazer's note remarks that courtesans are referred to at the end of the first sentence, and that "on April 1, women of the lower sort bathed in public in the men's public baths, and worshipped Fortuna Virilis." (Loeb Classical Library edition, p. 198.)

27   A case in point is surely this engaging one-act play,
the work of an experienced lady-poet with many other
romances[17] to her credit, which fails in its plot and
completely loses track of its ending. And another point:
a number of men were involved, to make sure Licinius
would be taken and the episode witnessed by many
pairs of eyes—how could they have let Licinius slip
out of their grasp? Why could he not have been grabbed
recoiling and withholding the box, just as if he had,
in fact, handed it over? They were posted around so as
to grab him, so that Licinius might be caught red-
handed either offering or withdrawing the box. This was
the woman's basic strategy, and these were the orders
issued to the troops on duty: so, the men, you claim
sprang forward too suddenly, I find did so just at the
right moment. Their positions, their assignments had
been devised to apprehend the poison, the plot, and the
culprit caught in the act. Could they have pounced on
him at a better juncture than at the precise moment
Licinius arrived, still holding the telltale box in his
hand? If Clodia's friends had waited until he had
given the box to her slaves and then streamed out of the
bathing establishment to take him by surprise in the
street, Licinius would have appealed to their honor as
fellow citizens and roundly denied having handed over
any such box. And how could they have reproved him
for that? By saying that they had seen him? But first,
that would be to bring down on their own heads the
suspicion of the very foul play they were accusing him
of. And next, they would be saying they saw something
that, from their places of concealment, they could not
possibly have observed. Therefore, they materialized at
the exact moment when Licinius had arrived, had
fumbled with the box, and was extending his hand to

17 *Velut haec tota fabella veteris et plurimarum fabularum
poetriae quam est sine argumento, quam nullum invenire exitum
potest!*

"For example: take this whole pretty little drama, the work
of a lady-poet who is an old hand at the game and has many
romances to her credit—how devoid of plot it is, how utterly lost
for an ending!" (Austin)
Fabula could suggest that Clodia wrote plays and also played
tricks and made fools of people, as well as refer to her own "fabu-
lous" reputation as a woman, about whom many stories were
repeated. At the *Ludi Megalenses,* plays were the chief public
entertainment.

deliver the poison. Well, this is the closing scene of a mad farce, not a play, the kind where no suitable ending comes to the author's mind, and so, someone wriggles loose, scampers off the stage accompanied by a flourish of castanets, and curtain.[18]

I fail to see why this group of woman-launched **28** commandoes let Licinius slip through their fingers, stumbling, wavering, retreating, why they did not hang on to him. Or why they did not make use of his personal confession, the open publicity, the outcry raised by the incident itself, to carve out the full shape and form of a charge involving so fiendish a crime. Were they afraid that so many powerful men could not subdue one weakling, so many swift-footed men of mettle one frightened fool?

No proof can be discovered in the actual events, not a shred of suspicious circumstance, no trace of a motive for the crime, and so the case has been moved bodily out of the realm of proof and inference, and those tokens, by which the truth is usually illuminated, and left to the discretion of witnesses. I must say, gentlemen, that I await these witnesses, not only without fear, but with a certain delighted anticipation. My heart leaps up at the prospect of seeing, first of all, the cool, young swains of a rich noblewoman, then those doughty heroes posted by their female general, in ambush inside the enemy garrison, a bath house. I intend to ask them how in the world they managed to hide themselves, and just where—whether some huge bathtub was the Trojan Horse that contained and concealed so many indomitable gallants fighting this female war. I will insist on their answering the question of why so many men did not either lay hands on that one sole weakling you see before you, or at least pursue him when he took to his heels. They will, in my opinion, never extricate themselves, once they have stepped into the witness box. They can be ever so clever at parties, with their smart chatter and quick repartee, eloquently droll over their drinks; still, the demands of the forum are one thing, and of the banquet hall quite another; the judges' bench calls for a different brand of intellect than the cushioned couch. The sight of a row of judges is not quite the same as that

---

18 *Aulaeum tollitur:* the curtain is raised, i.e., brought up to conceal the stage. This is the first mention of the drop-curtain in literature.

of a group of gay party faces. Far different is the streaming light of the sun in daytime from the fitful gleam of torches in the murk. Therefore, we shall smash into little pieces the lascivious absurdities of these fops, if they put in an appearance. Let them mark my words: they can busy themselves elsewhere, pursue popularity some other way, show off some other way, display their charms in the center of that lady's charmed circle, impress her with the amounts they spend, cling to her, lie at her feet as her humble servants. But let them spare the person and fortunes of an innocent man.

29   Now, on the advice of her distinguished and celebrated relatives, the slaves have been freed, and we finally come to an action the woman may be said to have performed under the advice and weighty influence of her relatives. But I would like to know just what the drift of this manumission is; for it means that a charge had been trumped up against Caelius, or that the normal lines of inquiry were destroyed, or that a fine reward was paid to the deserving slaves who had knowledge of so many secrets. Still, I am told, this was "a decision deemed wise by her relatives." Why would they not approve of it when you, my dear lady, state that you told them the plot had been discovered by you, not reported to you by others? And are we at all surprised to find Clodia the victim of that weird practical joke[19] we heard about recently, after the affair of the phony poison box? It is only what seems to fit in with that sort of woman, this business of the joke that was so widely talked about and heard of. You know in your own minds, gentlemen, what I mean, or rather mean not, to mention. If the trick was played on her, of course, it was not Caelius who was behind it—for what would he have to gain from it?—but it was the work of some other young man, not so much the dull as the untruthful sort. If it actually occurred, the episode is hardly amusing, however obscene. And, in my opinion, all the gossip and tattle in the world could never have proved it, unless the things redolent of indecent behavior tallied with her reputation.

And so, gentlemen, I rest my case. You now know what a weighty decision is yours, how significant is the matter assigned to you. You are investigating a charge of violence. This is a law of great importance to the empire, to the glory and renown of our fatherland, to

19 We know nothing more about this incident.

the welfare of all people. It is based on the law passed by Quintus Catulus at a time of armed conflict among citizens that nearly spelled the last days of the republic, the law that smothered the smoldering ashes of the flame that had blazed during my consulship. It is by this *lex de vi* that Caelius and his youth are being called to account, not for the damage done to the republic, but for the depraved desires of a woman.

And here, in this very place, the condemnation **30** that befell Camurtius and Caesernius is being pointedly mentioned. How absurd! Should I say absurd, or rather how remarkably arrogant? Do you really dare, representing a woman like her, mention men of that stripe? Do you dare arouse the memory of so flagrant an offense, one not extinguished, but merely buried over by the time that has elapsed? For on what charge and for what offense were they condemned? In fact, they merely avenged the very same woman's spite and resentment for the nasty trick Vettius played on her. To drag in the name of Vettius, to revive that old penny pornographic plot—is that the reason reference was made to the case of Camurtius and Caesernius? Although their antics could not be construed as actionable under the *lex de vi*, they were so compromised by the crime in question that it seemed impossible for them to wriggle loose from the meshes of the law.

But why is Marcus Caelius, of all people, haled before this court? No charge relevant to the investigative powers of this body has been brought against him, nor, in fact, one which, though it might lie outside the court's jurisdiction, might still be appropriate to your powers of censure. In early manhood Caelius devoted his time to the study of the liberal arts, by which we are prepared for participating in affairs of state, for honor, glory, and the responsibility of man's estate. Furthermore, his friendships with older men were made among those whose energy and self-control he desired most to emulate. The interests he shared with his contemporaries were such that made it clear he was following the same path as the finest and best of them. Growing in years and strength, he went to Africa as aide-de-camp of the proconsul, Quintus Pompeius Rufus, a man of exemplary moral fiber and deep devotion to duty. Not only were his father's estates in Africa advantageous to Caelius, but also he gained there the experience of provincial administration traditionally regarded, and rightly so, as useful for a man of his years. As you will learn from Pompeius' testimony, Caelius returned from this service as a young man most highly regarded by the proconsul. Next, he wanted to bring his public-spirited energies to the attention of the Roman people by means of some memorable prosecution, in accordance with the established custom, as well as with the example of those young men who had done so before him and gone on to become leading citizens and men of great influence in the state.

31   I might wish that his eagerness for distinction had fastened on some other target, but the time for such objections is long since past. He brought an indictment against my colleague, Gaius Antonius. The memory of Antonius' great services to the state proved to be of no value to the poor man, but the suspicions of his intended treason was a disaster. Afterward, Caelius was second to none of his contemporaries in successfully applying himself to the work of the forum, to business matters, as an advocate for his friends, in exerting his influence to the advantage of friends and associates. He actively and diligently performed in all matters where success depends on a man's conscientious, alert attention to business. And then, just at the turning point in his young career—confident of your sympathy and good judgment, I hide nothing from you —the young man's reputation veered perilously near the post, because of the novelty of acquaintance with the lady, the unfortunate proximity to her, and his inexperienced knowledge of pleasure. Desire for pleasure having been kept in check and held down unduly long in youth can often build up and burst out suddenly and uncontrollably. But he emerged from this life of indulgence, or from what people said were his dissipated ways—and they were, by no means, as wild as talk made them out to be—well, whatever it should be called, he extricated himself and got entirely clear of it. And now, so far removed is he from the unsavory reputation of being on friendly terms with that notorious woman, that he is busy fending off the attacks stemming from her hostility and rage.

To kill the intervening gossip about loose living and frivolous behavior, he then indicted my friend

Bestia on a charge of bribery. He did it quite against my wishes, and, although I protested loudly, he insisted on going through with it. Even now that Bestia has been acquitted, Caelius has promptly instituted new proceedings against him. None of us can reason him out of it; he is more headstrong than I could have wished. Of course, I am not speaking of wisdom, a quality hardly applicable, in any case, to this period of life: I speak of his excited spirit, his eagerness for victory, his burning intellectual desire for renown. In men of our age, such qualities as these ought to be kept at a low burning point, but in young men, as in healthy young plants, they are dependable signs of the characteristic strength and powerful energies in store. Young men of great natural powers have to be reined in from seeking glory, rather than spurred on to it; more pruning than grafting is called for at that time of life when the spirit blossoms with a profusion of powers. So, if Caelius seems to have boiled over with too much eagerness, or seems to be too ferocious or obstinate in initiating hostilities and continuing them; if the minor particulars of his conduct in these matters have offended any of you; if the flamboyant swirl of pronounced purple in his toga, his throng of admirers, his glitter and glamor, have put you on edge—do, I pray you, remember that this will taper off: that riper years, circumstances as they evolve, the days as they go by, will tone down these loud effects.

Therefore, gentlemen of the jury, save, for the good of the state, a good and gifted young man, well-trained in the liberal arts, a man of parts, and the friend of good men. To you and the state, I make this solemn promise and pledge: if I have not been found wanting in my country's needs, neither will this young man ever dissociate himself from my way of thinking. I promise this, not only confident of the close accord existing between him and me, but also because Caelius has bound himself to the state by the strongest ties. A person who has brought to trial a man of consular rank, saying that he had subverted the state, cannot possibly be himself a disruptive element in the state. Nor is it possible that a man who refused to allow a person acquitted of a charge of bribery to stay acquitted should ever bribe others without having to answer for it.

32

The state holds two hostages, gentlemen, in the form of the prosecutions conducted by Marcus Caelius, as guarantees of his good intentions, and pledges that it is secure from any danger from him. And so I earnestly beseech you, gentlemen of the jury, above all, in the very city where a scant two days ago Sextus Clodius was acquitted, a man you observed during these past two years to be always either an agent of, or a leader in, subversive activities, a faithless, cynical, desperate, shiftless derelict, foul-mouthed, foul-tongued, and dirty-handed: a man who, with his own hands, set fire to the shrines of the nymphs, where the public records of the census of the Roman people were housed; who damaged the portico of Catulus;[20] pulled down my house; burnt my brother's home; a man who, on the Palatine Hill and in sight of the whole city, aroused a mob of slaves to the pitch of massacre and to the conflagration of the city. Here, in the same city, do not suffer such a person to go unscathed, thanks to a woman's influence, while, at the same time, Marcus Caelius is sacrificed to the woman's lust. Do not, I beg you, allow the woman and her bridegroom of a brother to rescue a recognized robber and ruin a perfectly decent young man.

And when you have given due consideration to the fact of his youth, then bring before your eyes also the picture of the unhappy old father, here present in the court today, who counts so heavily on his son. This father's solace stems from hope for his son's future, his anxiety from the possibility that misfortune may befall him. This father who has thrown himself on your mercy and is subservient to your power you see here prostrate, not at your feet, but at the good graces of your moral instincts and human sympathy. Support and sustain this man, I implore you, in fond memory it may be of your own parents, or because of the joy you take in your own children. By assuaging the other's grief, you preserve either the spirit of natural piety or of filial affection in yourselves. Do not begrudge the one his natural death by dealing him a fatal blow before his appointed time; do not overwhelm the other, in the first flower of manhood and the strength of early

20 Adjoining Cicero's house on the Palatine. In 58 B.C., Clodius destroyed both the house and the portico, and in 57 B.C., burned the house of Cicero's brother, Quintus, in the same region.

life, swept off the scene without warning, as though caught up in some storm or whirlwind. Preserve the father for the son, the son for the father, and you will not appear to have cynically disregarded the empty old age of the one or to have not only failed to nourish the youth of the other, so full of promise, but to have struck at it savagely and brought it down. The person you save for yourselves, for his family and friends, for the state, you will possess evermore as a person dedicated, devoted, and deeply committed to you and your children. In future days, you will reap the rich harvest of all his work and all his energies, in the fullest measure.

In Defense of Ligarius

INTRODUCTION

In 50 B.C., Ligarius, then a lieutenant under Considius, the governor of Africa, was left in charge of the province when Considius returned to Rome to stand for the consulship. When the civil war between Pompey and Caesar began in 49 B.C., Ligarius was urged by Pompey's friends in Africa to take over the province as the commander of their party, but refused to do so. Varus soon arrived to take charge, and Ligarius served under him on the side of the Pompeian forces. He was eventually taken prisoner at Hadrumentum (modern Sousse, in North Africa, the scene of considerable action by German, Italian, and Allied forces in World War II). By Caesar's clemency, Ligarius' life was spared, but he was not permitted to return to Rome. Attempts were then made by Ligarius' friends to secure his recall from exile, but Quintus Tubero—himself a former partisan of Pompey, who had been pardoned by Caesar and restored to citizenship—brought charges against Ligarius for having fought against Caesar in Africa. In this speech, delivered in the forum in 46 B.C., before Caesar, Cicero asked that the same clemency shown to himself and Tubero be accorded Ligarius. The appeal was successful and Ligarius was pardoned fully and allowed to return to Rome.

The occasion was spectacular enough to command the interest of the later biographer Plutarch, who writes in his *Life of Cicero:*

So also it is related that when Quintus Ligarius was prosecuted for having been in arms against Caesar, and Cicero had undertaken his defense, Caesar said to his friends, "Why might we not as well hear a speech from Cicero? Ligarius, there is no question, is a wicked man and an enemy." But when Cicero began to speak, he wonderfully moved him, and proceeded in his speech with such varied pathos, and such a charm of language, that the color of Caesar's countenance often changed, and it was evident that all the passions of his soul were in commotion. At length, the orator touching upon the Pharsalian battle, he was so affected that his body trembled, and some of the papers he held dropped out of his hands. And thus he was overpowered, and acquitted Ligarius.*

Two years later, Ligarius was one of the men in the group that assassinated Caesar. Shakespeare, calling him "Gaius," describes Ligarius as the "sick" man in the group, afflicted with ague (or malaria: *acuta febris*):

Brutus	. . . Would you were not sick!
Ligarius	I am not sick, if Brutus have in hand
	Any exploit worthy the name of honour.
Brutus	Such an exploit have I in hand, Ligarius,
	Had you a healthful ear to hear of it.
Ligarius	By all the gods that Romans bow before,
	I here discard my sickness! Soul of Rome!
	Brave son, derived from honourable loins!
	Thou, like an exorcist, hast conjured up
	My mortified spirit. Now bid me run,
	And I will strive with things impossible;
	Yea, get the better of them. What's to do?
Brutus	A piece of work that will make sick men whole.
Ligarius	But are not some whole that we must make sick?
Brutus	That must we also. What it is, my Gaius,
	I shall unfold to thee, as we are going
	To whom it must be done.
Ligarius	Set on your foot,
	And with a heart new-fired I follow you,
	To do I know not what; but it sufficeth
	That Brutus leads me on.†

When the conspirators meet Caesar to accompany him to the Senate house, Caesar's words of greeting to Ligarius are:

. . . Gaius Ligarius,
Caesar was ne'er so much your enemy
As that same ague which hath made you lean.‡

* Translated by John Dryden.
† *Julius Caesar*, II, i, 11. 315 ff.
‡ Ibid., II, ii, 111-13.

In Defense of Ligarius

This is a novel accusation, Gaius Caesar, one quite **1**
unheard of until now, the charge my kinsman, Quintus
Tubero, has brought before you; he is stating firmly
that Quintus Ligarius was actually stationed in Africa!
Furthermore, Gaius Pansa,[1] a man of eminent character and a person no doubt confident of being on
familiar terms with you, has dared to corroborate this
statement of the case. I hardly know where to turn.
Naturally, I had come here quite prepared—inasmuch
as you, of course, could not be expected to have knowledge of the situation directly, or to have been informed
of it from other sources—quite prepared to take full
advantage of your ignorance, in order to get this poor
man off. But now that, thanks to the diligent work of a
hostile person, the hidden facts have been carefully
brought to light, the truth must, I suppose, be freely
owned up to; and I say this, particularly because my
good friend Pansa has brought out merely a part of
the question. Putting argument aside for the moment,
I presume that my words should be entirely addressed
to your spirit of forbearance, a source from which
many have been saved in time past, when they had
won from you, not their being absolved of guilty conduct, but their pardon for a pardonable error. And
Tubero, my unworthy opponent, you have at hand
something heartily wished for by every prosecutor, a
witness willing to admit to the charge; he admits to the
charge of having been himself a member of the very
same party that another excellent praiseworthy man
could be found in: I refer, Tubero, to your own
father.[2] Perhaps, it might be in order for you to make
a clean breast of your offense first, before you begin
attaching blame to Ligarius.

Indeed, Quintus Ligarius set out for Africa in the
diplomatic service, with Gaius Considius, when there
was, as yet, not the slightest suspicion of war; and in
that diplomatic mission he made such a good showing
to Roman citizens and to our allies alike that, when

[1] Gaius Vibius Pansa, a friend of Caesar, consul in 43 B.C.
[2] Quintus Tubero's father, Lucius Tubero, had also belonged to
Pompey's faction, as had Considius.

Considius left the colony, people were prepared to object strongly to the appointment of anyone other than
Ligarius as the governor of this province. Ligarius,
therefore, when his reluctance to accept got him nowhere, did, with misgivings, accept the command of
the province; and his unassailed integrity and trust-
worthiness in office earned him the deepest gratitude of
all our citizens and allies. War suddenly flared up—an
exigency that those in Africa heard was already upon
them before they could prepare to meet it. When the
news came, they searched for a leader, partly motivated
by sheer instinct, partly by blind fear, at first, frantic
to have someone protect them and then later, wanting
someone to look after their interests—for Ligarius,
considering his own situation and wishing to get back
to his family, refused to allow himself to become involved in the crisis. Meanwhile, Publius Attius Varus,[3]
the praetor in charge of Africa at that time, came to
Utica.[4] Contact with him was swiftly made, and he,
with a more-than-average display of ambition, arrogated the command to himself: if that could legitimately be called a command, which was conferred, not
by public counsel and order, but by the impromptu
acclaim of a mob of inexperienced people. Therefore,
Ligarius, who was desirous of being rid of all such
business as this, retired, shortly after Varus' arrival.

2   Up to this point, Gaius Caesar, Ligarius is entirely free of blame. He left his home, not only not
intent upon war, but without the slightest suspicion
that there would be any war. He first set out as an
ambassador in time of peace; in a completely peaceful
province, he so conducted himself as to advance the
cause of peace therein. Such a mission as the one he
embarked on should surely not grate on your mind.
But what about his remaining there? Even less so, I
would say; for his original setting out on this mission
had a noble purpose, his remaining on the spot, the
character of a fully justifiable necessity. So, both these
phases of action are free of any criminal imputation,
in the one case, his departure as our ambassador, in

---

[3] After being deserted by his troops at Picenum in Italy, Varus
assumed command in Africa for Pompey.
[4] After the Third Punic War and the destruction of Carthage,
this African city, founded by the Phoenicians, became the capital
of the Roman province of Africa.

the other, when, under urgent request, he was appointed to the post of governor of Africa. The third phase coincides with his retirement after the arrival of Varus in Africa; but, if this is a criminal offense, it is a crime of necessity, not of deliberate intention. Would he have rather stayed in Utica than Rome, have been with Attius rather than with his congenial brother, been with others rather than his own people, if he had been able in any manner to get away? Inasmuch as that very diplomatic mission itself had been fraught with interest and anxiety because of the remarkable attachment of the brothers, could Ligarius have been easy in his mind, separated from his brothers forcibly by war?

Therefore, Caesar, you have no indication of any will hostile to you; and notice, I beg of you, whose case, whose loyalty I am defending, for I proffer my own. Oh, that wonderful clemency of yours, embellished by the praise of all in writings and monuments to its honor, when Marcus Cicero in person defends another person before you for not being of the opposition which Cicero himself admits having belonged to, a Cicero who yet has no fear of your silent thoughts and does not shudder at the possibility that some one of his hearers may rush up and confront you with a charge of disloyalty against the speaker!

Just see how I do not shudder, and how clear a light from your liberality and wisdom shines before me as I plead in your presence. I shall plead in as loud and clear a voice as I can summon, so that the Roman people may bear witness to this fact through their ears. The war once begun, and, in fact, for the most part, fought, coerced by no force, but by my own judgment and free will, I joined sides with those armies assembled against you. And to whom, pray, am I saying this? To the very man who, when he had knowledge of my actions, despite this, and before he even saw me, nevertheless restored me safely to the republic; who sent letters to me in Egypt, assuring me I should carry on as the very same person I had been previously; a man who, as the one *imperator,* commander-in-chief of the entire realm of the Roman people, allowed me to assume also the title of *imperator* which I had earned; a man by whom, when this selfsame Gaius Pansa brought the message to me, had made over to me the wreathed emblem of the fasces for as long as I should

deem it right to retain them; and a man, finally, who
considered that he was conferring immunity on me,
only if he granted it not without some token of honor.

I draw your attention, Tubero, to the way I, unhesitatingly admitting my own conduct, would hardly
dare make such a confession on behalf of Ligarius.
Of course, were I to say, Tubero, the same kinds of
things about Ligarius, Caesar would undoubtedly pardon him, just as he once pardoned me; Caesar, the
man whose energy and renown I bespeak, because of
our being closely related, or because I fully appreciate
his intellectual powers and his skillful cultivation of
oratory, or because I think that the praise of a young
relation ought to redound somewhat to my credit.

But I ask the question: who imputes it a crime
to have been in Africa? Well, the very person who both
wanted to be in the selfsame place and complained of
being[5] prevented from so being by Ligarius, and who
undeniably joined in armed combat against Caesar.
What indeed, Tubero, did your drawn sword perform
on the fields of Pharsalus?[6] Whose side was the edge
of your blade menacing? Who felt the impact of your
weapons? Against whom were your eyes, your hands,
your belligerent spirit, your tactics directed? What
were you desirous of grasping, and what hopes did you
entertain? What was it that you wanted so very much?
Well, I will desist from pursuing this line of questioning
further; I see the young man appears somewhat ruffled.
Let me return to my own case. After all, I was engaged on the same side as he, against Caesar.

4   Besides, my dear Tubero, what else have we need
of, except, perhaps, to be able to respond to the situation in the way that Caesar could—not seeming to be
quite capable of that ability of his to drop our grudges?
As for those very men who went unpunished, Caesar,
simply and solely thanks to your forgiveness, can this
trial by words sharpen your impression of their cruelty
toward you? Indeed, in this case before us, Tubero, I
crave a good portion, not only of your prudence, but

5 After Varus had assumed command in Africa, Lucius Aelius
Tubero, who had been appointed governor of the province,
arrived in the harbor of Utica, accompanied by his son Quintus.
Varus issued an order that neither father nor son be allowed to
land. Presumably, Ligarius carried out this order.

6 The battle fought near Pharsalus in Thessaly resulted in Pompey's defeat in the civil war.

your father's, because such a man, highly endowed, not only with natural intelligence, but with trained knowledge, failed to see what this case presented. Had he seen that, he would have preferred prosecution in any way but the one you have chosen.

You maintain that Ligarius admits his culpability. But this is hardly sufficient, for, either you are prosecuting someone who has a case to defend or, as I would insist, a better case than you have, or as you would put it, as strong as yours. These are remarkable matters, but I may say that they are rather ominous. Such an accusation has the force, not of merely condemning Ligarius, but of putting him to death. No Roman citizen has prosecuted a fellow citizen with this aim before you, Tubero; those are the procedures of foreigners, of shifty-minded Greeks or uncouth barbarians. What else is it than this, that you are pressing for in the case? That Ligarius be kept from Rome, from his own household and family, not be allowed to live with his excellent brothers, not even with his uncle, Titus Brocchus, not with his sister's son, not with us, his friends and associates, not to live in his native land; this is what you are aiming at, is it not? Could a man "live" in that condition? Could he be more in need? He is forbidden to be in Italy; he is in exile. Therefore, I say you want to deprive the man, not of his country, which is refused to him, but of his life. And that sort of measure none would urge against even a dictator who punished by death those whom he hated. The dictator Sulla proscribed citizens, even though no one else was in favor of it, and even set a price on their heads. But this very cruelty was avenged many years afterward by Caesar, the man you are hoping will be as cruel, for Caesar prosecuted the agents of Sulla.

Of course, you will say that you are not asking for this at all. Still, it comes to this in my opinion, Tubero. I have known you and your father, I have known your family and your name. All the best, commendable interests of your whole family in virtue, in humanity, in learning, are long since familiar to me. Therefore, I of course, realize that you are not bloodthirsty; but you do not consider carefully enough the consequences of your action. As it now stands, you appear to be far from satisfied with the punishment so far visited upon Quintus Ligarius, and, therefore, what remains beside

5

this except the death penalty? If, in fact, he is already in exile, as he is, what more are you demanding? That he not be granted a pardon? But that seems much more depressing and much more strict. What we ourselves plead for prayerfully and tearfully, prostrate at the feet of the judge, not relying so much on our rights in the case as on his spirit of humane forgiveness —to keep us from gaining that request, will you fight to keep us from winning it, and break in on our sorrow and prevent our lying at the feet of the judge and assuming the attitude of suppliants? When we did this in Caesar's home, as we truly and successfully did, suppose you had suddenly rushed in and begun to shout: "Caesar, take care not to pardon him, be careful not to take pity on brothers appealing to you on behalf of their brother's salvation!" Would you not seem to have shed every vestige of human instinct? How much more difficult is this, to have you strike out publicly against what we sought in Caesar's home and to have you sweep away the refuge of compassion in the midst of the intense suffering of many victims!

Caesar, I will express plainly what I feel. If, in this situation of fortune, your clemency had not been of so high an order, proffered by you and through you alone—and I am fully aware of what I am about to say—the great victory you won in the field would have recoiled on you in a bitterly resentful tide of grief. How many there were in the ranks of the victorious who wanted you to be cruelly unsparing, even though they might themselves have been in the ranks of the conquered! How many there were who would interfere with your clemency, because they wanted no one to be pardoned! And notice how, of course, these Tuberos, father and son, whom you have pardoned, are unwilling that clemency be accorded others. What if we could prove to Caesar that Ligarius had not even been in Africa, if we wished a well-intended and humane lie, unfortunate as that is, to benefit the state at a time of dire emergency? Still, no man would have the right in so severe a crisis and danger to undeceive the citizens; and, even if it were someone's, it certainly would not be his who had been in the identical situation and plight. Still and all, it is one thing to be unwilling that Caesar should err and quite another thing to be unwilling that he show mercy. Then you might well

ay, "Caesar, don't trust him; he was in Africa, he bore
arms against you!" But, as it is now, what are you say-
ng except, "Beware of being lenient"? This is not the
one for one man to take toward another. And he who
employs it in your presence, Caesar, more readily dis-
cards his own claim to human kindness than wrenches
away yours.

But the first approach and demand of Tubero here
was, I presume, that he wanted to be heard himself on
the subject of Ligarius' crime. I have no doubt that you
rather wondered whether he who had been in the
same situation was introducing some new matter, or
whether he was not speaking of someone else. Your
word for it, Tubero, was "crime," was it? Why so?
His case has so far been lacking in a name like that.
Some call it error, others timidity; looking at it in a
darker light, there are those who would call it ambitious hope, overeagerness, hostility, stubbornness;
those who view it most gravely would say it was sheer
recklessness; but except for you, no one has referred
to it as crime. To me, indeed, if the true and proper
term is sought for our distress, it would seem that a
certain fatal calamity came down on us and took possession of our minds, and that no one ought to marvel
that human plans have been overwhelmed by divine
necessity. Let us grant that they are unhappy, although,
as a matter of fact, since Caesar is the triumphant man,
we cannot claim as much. But I do not refer to ourselves; rather, I speak of those who have died. They
may have been overzealous, they may have been angry,
they may have been obstinate; even so, in truth, let us
grant that the now-dead Gnaeus Pompey and many
others fell far short of the crimes of perpetrated evil,
of passion, of parricide. When has anyone heard such
a charge originate with you, Caesar, or heard that your
victorious weapons craved anything other than that
bitter resistance to you be ended? And what is the
import of this? Simply, that you wanted peace to reign
and acted, did you not, to that end whether you were
dealing with avowed diehards or with reliable citizens?

Your exceedingly praiseworthy actions toward me
would not have seemed such, if I thought of myself
as a rascally diehard saved by you. For how could
you be so deserving a benefactor of the republic, if
you had wanted so many convinced enemies of the

state to go unscathed and be restored to their status? You considered that secession in its beginnings, Caesar, to be not out-and-out war or implacable hostility, but a form of civil discontent, in which both parties sought the welfare of the state, but veered away from the common welfare, partly in the schemes they arrived at, partly in their analysis of the objectives. The high standing of the leaders was about equal, but that of the followers was not; the issue was at the time somewhat in doubt, because there was some truth in what either side maintained. Now that side ought to be judged the better, which the gods have also helped. Your forgiving spirit having now made itself known, who will not applaud that victory, in which no one has perished except in armed combat?

7   But to omit the general problem, let us now come to the particular case at issue. In the long run, which, Tubero, do you think was easier, for Ligarius to get out of Africa, or for you not to go to Africa? "Could we have done so?" you would ask, "when the Senate had forbidden it?" If you ask me, No, not at all. But still, the same Senate had dispatched Ligarius on his diplomatic mission. And he obeyed, at a time when it was necessary to obey the Senate; you obeyed at a time when no one obeyed who chose not to. And do I blame you for that? Not in the slightest, for it would not have become one of your background, name, family, and upbringing to have done otherwise. But this I do not concede, that you should reproach others for the very same things which you take credit for having done yourself. Your father Lucius Tubero's decision was cast up for him by decree of the Senate, when he himself was in fact not at hand, but being kept away by sickness, had decided to excuse himself. These things I came to know through all the many and necessary ways in which Lucius Tubero and I were thrown together; we were educated together, we were comrades in arms, then relations by marriage and finally lifelong associates; it was a strong bond between us, that we had followed the same course of studies. I, therefore, know that Tubero wanted to stay at home, but a certain person, whose name I shall not mention, so acted, presenting the name and sacred cause of the republic in so grave a light, that even though Tubero may have felt otherwise, he still could not withstand

the pressure of those very words, and yielded to the authority of this most upright person; or rather, he obeyed. He set out in the company of those with whom he had common cause. Slowly, he proceeded on his journey, and therefore reached Africa only after it had been taken by the enemy. Hence, the criminal charge that was brought up against Ligarius, or rather the angry resentment. For if it is criminal to have wished for something, no less great an offense is it that you wanted to hold Africa, the keystone of all our provinces, a place born to wage war against this city of ours; that you wanted to obtain it for yourselves rather than let someone else have it. This someone else, even so, was not Ligarius; Varus declared that he held the supreme authority, and certainly he flourished the fasces, the emblems of power. But in whatever way he may have flaunted that authority, does this case of yours really stand up: "We were not admitted into the province?" What if you had been? Would you have handed it over to Caesar's power or kept it yourselves, as a weapon against Caesar?

Observe, Caesar, what freedom of speech, or perhaps better, boldness, our liberal spirit grants us. If Tubero should answer that his father had delivered to you that Africa where the Senate's lot had dispatched him, I will not hesitate to denounce his scheme in the most serious terms, and in the presence of you in whose interest it was that he did this. For that business was not one to be approved of, even though it may have suited your wishes. But I leave all this out, not so much to refrain from offending your very patient ears, as not to make Tubero appear to be on the verge of doing something he never contemplated doing. You were all coming to Africa, the one province of all most resistant to your victory, in which there was a very powerful enemy of your cause and an unfriendly alliance, solid and strong. I put the question: what were you intending to do? Although, should I doubt your intentions, when I observe what you have done elsewhere? You were prevented from setting foot in your province, and stopped with heavy injury. How did you support that? To whom did you report your complaint of the injury that befell you? Of course, to him on whose authority you had come into the confederacy of war. But if you entered the province in the cause of Caesar, you should

8

surely have returned to him when you were excluded
from the province. You went to Pompey. And what,
therefore, is your quarrel with Caesar, though you
would accuse him, by whom you complain you were
prevented from waging war against Caesar? And yet,
you may boast of your work so far as I am concerned,
of this, even though it is a lie, that you have conveyed
the province to Caesar. Even if you were kept from it
by Varus and certain others, I will declare that the
blame is really Ligarius', for he deprived you of so
major an opportunity for congratulations.

9   But observe, Caesar, the consistency[7] of so distinguished a man; although I myself might approve, as
I do approve, still, I would not keep reminding you
of it, unless I had recognized that that virtue is customarily praised by you very highly. Was there ever in any
man such a high degree of consistency? I call it consistency: I am not sure whether I ought not rather call
it patience. For how many times had someone kept at
it, to make his way back to those very people, by whom,
in civil strife, he was not only not received, but rejected cruelly? A certain greatness of spirit must be
granted to a man no disagreeable opposition, no force,
no danger, can check, once his cause has been decided
upon and his mind made up. For even if other things
had been equal between Tubero and Varus—honor,
nobility, impressiveness, native talent, which they were
not—this was surely to Tubero's highest credit: the
fact that he had come to his province with the power
of the Senate legally invested in him. And excluded
from it, he did not repair to Caesar, who might have
been angered, or to his own home to lapse into idleness,
or to some other region at random, so as not to seem
to renege on that cause in which he had enlisted;
instead, he proceeded to Macedonia, to the camp of
Gnaeus Pompey and that very same side in the struggle,
by which he had been forcibly rejected. And what
next? Since the whole affair had made little impression
on the mind of the man you had then approached, you
were considerably less enthusiastic for the cause, I
imagine. You were on his side, within his lines, but
your thoughts were shrinking away from commitment

7 Cicero stresses the contrast between Tubero, who had readily
abandoned the cause of Pompey, and Ligarius, who had obstinately
clung to that cause.

to the cause. Did you really want to win the war? As usually happens in civil war, you, like the rest of us, were caught up in the fever of conquering. I, indeed, was an advocate of peace, but at a late point only, just before Pharsalus: it was a foolish thing to contemplate peace when you saw the battle lines drawn up. We all wanted to win, I say, you most especially, having gotten yourself into a position where you must perish if you did not win. Although, as the situation now stands, I have no doubt that you prefer this safety to that victory.

I would not say all this, Tubero, if either you *10* regretted your consistent application or Caesar regretted his kind deeds on your behalf. Now I ask whether you are revenging your injuries or the republic's. If the republic's, what do you have to say to your persevering in that cause? If yours, see that you make no mistake, in thinking that Caesar would be angry at your enemies, when he has, in fact, just pardoned his own.

Therefore, do I seem to you to be engaged in the cause of Ligarius? Do I speak of his deeds? Whatever I have said I wish to be referred to one thing of primary importance, the matter of human kindness, clemency, pity. I have, Caesar, conducted many cases while the pursuit of advancement in office kept you in the forum, but never one in this manner: "Pardon this man, O gentlemen of the jury: he erred, he lapsed, he did not think. He will not do it again." This is the way to appeal to a parent, not to a judge. To the latter, one should say, "He is not guilty, he did not think of it; the witnesses are false, the crime wrongly alleged." Say that you, Caesar, were the judge *de facto* in Ligarius' case, ask in whose protection he has been: I keep silent so as not to adduce things which might carry weight with a judge. "Having set out on a diplomatic mission before the war, having been left behind during a time of peace and overtaken by the war, and for all that, far from bitterly disposed, he is entirely yours, heart and soul." So it might be argued before the judges, but I speak as if to a parent: "He went astray and acted rashly, and he is sorry for that. I appeal to your good instincts for mercy and seek allowance for the oversight and ask that he be granted a pardon." If no one had succeeded in gaining pardon from you, then I am speaking out of turn; but, if many

have, may you offer the same help to us as the hope
you have given to many. Or is there no cause for hope
in Ligarius' case, inasmuch as the occasion for pleading
for him is given to me, instead of to someone else? And
yet, the hope does not rest in this speech of mine nor
in the zealous efforts of your kinsmen who have
petitioned you on behalf of Ligarius.

11   I have seen and come to know what you regard as
of chief importance when many set to work for the
freeing of some one man. The actual grounds of the
petitioners are more important to you than the appearance and looks of the men. You do not regard so much
the fact that it is your kinsman who pleads before you
as the thing that he is laboring to present. So you
confer on your kinsmen so many advantages that they
seem to me meanwhile better off than you yourself are,
who grant so many honors to them; but yet, as I have
said, I see that the specific issues at stake weigh more
heavily with you than the sincere tones of our pleas,
and that you are impressed, most of all, by those whose
grief as petitioners you see to be entirely justified.

In preserving the innocence of Quintus Ligarius,
you will earn the thanks of many of your kinsmen and
close friends; but do, I pray you, consider this as you
customarily do, in terms of the genuine reasons of the
petitioners. I can present to you in his support the
bravest men, most loyal to you, the Sabines, and the
whole Sabine province, the flower of Italy and sturdy
stock of the republic: you know they are of the best sort.
Notice the solemnity and grief of them all: of this
Titus Brocchus, your opinion of whom I have no doubts
about—you see tears, degradation, dejection written
on his countenance and on his son's. What shall I say
is respect to Ligarius' brothers? Do not think, Caesar,
that I am arguing a case concerning the civil status of a
single person only: either three Ligarii are to be retained by you in the state or three driven out of it. For
any place of exile would be more desirable for them
than the native land, house, home, and household gods,
if one of the brothers went into exile. If they act
piously, fraternally, and as truly aggrieved, let their
tears, their reverence, their fraternal affection impress
you. Let that voice of yours which has won out, prevail;
for we heard you say that you thought all who were
not against you were your friends, whereas we thought

those were our enemies unless they were with us. Therefore, you see this outstanding representative, and this household of the Brocchi, this Lucius Marcus, Gaius Caesetius, Lucius Corfidius, all these Roman knights here present clothed in mourning garb, men not merely known to you, but standing high in your favor. And toward some we were angry, some we harassed and solicited, some we even threatened. Save them then for your own, so that, as in the case of other things you have said, this also may be found to be absolutely true.

But if you could see deep inside the unanimity of the Ligarii, you would judge that all the brothers were on your side. Or can anyone doubt that if Quintus Ligarius had been able to be in Italy, he would have been of the same opinion as his brothers? Who is there who has not known the unanimous agreement of these three, breathing almost as one in their near-equality of age? Who does not realize this; namely, that you could imagine anything else happening before these brothers would pursue different convictions and aims? By free will, therefore, all were with you, but one of them was carried off course by the storm, one who, had he been able, would have been like those whom you still wanted to be saved. But granted that he went to war and dissented, not only from you, but from his brothers; they, your allies, plead with you. Indeed, when I became interested in these proceedings, I held in memory what sort of a man Titus Ligarius had been[8] respecting you and your high office. But it is a minor matter for me to recall this merely: I hope that you who forget nothing except the wrongs done you, since this is the nature of your character and genius, also remember something about his career as quaestor, especially, when you reflect back upon the behavior in certain other quarters. Therefore, this Titus Ligarius, who then did nothing—for he had no inkling of these eventualities—except what you would consider expected of your eager servant and reliable man, now seeks the welfare of his brother as a suppliant before you. And when, duly aware of Titus' performance of his duties, you have conferred pardon on both Quintus in exile

12

---

8 Titus Ligarius was helpful to Caesar in 56 B.C., when Caesar obtained an appropriation for his Gallic wars. Cicero had also favored this appropriation.

and on his two brothers, you will have restored three excellent and wholehearted men to themselves, not only to these many and very talented citizens, not only to us, your close friends and relations, but also the republic.

Do, therefore, what you recently did in the Senate for a man of the most outstanding degree—do the same in the public forum for these best of brothers, most acceptable as they are in the eyes of all men here present. You readmitted us to the Senate: give back this Ligarius to the people whose good will you have always held most dear. And if that day was a most splendid occasion for you and a deeply gratifying occasion for the people, the day you pardoned Marcellus,[9] do not,

---

[9] Marcus Claudius Marcellus, consul in 51 B.C., also a "Pompeian," had been pardoned by Caesar in 46 B.C. in an impressive scene in the Senate. Cicero was so moved by the clemency accorded his good friend, that he broke his vow of silence and rose to deliver *ex tempore* the speech *For Marcellus.*

A similar occasion, an appeal to Caesar to grant a pardon, was the ruse employed on the Ides of March in 44 B.C.:

Brutus   I kiss thy hand, but not in flattery, Caesar;
              Desiring thee that Publius Cimber may
              Have an immediate freedom of repeal.
Caesar   What, Brutus!
Cassius   Pardon, Caesar; Caesar, pardon!
              As low to thy foot doth Cassius fall,
              To beg enfranchisement for Publius Cimber.
Caesar   I would be well moved, if I were as you;
              If I could pray to move, prayers would
                   move me;
              But I am constant as the northern star,
              Of whose true-fixed and resting quality
              There is no fellow in the firmament.
              The skies are painted with unnumbered
                   sparks,
              They are all fire and every one doth shine;
              But there's but one in all doth hold his
                   place.
              So in the world: 'tis furnished well with
                   men,
              And men are flesh and blood, and appre-
                   hensive;
              Yet in the number I do know but one
              That unassailable holds on his rank,
              Unshaked of motion; and that I am he,
              Let me a little show it, even in this:

Caesar, I implore you, hesitate to strive for the same
kind of glorious praise as often as possible. Nothing is
so popular as goodness, and none of your many virtues
surpasses the pleasure and respect your clemency evokes.
Men come closest to the gods when they confer salvation on their fellow men. Your destiny holds nothing
greater, your nature nothing better than the fact that
you wish to save as many men as possible. The case
before you might call for a long speech, but your
natural instinct prizes a short one. Therefore, since it
would be more useful for you yourself than for me or
anyone else to speak to you, I will end my presentation.
Let me only remind you that if you grant a saving
pardon to this man now absent, you will be conferring
it on all who are actually present here.

	That I was constant Cimber should be banished,
	And constant do remain to keep him so.
Cinna	O Caesar,—
Caesar	Hence! Wilt thou lift up Olympus?
Decius	Great Caesar,—
Caesar	Doth not Brutus bootless kneel?
Casca	Speak, hands, for me!
	[*They stab Caesar*]
Caesar	*Et tu Brute!* Then fall, Caesar!
	Dies *

* *Julius Caesar,* III, i, ll. 52–77.

THE DREAM
OF SCIPIO

INTRODUCTION

In many different orations, as well as in his philosophical essays and other writings, Cicero often brings up the name of Scipio the Younger. The name itself was to be a kind of shorthand title to glory: PUBLIUS CORNELIUS SCIPIO AEMILI-ANUS AFRICANUS MINOR NUMANTINUS describes what this Roman did and who he was. Born around 185 B.C., the natural son of Lucius Aemilius Paulus, he was adopted into the Cornelian gens by Publius Cornelius Scipio, the elder son of the great Africanus, and more than fulfilled the promise implicit in this beau geste by becoming the final conqueror of Carthage in 146 B.C. His adoptive grandfather had delivered the crushing defeat to Hannibal at Zama in 202 B.C. that ended the First Punic War. In Spain, first as an administrative official and later as a military commander, Scipio was instrumental in reasserting strong Roman control over the province; by the successful siege and destruction of Numantia in 133 B.C., he completed its subjugation to Rome. Scipio's political career was distinguished by his being elected consul when he was thirty-seven, long before the legal age, during the year he was a candidate merely for the office of aedile. After celebrating his triumph over Carthage, he was elected censor, and subsequently undertook a two-year diplo-matic mission to Egypt, Syria, Pergamum, and Greece, to consolidate Roman interests in those countries.

He married Sempronia, the sister of Tiberius and Gaius Gracchus, but always stood opposed to the popular reforms the Gracchi championed. He expressed no sorrow over the death of Tiberius Gracchus in 133 B.C. In 129 B.C., when it was clear that Scipio had thrown all the weight of his authority and prestige on the conservative side to maintain a balance in the republic between the forces of the patricians and the plebeians, by such acts as his rejection of Carbo's proposal to legalize the re-election of tribunes, popular disorder broke out against him, prompted by Carbo's accusation that he was an enemy of the people. When Scipio one day reaffirmed his position and re-expressed his approval of the death of Tiberius, voices shouted "Down with the tyrant!" He went home that evening intending to compose a speech to be given the following day, but the next morning was found dead in his room. Subsequently, Carbo committed suicide, presumably to forestall prosecution for the murder.

Scipio the Younger was a man of letters as well as a man of action. He was a distinguished orator and a cultivated man, with a marked interest in Greek philosophy and literature. He formed around himself a literary circle, whose aura is well captured in Cicero's essays *On Old Age* and *On Friendship,* as well as in the dialogue-treatise *On The Republic,* of which "The Dream of Scipio" comprises the final section. In this group were such men as Polybius the historian, the orator Laelius, Lucilius, the founder of the genre of Roman satire, and Terence, the brilliant young dramatist.

The combination of interests and talents which Scipio made memorable on the scene of Roman politics during difficult days for the republic must have seemed to Cicero, nearly a hundred years later, relevant to his own. As a political leader and administrator, Cicero had met the crisis of the conspiracy in 63 B.C., and upon his return from exile, faced successive challenges in the strategic use of his authority and influence against the gradual gaining of power by the popular leader Caesar. Cicero also tried, in office and out, to achieve the balance of power between the contending classes, the "concord of orders" that would keep the Senate in command of the complex forces that were to end by altering the constitutional and legislative nature of the Roman republic into the all-powerful executive state that Caesar symbolized and left as his legacy to Augustus. Cicero's practical role in determining events was relatively minor: from the time of his return in 57 B.C., until his death in

43 B.C., he had more time for reflection than action. He began the composition of the lengthy treatise in dialogue form, *De Re Publica* in 54 B.C. and finished it in 51 B.C. In the dialogue, Scipio is the principal speaker, as he and Laelius and other friends conversationally debate the philosophy and practice of government. Modeled, to some degree, on Plato's *Republic,* the discussion shows its Roman spokesmen much more concerned with the practice of politics and the history of their own government. We have only some sections of the first five books to judge by, but the emphasis clearly falls on the historical lessons Rome had learned about government, rather than on ideal doctrine. Portions of the whole dialogue were rediscovered in the nineteenth century, but the last book, comprising the Dream of Scipio, survived intact, the basis of a learned commentary by the fourth-century scholar, Macrobius.* Chaucer's account of his own dream in *The Parlement of Foules* starts from his reading of *Scipio's Dream* with Macrobius' commentary. As a brief composition, dramatically portraying the destiny of the immortal soul, the Dream was uncannily well-suited to the interests of Christians; together with Macrobius' rather arcane, Neoplatonic commentary on its meaning, it enjoyed a great success, and exerted wide influence on medieval and renaissance humanists. The dream device itself was apt and picturesque—even Kepler made use of it to set forth, in fictional disguise, notions about flight through outer space.† Dante's poetic vision of the voyage of the soul to its ultimate destiny is surely the largest and most complex revision of Cicero's momentary fantasy.

A generation after Cicero's work appeared, Virgil, in the Sixth Book of the *Aeneid,* enhanced the encounter of Aeneas and Anchises with a panoramic vision of Roman political destiny. And some three hundred years earlier, Plato had ended his elaborate dialogue, *The Republic,* with the Vision of Er the Pamphylian, who had sojourned in the realm of the hereafter long enough to become convinced of the immortal destiny of the soul. Plato's figurative man in the apocalypse had seen that men could choose their course of life and that their decisions, once taken, were irrevocable.

* Stahl, W. H., in *Macrobius: Commentary on the Dream of Scipio* (New York: Columbia University Press, 1952), discusses this tradition.
† Nicolson, Marjorie H., in *Voyages to the Moon* (New York: The Macmillan Company, 1948), discusses Kepler's "Somnium" and the literature of space-flight in the seventeenth and eighteenth centuries.

Much matter is contained in condensed form in the brilliant dream Cicero imaginatively assigned to Scipio. The filial interview is, like Plato's Vision of Er, a narrative climax after long pages of sociological and philosophical analysis. It offers a well-organized account of the Ptolemaic conception of the geocentric universe, which passed for scientific truth in Cicero's day. The mood is, to some extent, one of disenchanted realism: Scipio is invited to see his life in broad perspective and to appreciate the fact that, however important a man may seem or be, his life is a temporary and minor event on this planet. The good life is, of course, there for him to choose, but the good of life on earth is to be valued at something less than the cosmic rate. This notion, that man is not all-important, but rather, a small, single aspect of the eternal, adds a somber glow to Cicero's bright fantasy. The great Scipio Africanus Major could no doubt have ruefully verified it when, in later years, he had again met Hannibal at the court of King Antiochus in Ephesus and both men, one in exile, the other in disfavor, compared notes on their careers. The Younger Scipio, at the dramatic date chosen by Cicero for this dialogue, the Latin Holidays in 129 B.C., could deploy his thoughts in leisurely talk—but it was precisely during these days that Carbo was instigating the popular resentment that would overwhelm him.

The Dream of Scipio is also Cicero's dream. Cicero's claim, in 44 B.C., that he had written *On the Republic*, "while still holding the rudder of the ship of state" in his hands, was merely a pardonable exaggeration. His day had passed. His political star had set, and while he still had a rehabilitated prestige to put at the service of the state, it was, in fact, the assumption of power by others that gave him the leisure to reflect on the problems of Roman government and their historical development, and the time to write such books as his discursive *On the Republic*. But, like Scipio in the dialogue, Cicero was able to confront relativity in human affairs from the vantage point of convictions about the good life. The *Somnium* is a very Roman product, the climax of a practical and sensible discussion of political realities, animated by a stirring sense of the grandeur that was Rome's mission to her statesmen. Its design is impressive, its architecture vast and complex. The purpose behind it challenges the human will:

There is a sure place prepared in heaven for all who have cared for their fatherland, preserved it, contributed to its growth; increased it: a place where they may enjoy eternal life in everlasting bliss. There is nothing more acceptable to the chief of the gods who rules over the cosmos, of all the things that happen on earth, than the councils and gatherings of men who associate together in respect for law and justice, that is, the organizations called states. Their rulers and preservers have come from heaven and will return here.

Paradise is politics. Those who choose their country's good over their own, know a form of beatitude; those who cannot look beyond themselves to the world of their fellow men, do not end as such prominent spirits. The statesman who exercises his capacity for choosing the good life is kidnapped, once and for all. Conscientiously, the elder Scipio had insisted on the transitoriness of all things, in relaying the vision to his descendant. But the memorable truth about the purpose of the statesman's life is as significant as was the history of the two lives of the two Scipios. Cicero had himself done what he could to keep that purpose clear, both in his life and in his writing. A man can awaken from a dream without losing sight of its benefits.

The Dream of Scipio

When I went to Africa, as military tribune to the Fourth Legion, as you know, in the year of the consulship of Manius Manilius, my first wish upon arriving was to meet King Masinissa, our family's deservedly close friend. When I entered his headquarters, the old king embraced me, shedding tears of joy; after a moment, he raised his eyes toward heaven, saying:

"I offer my thanks to you, O highest sun, and to the other inhabitants of heaven for letting me see, before I take leave of my life, a Publius Cornelius Scipio in my kingdom and in this tent, one whose very name revives my spirits. The memory of that splendid unconquerable hero has never dimmed in my mind."

We proceeded to discuss at length many matters, as I asked him questions about his kingdom and its affairs and he questioned me about our commonwealth. We spent that whole day in conversation.

After I had been welcomed in royal fashion we prolonged our talk far into the night, for the old man wanted nothing more than to talk about Africanus, and to review in memory, not only his deeds, but his words. When we separated to go to bed, I felt tired from my long journey and from the lateness of the hour and sank immediately into a deeper sleep than usual. In that sleep Africanus appeared before me in the form that is more familiar to me from his portrait than from his own person. His manifestation in my dream was undoubtedly due to our having talked of him so much, for it often happens that the subject of our conversations and thoughts carries over into our dreams—as Ennius writes of Homer's appearing to him after the waking hours during which he customarily talked about and thought of him. Trembling, I recognized Africanus, who addressed me as follows:

"Do not start away; dismiss all fear from your heart, Scipio, and store up in your mind what I have to say to you. You see, do you not, that city which was compelled by me to become obedient to the Roman people, now renewing its former wars and refusing to remain quiet?" He was pointing out Carthage from the high and brilliant place where he stood surrounded by radiant stars.

"You now come to attack it, as a mere soldier. But within two years' time, you will overthrow it, as consul, and, thereby, earn the cognomen you have so far borne as an inheritance from me, Africanus. After you have destroyed Carthage, moreover, and have celebrated your triumph, and held the office of censor, you will proceed on missions to Asia, Egypt, Syria, and Greece. In your absence, you will be chosen consul a second time; then you will win your greatest war, and will raze Numantia. But when you are riding in triumph to the Capitoline Hill, you will find that the state is being sorely tried by the revolutionary schemes of my grandson, Tiberius Gracchus.

At this juncture, you, Africanus, must show the light of your spirit, of your character, and of your intelligence to your fellow countrymen. I foresee, at that time, two different paths, as it were, of fate lying before you. When your lifespan has lasted through seven times eight revolutions of the sun—each of these two numbers being deemed fraught with significance—which in their course have brought you to this critical time of life, the whole state will turn toward you alone and toward your name. The attention of all will be focused on you; the Senate, all loyal citizens, your associates, the Latins: you will be the one person on whom the welfare of the republic depends. To put it briefly, you will have to assume the role of dictator and reconstitute the state, if you manage to escape destruction at the impious hands of your own kinsmen."

At this, Laelius cried out and the others groaned aloud, but Scipio smiled at them calmly and said, "Shhh! Please do not rouse me from sleep; listen a while longer to what I heard."

"Africanus, so that you may be all the more ready to safeguard the republic, consider this. There is a sure place prepared in heaven for all who have cared for their fatherland, preserved it, contributed to its growth; increased it: a place where they may enjoy eternal life in everlasting bliss. There is nothing more acceptable to the chief of the gods who rules over the cosmos, of all the things that happen on earth, than the councils and gatherings of men who associate together in respect for law and justice, that is, the organizations called states. Their rulers and preservers have come from heaven and will return here."

Alarmed as I was at the prospect, not of my own death but of the treachery in store for me from my own kinsmen, I nevertheless inquired whether my father Paulus himself still lived, and others whom we had thought had died.

"Yes, I assure you," he said, "they do live, for they have escaped the bondage of their bodies as though they had escaped from prison. That life of yours is called life, but it is death. Look there: do you not see your father Paulus coming toward you?"

When I saw him, I burst into tears, but he embraced me and kissed me and bid me weep no more. As soon as I had regained my composure and was able to talk again, I asked, "O most revered of fathers and best of men, if this is truly the realm of life, as I hear Africanus say, why, I beg of you, must I tarry longer on earth? Why do I not hasten to come among you?"

"That is not the way things are," he answered. "This whole space you see is god's temple, and unless he has freed you from the confinement of your body, the pathway here does not lie open to you. Life was given to men, so that they might occupy that globe which you see in the center of this realm, and which is called the earth. They have been endowed with souls from those everlasting fiery elements which you call the stars and the constellations, the circular spheres animated by divine mind which complete their circuits and orbits with marvelous swiftness. Therefore, Publius, both you and all righteous men must let the soul be kept in the custody of the body and not allow it to emigrate from human life unbidden by him who has endowed you with this soul, or you will seem to have shunned the gift of humanity allotted you by god. Instead, Scipio, as your grandfather and as I who brought you to birth have done, cherish justice and righteousness. Significant as these qualities are in relation to one's parents and kinsmen, they are of the utmost importance in one's responsibility to his country. That pattern of life is the path to heaven and to the company of those who have lived their lives and now, released from their bodies, inhabit the region you see over there (a brightly glowing circle, glowing with glorious light among the flames) which you call, deriving the name from the Greeks, the Milky Way."

As I gazed out from this region, all things appeared marvelously resplendent to me. Here were the stars we never see from earth, in magnitudes that we can never envisage: the smallest was the planet most distant from heaven and nearest the earth, which shines by reflected light. The starry spheres easily surpassed the earth in size. And in truth, the earth now appeared so small to me that I saw with chagrin how small was our empire, by means of which we have gained possession of a tiny point.

As I gazed with fixed fascination on the earth, Africanus said, "How long will your mind be trained on the ground? Will you not look up around you at the vast temple you have entered? Here are the nine circles, or spheres, interconnected. The one that is outermost and contains all the others, itself the highest god watching over and governing all the rest, is the celestial sphere. In it, are set the fixed stars, which revolve in their eternal courses through the heavens. Within and below it, are the seven planets, that turn in the opposite direction to the heavens. The farthermost of these spheres is the one we on earth call Saturn. Next below it, is the planet Jupiter, whose bright influence is benign and healthful for the human race. Then comes the golden-red hue of the planet that bodes ill to men on earth, which you call Mars. Next below, at the mid-distance between heaven and earth is the orbit of the sun, the leader and prince and ruler of the other lights, the rational principle and controlling power of the universe, and so large that he fills and illuminates all with his light. Like faithful companions, Venus and Mercury follow him in their respective orbits, and at the lowest juncture, spins the orbit of the moon, whose light is kindled by the rays of the sun. Everything lying below this point is mortal and perishable except the souls of men, which are the gift of the gods, and above the moon, all things are everlasting. The ninth body, lying at the center, the earth, is the lowest and remains motionless. All things of weight fall toward it by the inherent nature of their gravity."

I surveyed the scene in rapt wonder. Then, coming back to myself, I asked, "What is this lovely and full sound that greets my ears?"

"It is the music of the spheres," he answered, "produced by the motion and flight of the planets in their courses, separated, as they are, at varying intervals and yet, systematically arranged in true proportions that effect a pattern of tempered harmony, combining the high and the low tones. Motions as mighty as these could not be set going in silence; nature has arranged that at one far end the high tones will sound, and at the other the low tones. This is the reason that the highest point of heaven, the starry path, whose motion is swifter, glides with a high and piercing accompaniment of sound, but the lunar orbit, the lowest, with a deep sound. The ninth circle, the earth, remaining ever still, stays in one place, and occupies the central position in the universe. The eight spheres, two of which have the same velocity, produce seven tones at separate intervals—the key number for virtually everything. The learned men who have rediscovered it on stringed instruments and in the voice have thereby won for themselves a return to this place, as have other men who have recognized the importance of physics and astronomy and devoted their surpassing genius to heavenly wisdom in human life. Overflowing with this sound, men's ears have grown deaf to it, and no other physical faculty has become more blunted. So it is, for example, with the inland race who live near the Cataract of the Nile, where it plunges down from steep cliffs: because of the grandeur of the noise, they have lost the faculty of hearing it. And of course, this bank of sound created by the onrushing revolution of the whole universe in motion is so voluminous that men's ears cannot detect it, just as you are incapable of looking directly into the sun, because your eyesight and faculty of vision is overwhelmed by his rays."

Marveling at this, I, nevertheless, kept turning my eyes toward the earth again and again. Africanus continued: "I perceive that you, even now, fix your gaze on the settled abode and dwelling place of men. But if it appears to you as small as it actually is, train your eyes ever on the heavenly realm and banish human thoughts from your mind. After all, what renown, what fame worth seeking can you gain from the lips of men? You see how few and far between, and how cramped are the places where they live, and that between those blisters and spots where there is habitation, vast unpeopled tracts intervene. You see how they who dwell on earth are so cut off from one another that communication between them is hardly possible; and how the earth's inhabitants stand obliquely, or at right angles, or at opposite angles to you—and from them, you can surely expect to elicit no fame.

"Moreover, you can distinguish the same earth wrapped and encircled with ribbon-like zones, the two of which, most widely distant from one another and verging toward the opposite poles of heaven you see are glazed with ice, whereas the central zone, which is the largest, is subject to the blazing heat of the sun. Of the two temperate and habitable zones, one is the southern antipodes, whose people walk upside down and in no way pertain to you. The other zone, lying to the north which you inhabit—see how small is the part of it that affects you—comes under the care of you Romans. Narrow and steep in the center, broader at the sides, it is like a small island surrounded by the sea you on earth call the Atlantic, or Great Sea, or the Ocean. Despite its grand name, you see how tiny it is. Reaching out from these inhabited and known regions, has your name, or that of anyone, been able to scale the mountain ranges of the Caucasus that you see there, or make the passage across the waters of the Ganges, over there? Who among the inhabitants of the most distant parts of the earth, north, south, east, or west, will hear your name? Being deprived of an audience such as this, you see how narrow is the compass wherein your fame may expand. As for those who still speak of us, how long will they be speaking?

"And should the progeny of our future descendants wish to pass on in an unbroken line to posterity the noble reports they have inherited from their fathers about any one of us, the earth is subject to inundations and holocausts that are bound to descend on it sooner or later: the fame we achieve cannot be long-lasting, much less everlasting. What concern is it of those born in later years that mention be made of you, when there is no longer anyone among them from the preceding generation? Our predecessors were no less numerous and they were assuredly better men, when you compare them with those who now sing our praises, but among whom none will achieve the distinction of being remembered for more than a single year. You know how men commonly calculate the year, with reference only to the sun's return, the journey of that one star. In fact, it is only when all the stars have returned to their original positions, and the heavens once more assume the same configuration they first had, that the great revolving year can be called complete. I hardly venture to say how many are the ages of man covered within one great year. Once upon a time, men perceived that the sun's light was failing and being eclipsed, when the soul of Romulus soared into these very temples of heaven. And when, once again, in the very same direction and at the very same time, the sun's light begins to diminish, and when all the stars and constellations have been summoned back to their point of origin, then you may know that the great year is fulfilled. And you must realize that the twentieth part of that year has not yet been traversed.

"But if you abandon all hope of returning to this realm, the paradise of great and glorious men, what is the value of a reputation among human beings that can barely last for the slender part of one great year? Rather, look aloft, and contemplate this domain and eternal home. Do not hand yourself over to what men may say of you or place your hopes in human rewards for your achievements. Virtue should draw you by her own allure to the ultimate honor. Let other men see what it is they have to say of you; they will say it in any case. All such reputation is confined to the narrow limits of that earth you see below you. It has never lasted indefinitely, but sinks into the grave with the men who voiced it and is quenched by the forgetfulness of posterity."

After he had said this, I replied, "If, indeed, Africanus, they, who have earned their country's respect, have, as it were, this open path to the entrance of heaven, I, who have from childhood onward, followed in my father's footsteps and in yours and not failed to live up to your greatness, will strive still harder now that so great a goal has been revealed to me."

And he answered, "Do so commit yourself. Remember that it is not you, but your body, which is mortal. You are not the person your outward appearance makes manifest; the essential person in everyone is his spirit, not the form that can be pointed to with a finger. Know, therefore, that you are a god, if it is god who flourishes in life, who thinks and feels, who remembers, who foresees, who so rules, governs, and moves the body it is in command of as the highest god governs this cosmos. Just as the eternal god impels the cosmos, which has its mortal elements, so an everlasting spirit impels your frail body.

"What is always in motion is eternal. But what transmits motion to another body and is itself kept in motion by another, must see the end of its life when it sees the end of its motion. Only the self-moving principle never abandons itself and never ceases to move. For all other things that move, this is the source and first cause of their motion. But there is no beginning of the first beginning: all things rise from the first principle, but it cannot be brought to pass by anything else. For it would not be the first principle if it had its origins from something else; and never arising, it never declines. Were it to be destroyed, it could not be generated by something else, nor create anything, for all things derive from the first principle. So it happens that the beginning of motion comes from that which is itself self-moving, which cannot be born and cannot die. Otherwise, the whole firmament would fall and universal nature would dissolve and lack recourse to any power by which its motion might be generated.

"Since it is apparent, therefore, that the self-moving principle is eternal, who will deny that spirit has this attribute? All inanimate things are kept in motion by an external impulse, but the animate moves by virtue of its own inner power. And this is precisely the character and strength of the spirit. If it is, therefore, the one entity out of all others that is self-moving, assuredly, it is not born, and it lives forever. So train your soul on the best pursuits. The highest concerns, moreover, are those related to the well-being of the state, and a spirit exercised and engaged in these commitments will soar all the more swiftly to this domain as its ultimate home. It will do so even more rapidly, if during the time it is enclosed in the body, it thrusts itself out to contemplate the things that lie beyond and gains as much distance from the body as possible. The souls of men addicted to the pleasures of the body, who have offered to be, as it were, their servants and, influenced by the desires that counsel compliance with pleasure, have flouted the laws of men and gods—when such souls fall away from their bodies, they continue to hover close over the earth, and do not return to this realm, without spending eons in torment."

Africanus withdrew, and I awoke from sleep.

THE LIFE
OF CICERO

Marcus Tullius Cicero was born in Arpinum, an ancient municipality in the central Italian region of Latium, on January 3, 106 B.C. Of his mother, Helvia, we know little, except that she came of a "good" family. Cicero's father may have been a distant descendant of the Volscian ruler Attius Tullius, who had received Coriolanus in exile from Rome in 491 B.C. He was a member of the equestrian order of middle-class Roman citizens, membership in the order consisting of the minimum property qualification of 400,000 sesterces ($20,000). The elder Cicero maintained a house in Rome as well as the family estate at Arpinum, but because of poor health spent most of his time at Arpinum as a kind of country squire, bending his mind to the study of literature and philosophy. Cicero speaks of his birthplace with affection and pride: in later life it was one of his retreats from the scene of professional and political action, like the villas at Tusculum near Rome or near the sea where he went to rest and reflect.

Arpinum was also the birthplace of the great democratic soldier and leader, Marius, seven times consul of Rome, who was born near this town in 157 B.C. Marius had served under Scipio Africanus the Younger, and soon after the beginning of his political career married Julia, the sister of Gaius Julius Caesar, the father of Julius Caesar. Both Cicero of Arpinum and Julius Caesar, the nephew of the great Marius of Arpinum, were destined to become significant figures in the political epoch that brought Roman history to a complex and critical turning point in the years from 70 to 44 B.C.

The education of Cicero and his younger brother, Quintus (born around 102 B.C.) was placed in the hands of capable teachers of rhetoric, literature, and philosophy. Quintus emerged from his humanistic training with a marked preference for the military career, and eventually became a legate of Julius Caesar in the Gallic campaigns. When asked why he did not, like his brother, makes speeches in the forum, Quintus is supposed to have observed, "one orator in a family is enough." Cicero's teachers included Archias, the Greek poet and humanist, Phaedrus, the Epicurean philosopher, Diodotus, the Stoic philosopher, and Philo, the Skeptic philosopher. He studied rhetoric with Molon of Rhodes, and law, first with the eminent elder authority Quintus Mucius Scaevola, then with his nephew Scaevola the *pontifex maximus*, also a famous legal scholar. Before entering public life Cicero completed his military training, and at the age of seventeen, served in the Social War against the Samnites, first under Strabo, and then under Sulla, the rival of Marius. He did not take part in the conflict between Marius and Sulla.

At the age of twenty-five, Cicero made his first public speech in the forum, in defense of Sextus Roscius, who had been "framed" on a parricide charge and was acquitted, thanks to Cicero's presentation of evidence and powerful argument of the case. He next defended a woman of Arezzo, about to lose her property and freedom because of Sulla's confiscations in the territory. These cases deserve mention as an illustration of Cicero's willingness to speak out on behalf of victims of the powerful dictator's policy.

Two subsequent years of travel, recuperation, and further study in the Near East and Athens brought Cicero into contact with several influential teachers, among them Antiochus, then head of the Academy in Athens. Antiochus combined in his teaching, various doctrines of the Platonic, Aristotelian, and Stoic schools, and Cicero may have been influenced by Antiochus' example to create his own working synthesis of thought in his later philosophical writings. These years of advanced training and study are best described by Cicero himself in a dialogue written in 46 B.C. called the *Brutus* (and dedicated to Brutus), in which he traces the

history of eminent public speakers in Roman political life
from the early generations to his own day:

. . . At this time my body was exceedingly weak and emaci-
ated; my neck long and slender; a shape and habit which I
thought to be liable to great risk of life, if engaged in any
violent fatigue, or labour of the lungs. And it gave the greater
alarm to those who had a regard for me, that I used to speak
without any remission or variation, with the utmost stretch of
my voice, and a total agitation of my body. When my friends,
therefore, and physicians, advised me to meddle no more
with forensic causes, I resolved to run any hazard rather than
quit the hopes of glory which I had proposed to myself from
pleading; but when I considered, that by managing my voice,
and changing my way of speaking, I might both avoid all
future danger of that kind and speak with greater ease, I
took a resolution of travelling into Asia, merely for an opportunity to correct my manner of speaking; so that after I
had been two years at the bar, and acquired some reputation
in the forum, I left Rome. When I came to Athens, I spent
six months with Antiochus, the principal and most judicious
philosopher of the old Academy; and under this able master,
I renewed those philosophical studies which I had laboriously
cultivated and improved from my earliest youth. At the
same time, however, I continued my rhetorical exercises
under Demetrius the Syrian, an experienced and reputable
master of the art of speaking. After leaving Athens, I traversed every part of Asia, where I was voluntarily attended
by the principal orators of the country, with whom I renewed
my rhetorical exercises. The chief of them was Menippus of
Stratonica, the most eloquent of all the Asiatics; and if to
be neither tedious nor impertinent is the characteristic of an
Attic orator, he may be justly ranked in that class. Dionysius
also of Magnesia, Aeschylus of Cnidos, and Xenocles of
Adramyttium, who were esteemed the first rhetoricians of
Asia, were continually with me. Not contented with these, I
went to Rhodes, and applied myself again to Molo, whom I
had heard before at Rome; and who was both an experienced
pleader and a fine writer, and particularly judicious in re-
marking the faults of his scholars, as well as in his method
of teaching and improving them. His principal trouble with
me was to restrain the luxuriancy of a juvenile imagination,
always ready to overflow its banks, within its due and proper
channel. Thus, after an excursion of two years, I returned to
Italy, not only much improved, but almost changed into a
new man. The vehemence of my voice and action was considerably abated; the excessive ardour of my language was
corrected; my lungs were strengthened; and my whole con-
stitution confirmed and settled.

Two orators then reigned in the forum (I mean Cotta and

Hortensius), whose glory fired my emulation. Cotta's way of speaking was calm and easy, and distinguished by the flowing elegance and propriety of his language. The other was splendid, warm, and animated; not such as you, my Brutus, have seen him, when he had shed the blossom of his eloquence, but far more lively and pathetic both in his style and action. As Hortensius, therefore, was nearer to me in age, and his manner more agreeable to the natural ardour of my temper, I considered him as the proper object of my competition. For I observed that when they were both engaged in the same cause (as, for instance, when they defended Marcus Canuleius, and Gnaeus Dolabella, a man of consular dignity), though Cotta was generally employed to open the defence, the most important parts of it were left to the management of Hortensius. For a crowded audience and a clamorous forum require an orator who is lively, animated, full of action, and able to exert his voice to the highest pitch. The first year, therefore, after my return from Asia, I undertook several capital causes; and in the interim I put up as candidate for the quaestorship, Cotta for the consulate, and Hortensius for the aedileship. After I was chosen quaestor, I passed a year in Sicily, the province assigned to me by lot; Cotta went as consul into Gaul; and Hortensius, whose new office required his presence at Rome, was left of course the undisputed sovereign of the forum. In the succeeding year, when I returned from Sicily, my oratorical talents, such as they were, displayed themselves in their full perfection and maturity.

I have been saying too much, perhaps, concerning myself; but my design in it was not to make a parade of my eloquence and ability, which I have no temptation to do, but only to specify the pains and labour which I have taken to improve it. After spending the five succeeding years in pleading a variety of causes, and with the ablest advocates of the times, I was declared an aedile, and undertook the patronage of the Sicilians against Hortensius, who was then one of the consuls elect.*

On his return to Rome to resume his career in law and politics, Cicero married a wealthy woman, Terentia. Their daughter, Tullia, the "Tulliola," to whom Cicero was deeply devoted, was born around 78 B.C. Her death at the age of thirty-one was an overwhelming personal sorrow for Cicero. Cicero's father died in the year 65 B.C. and his son Marcus Tullius was born the same year. He had an undistinguished career, but thirteen years after Cicero's death he was elevated by Augustus to the consulship in a belated gesture of honor to his father.

* *Brutus*, or *De Claris Oratoribus*, Chapters 91–93, translated by J. S. Watson.

Cicero qualified for the successive offices by which one could rise politically in Rome to the ranks of the nobility,* starting as a quaestor in Lilybaeum in Sicily in 75 B.C., then becoming curule-aedile in 70 B.C. His career as legal advocate brought him to the defense of Marcus Fonteius on charges of extortion in Gaul, the year after his prosecution of Verres for extortion in Sicily. Holding the office of praetor in 66 B.C., he presided over cases in the extortion courts. In 66 Cicero also delivered his speech for the Manilian Law, recommending the transfer of the Near East command against Mithridates from Lucullus to Pompey. In another extant speech from the same year, he defended Aulus Cluentius, on trial for charges of poisoning. The year previous, Cicero had made two speeches on behalf of Gaius Cornelius, a tribune and leader of the democratic party, and in 65 B.C., he was considering the defense of Catiline on charges of extortion. This brief review of unfamiliar names and cases indicates how, in his early career, Cicero was on the "democratic" side of Roman politics. After his election to the consulship in 63 B.C. and his checking of the conspiracy of Catiline, he swung to the "republican," or conservative, as distinct from radical, side, advocating a policy of constitutional government under senatorial leadership which he hoped would align the "orders," or rival classes of aristocrats, plebeians, and equestrians, and promote effective legal administration of Roman government. At this point also is to be dated a remarkable document about the workings of Roman politics and the snobbish rivalry with which Cicero had to contend as an aspirant for high office in a nation whose rulers were largely drawn from the ranks of the nobility. It is a letter purported to be from his brother Quintus to Cicero at the time when he was a candidate for the consulship. Whether from the hand of Quintus or not, it does treat very directly the predicament of a non-aristocrat striving for political recognition in a Rome peopled by proud families, and reveals the tactical program of a candidate for elected office in any politically free state.

---

* Sir Ronald Syme epitomizes the complicated history of Roman status as follows: "The consulate did not merely confer power upon its holder and dignity for life: it ennobled a family forever. Within the Senate, itself an oligarchy, a narrow ring, namely the *nobiles,* or descendants of consular houses, whether patrician or plebeian in origin, regarded the supreme magistracy as the prerogative of birth and the prize of ambition." *The Roman Revolution,* Oxford, 1939, p. 10. Cicero discusses the situation of a newcomer (*novus homo*) striving for the consulship in the oration, *Pro Murena.*

Gaining the support of the "Optimates," or conservative aristocrats, Cicero won election to the consulship, the dominant feature of the year's executive action being of course the crushing of the Catilinarian conspiracy. In addition to the Catilinarian orations and the speech in defense of Murena, Cicero also delivered during his consular year four speeches in the Senate against the agrarian law sponsored by the tribune Rullus, and a speech in the assembly in defense of Rabirius, charged with being implicated in the death of Saturninus in 100 B.C. The significance of these cases lies in their being Cicero's answer to Caesar's bid for power; both were instigated by him, the agrarian measures intended to undercut Pompey's position, and the trial of Rabirius (for having put to death Saturninus when he had no constitutional right to declare the man a public enemy) would have its dangerous parallel for Cicero's execution of Catiline's accomplices. Cicero counted on the support of the nobles in these skirmishes with Caesar, the self-appointed champion of the people's party.

The political lines now drawn, Cicero continued to try to advance the cause of Pompey, and to work with him, the supposed leader of the "Optimates." The nobility as a whole were still envious of Cicero's success and fame in public life and soon, he was to find himself deserted by those whose cause and political position he had been trying to reinforce and, indeed, rehabilitate, in the face of the obvious fact of Caesar's increasing dominance. Caesar was adroit and amenable, a man whose abilities Cicero respected and whose personality he found sympathetic; Pompey a difficult, self-righteous man and a rather dull-witted snob. The First Triumvirate, formed in 60 B.C. among Caesar, Pompey, and Crassus, achieved a temporary balance of forces, Crassus supplying the money, Caesar the brains, and Pompey the prestige. It could have been the First Quattuorvirate, for Caesar invited Cicero to join the other members of the coalition. When he refused, Caesar offered him a post in the commission for the division of the Campanian lands, but, here again, Cicero refused to be an accessory to Caesar's political schemes. Caesar won election to the consulship in 59 B.C. and secured the passage of a law revoking the allocation by the Senate of an insignificant proconsular province and conferring on him instead the important provinces of Gaul and Illyricum. Before starting off on his decisive nine years of "Gallic Wars" in 58 B.C., Caesar then helped a vicious young aristocrat named Publius Clodius Pulcher to transfer himself to the plebeian order, for the purpose of being elected tribune in 58 B.C. Clodius was bent upon revenging himself against Cicero, who had given evidence against him in the scandalous Bona Dea affair of 62 B.C., when Clodius had been on trial for sacrilege. As tribune, he now passed a law exiling anyone who had put citizens to death without a trial. Confronted by the piece of legislation aimed directly at him, as the presiding consul in 63 B.C. when the conspirators had been executed, Cicero also found himself deserted by the nobles in the Senate. He left Rome at the end of March, 58 B.C., for exile.

From May to November, Cicero spent many months of exile in Thessalonica (modern Saloniki) in northeastern Greece. Eventually hearing of Pompey's disgust with the arrogant demagogic tactics of Clodius, Cicero traveled westward to Dyrrhachium (Durazzo) on the Illyrian coast to await recall, and left there for Italy on August 4, 57 B.C. Arriving in Brundisium (Brindisi) Cicero found that he had been officially recalled by a law passed in the assembly the very day of his departure:

> I arrived at Brundisium on the 5th of August. There my dear Tulliola met me on what was her own birthday . . . On the 8th of August, while still at Brundisium, I learnt by a letter from Quintus that the law had been passed at the *comitia centuriata* with a surprising enthusiasm on the part of all ages and ranks, and with an influx of voters from Italy. I then commenced my journey . . . On my arrival at the Porta Capena the steps of the temples were already thronged from top to bottom by the populace; and while their congratulations were displayed by the loudest possible applause, a similar throng and similar applause accompanied me right up to the Capitol, and in the forum and on the Capitol itself there was again a wonderful crowd. Next day, in the Senate, that is, the 5th of September, I spoke my thanks to the senators.
>
> (*To Atticus,* vol. IV, no. 1, Sept. 1957, translated by E. S. Shuckburgh)

Among those who greeted Cicero cordially on his return was Crassus the triumvir, who dropped his grudges, according to Plutarch's account, because of his son's great admiration for Cicero. Having incurred the loss of all his own money and property by being forced into exile and been made dependent on Terentia's money and what he could borrow from friends like Atticus, Cicero was eventually compensated for the loss of his house on the Palatine which Clodius had burned and vandalized, consecrating the site for a temple to Liberty, and for the loss of the villas that Clodius had destroyed.*

Aware of the rivalry between Pompey and Caesar, Cicero moved back into the political forum with speeches critical of Caesar's action during his consulship. He also made a proposal in the Senate that a discussion be held to reappraise Caesar's distribution of the Campanian land, a proposal which alarmed Caesar enough to prompt him to call the Conference of Luca in 56 B.C., at which he met with Pompey and Crassus for the purpose of reaffirming the Triumvirate. Pompey and Crassus became consuls for the year 55 B.C., but after the death of Caesar's daughter Julia, whom Pompey had married in 59 B.C., the attachment between him and Caesar was further weakened and cooperation between Pompey and Cicero renewed. Pompey encouraged Milo to harass Clodius, Cicero's tormentor, in a continuing series of strong-arm tactics, which ended in Clodius' murder in January, 52 B.C., at the hands of Milo and his gang. At the trial of Milo, Cicero was intimidated by the crowd and did not deliver his speech in defense of Milo, but wrote it out later and published it. Milo was condemned and went into exile at Marseilles.† In the course of the year 53 B.C., both Crassus' son—whose death Cicero deeply laments in a letter—and Crassus were killed in military action on the Mid-Eastern front.

In 52 B.C., Cicero set out for the province of Cilicia, which had fallen to his lot to govern under the provisions of a law passed by Pompey. With Quintus as his military legate, Cicero made his main task that of rehabilitating the ruined economic conditions of the province. Previous governors had supported a high interest rate for Roman moneylenders that had left the Cilicians virtually bankrupt.‡ Attempts to help

---

* These affairs are fully presented in Cicero's orations, *Concerning His House* (*De Domo Sua*) and *Concerning the Responses of the Sooth-sayers* (*De Haruspicum Responso*).

† In 48 B.C., he joined with Caelius in a harebrained resistance movement against Caesar during the civil war. Caelius was killed in a skirmish at Thurii (modern Sibari on the Gulf of Taranto). Milo was captured and executed at Cosa (modern Ansedonia, near Orbetello on the coast ninety miles north of Rome. Cosa is, at present, the site of the great archaeological explorations being conducted by Frank E. Brown, Director of the American Academy in Rome.).

‡ Brutus, for instance, charged interest at the rate of 4% *a month*, compounded annually. Cicero writes about the usurious demands of Brutus and of Pompey in letters to Atticus (vol. V.21 and vol. VI.1, Feb. 13 and 22, 50 B.C. from Laodicea).

the people of the province regain economic stability, the regular administration of justice, and the activities of one military campaign (in which the Roman troops under his campaign were victorious) kept Cicero occupied in Cilicia until 50 B.C., when he again returned to Brundisium on November 24, en route to Rome. There he learned that the civil war, long brewing between Pompey and Caesar as rivals for the supreme power, could no longer be stopped.

After the outbreak of the war in 49 B.C., Pompey placed Cicero in charge of the Campanian coast. Caesar continued to make overtures to Cicero to join his side, but Cicero refused and instead eventually joined Pompey's forces in Greece. He was prevented by illness from being present at the Battle of Pharsalia, in which Pompey's main elements were routed, and he himself fled to Egypt where he was murdered. After the debacle, Cicero was offered command of the troops at Corcyra, and when he declined it, was threatened with death by Pompey's son. By now, however, Cicero had concluded that it was useless to continue the struggle against the superior forces of Caesar, and sailed back to Brundisium, where he stayed until August 12, 47 B.C., when he received a letter of accommodation from Caesar and returned to Rome to live under Caesar's dispensation. He kept in the background of the political scene, for the most part, delivering only three speeches, *On Behalf of Marcellus* and *On Behalf of Ligarius*, both of which resulted in Caesar's offering amnesty to the two men in question who had been on Pompey's side in the civil war. And an oration on behalf of King Deiotarus, ruler of Galatia, also a former ally of Pompey, who by this defense, regained the possessions Caesar had deprived him of.

In 46 B.C., Tullia was finally divorced from her third husband, Dolabella, conventionally described as a "profligate libertine," and, only a few months later, died in childbirth. Cicero had earlier this year divorced his wife Terentia, and married his wealthy young ward, Publilia, but when the latter failed to share his grief over the death of Tullia, Cicero divorced her. Throughout these years, Cicero had been busy with his writing, composing the philosophical essays and dialogues on rhetoric that he hoped would interest Roman readers and bring him the literary recognition he yearned for, political fame apparently being denied him.

But after the assassination of Caesar, Cicero was to enjoy, if that is the term, one last blaze of political glory. He did not play any part in the conspiracy that effected the murder of Caesar, but he welcomed the event and aligned himself with the cause of Brutus and Cassius. Brutus had always been his friend and associate, and Cicero believed that in disposing of the dictator, the conspirators had given the Roman "republic" an opportunity to survive. On March 17, 44 B.C., Cicero delivered a speech in the Senate proposing a general amnesty. While continuing his work on the philosophical and literary essays, Cicero tried to gauge the political wind and found his opinions being sought by the young Octavian, and, in general, his voice being listened to by his fellow Romans, as well as his support being sought by Brutus. It was a very difficult and unpredictable state of affairs, the rivalry between Octavian and Antony over the claims of which was the proper "heir" of Caesar seeming to sap their strength and augur well for the "Republicans" under Brutus. Cicero's son, Marcus, like the young Horace, was an eager partisan of Brutus' cause, as the latter in Greece tried to marshal his forces for a showdown against the Italy-based troops of Antony and/or Octavian. Octavian proved to have the stamina for the political infighting and maneuvering necessary to keep Antony from dominating the situation exclusively; he convinced the Senate and influential persons like Cicero, for instance, of the right of his claim to Caesar's political legacy. Cicero's regard for this young aristocrat estranged him from Brutus, but equally failed to materialize in any judicious restoration of constitutional government at Rome.

Cicero had planned a voyage to Greece to see his son Marcus and by August 1 of 44 B.C. had gone as far as Syracuse in Sicily. He was apparently undecided still, as to whether to support the cause of Brutus outright or keep on hoping that his influence with Octavian would bear longer-lasting results. On this voyage, he was driven back by unfavorable winds to Leucopetra and, hearing what he thought was better news about Octavian's dominance at Rome, he returned to the capital on August 21. He did not attend the meeting in the Senate on September 1, and was bitterly attacked by Antony for not being present. The next day Cicero replied with his First "Philippic," and then left Rome for Tusculum where he composed the Second "Philippic," a venomous attack on the personality and career of Antony— the speech was not delivered, but written out and widely circulated. It brought down the vengeance of Antony on Cicero. Subsequently, Cicero went on to compose the rest of the fourteen speeches modeled after Demosthenes' famous warnings against the tyranny of Philip. Antony had, meanwhile, left Rome for Cisalpine Gaul and Cicero returned to Rome on December 9 and, from then on, acted as the leader of the "Republican" party in the Senate. His plan now was to make use of Octavian, until new legions had been raised which would follow the Republican commanders, although Cicero was promptly accused by Brutus of truckling to the young Caesarian. It was during these months that Cicero delivered the rest of his "Philippics" and corresponded energetically with provincial governors and military commanders trying to evolve a common plan of operation and to keep up the morale of the "Republican" side.

But unwittingly, he was a man more used against than using. Antony and Octavian settled their immediate differences and coordinated their plans for an assault on the Republicans. At a secret meeting near Bologna, in October, 43 B.C., they formed the so-called Second Triumvirate,* initiating it with a proscription list of two hundred persons to be murdered. Antony and Lepidus bargained with Octavian for Cicero as the first name on the list, and Octavian assented. Lepidus, in turn, handed over the name of his brother Paulis, and Antony agreed to the murder of Lucius Caesar, his mother's uncle. The Triumvirate was ratified by the Senate on November 27, 43 B.C. When Cicero realized the danger he was in, he reluctantly formed his plans to leave Italy, together with his brother Quintus and his nephew. Cicero himself got as far as Astura on the coast, but Quintus was caught on the road, having started later, and he and his son were murdered. On December 7, 43 B.C., Cicero was trapped in his house near Astura and murdered by the thugs Antony had dispatched for the purpose. Antony ordered that Cicero's head, which had spoken, and the hands, which had written the *Philippics,* be brought to Rome and impaled in public view on the Rostra in the forum. Fulvia, Antony's wife (and the widow of Clodius), thrust a hairpin through Cicero's lifeless tongue just before the head and hands were affixed to the Rostra.

* For "the First Triumvirate," see above, p. 312.

SELECTED
BIBLIOGRAPHY

Cicero edited by T.A. Dorey (New York: Basic Books, 1965)
A collection of seven different essays by leading classical scholars.

Cicero and the Roman Republic by F. R. Cowell (London: Sir Isaac Pitman and Sons, 1958), available in a Penguin paperback edition.
A social, political, and economic survey of Cicero's position in Roman history.

The Roman Revolution by Sir Ronald Syme (Oxford: Oxford University Press, 1939), available in an Oxford paperback edition.

Cicero of Arpinum by E. G. Sihler (New Haven, Conn.: Yale University Press, 1914), sub-titled "A Political and Literary Biography."

Cicero and His Friends by Gaston Boissier, first French edition of *Cicéron et ses Amis* was published in Paris; the English translation was published in 1897.
A study of the personalities figuring in Cicero's correspondence.

Cicero by Anthony Trollope (Longman, Brown: London, 1880).

Written near the end of Trollope's life, this is a biography of Cicero the man and writer.

The World of Rome by Michael Grant (New York: New American Library, 1961).

A re-creation of Rome's and Cicero's world.

This Was Cicero by H. J. Haskell (New York: Fawcett Premier, 1964).

A biography of Cicero.